Master Singers

Master Singers

Advice from the Stage

Donald George
and
Lucy Mauro

OXFORD
UNIVERSITY PRESS

OXFORD
UNIVERSITY PRESS

Oxford University Press is a department of the
University of Oxford. It furthers the University's objective
of excellence in research, scholarship, and education
by publishing worldwide.

Oxford   New York

Auckland   Cape Town   Dar es Salaam   Hong Kong   Karachi
Kuala Lumpur   Madrid   Melbourne   Mexico City   Nairobi
New Delhi   Shanghai   Taipei   Toronto

With offices in

Argentina   Austria   Brazil   Chile   Czech Republic   France   Greece
Guatemala   Hungary   Italy   Japan   Poland   Portugal   Singapore
South Korea   Switzerland   Thailand   Turkey   Ukraine   Vietnam

Oxford is a registered trade mark of Oxford University Press
in the UK and in certain other countries.

Published in the United States of America by
Oxford University Press
198 Madison Avenue, New York, NY 10016

© Oxford University Press 2015

Library of Congress Cataloging-in-Publication Data
George, Donald, author.
Master singers : advice from the stage / Donald George and Lucy Mauro.
pages   cm
Includes bibliographical references and index.
ISBN 978-0-19-932417-0 (hardback : alk. paper)—
ISBN 978-0-19-932418-7 (pbk. : alk. paper)
1. Singing—Vocational guidance.   2. Singers—Interviews.
3. Singers—Biographies.   I. Mauro, Lucy, author.   II. Title.
ML3795.G45   2014
782.1'143—dc23   2014020359

1 3 5 7 9 8 6 4 2

Printed in the United States of America
on acid-free paper

CONTENTS

List of Portraits of the Artists   *vii*
Foreword by Brian Zeger   *ix*
Preface   *xiii*
Acknowledgments   *xv*

1. On the Craft of Singing   *1*
2. On the Operatic Stage   *34*
3. On the Recital and Concert Stage   *69*
4. On Maintaining a Career   *88*
5. On Teaching and Studying   *115*
6. Extras from the Experts   *140*

References   *159*
Index   *161*

PORTRAITS OF THE ARTISTS

Stephanie Blythe   7
Lawrence Brownlee   15
Nicole Cabell   25
Joseph Calleja   31
David Daniels   40
Joyce DiDonato   46
Christine Goerke   56
Denyce Graves   66
Greer Grimsley   72
Thomas Hampson   77
Alan Held   85
Jonas Kaufmann   91
Simon Keenlyside   100
Kathleen Kim   105
Ana María Martínez   113
Lisette Oropesa   123
Eric Owens   127
Dimitri Pittas   134
Ewa Podleś   144
Jennifer Rowley   149
Gerhard Siegel   154

FOREWORD

It will come as no surprise to those interested in singing that there are as many points of view in *Master Singers: Advice from the Stage* as there are contributors. The parable of the blind men and the elephant comes to mind: the man who encounters the trunk takes the elephant for a kind of serpent; the one who pats the elephant's broad side describes a warm, wrinkly wall. There is a wide spectrum of points of view here, vividly expressed and from the heart. This multiplicity of voices is no accident. In tracing the mysterious alchemy that transforms a black dot on a page to a living, vibrating sound, so many elements come into play: a singer's musical understanding, the vocal instrument they were born with and what their technical craft has made of that endowment, their insights into language and text, and their dramatic skills.

The authors have assembled a broad array of artists to address these questions, ranging from artists with wide-ranging and long careers (Ewa Podleś and Thomas Hampson) to younger singers (Kathleen Kim and Lisette Oropesa). One senses in the more veteran singers—I'd also include Eric Owens and Simon Keenlyside in this category—an awareness of the danger of facile answers and a real wariness of one-size-fits-all nostrums. Here some of the younger singers, including Nicole Cabell and Lawrence Brownlee, are refreshingly direct. They're open-hearted in sharing what works for them and open-minded in their quest for the truths that experience will bring.

The interviews begin with the bedrock of singing: vocal technique. There's lots of good advice here, though the reader is always aware that putting kinesthetic feelings into words is not easy and that the same words will not mean the same things to two different singers, especially if they're looking for insights on breathing, support, resonance and release. Perhaps Ewa Podleś has the last word here: she will not respond to questions about vocal technique because "they seem to be too personal and... especially for young singers, such answers can be more harmful than useful. Questions regarding the technique of singing should be answered and discussed live, during a direct meeting, with a possibility of immediate demonstration."

Fair enough, but no one is suggesting that this book take the place of private study. Even when a singer is thriving vocally, the introduction of new vocabulary to describe sensations can be revelatory. On breathing, two of my favorites are Joyce DiDonato's "Air should drop like a weight 360 degrees around your midsection from your tailbone all throughout your side ribs like an inner tube," and the always musically grounded Eric Owens's "The breath should be part of the phrase and not a gasp...but as a note itself in the phrase." For those overly concerned with "getting it right," the iconoclastic Simon Keenlyside offers this: "Experiment is the name of the game! There are a few basics and the rest, to my mind, is trial and error....And if it don't work, don't do it."

The next topics move toward employing vocal technique in the service of music and words, and now it gets *really* interesting. Most of the contributors agree that good diction depends on a basis of well-produced and artfully linked vowels, though consonants also get their due. Lawrence Brownlee voices perhaps the most succinct suggestion: *Si canta come si parla.* Of course, this brings up many other questions. For example, do singers growing up in today's world, where language on stage, film, and television is projected universally by microphone, know what supported lyric diction feels and sounds like?

There's more unanimity of opinion on diction than in describing ideal vocal placement. Here the parable of the blind men and the elephant really comes into play. Many singers advocate "forward" placement, but Jonas Kaufmann counters, "I do not feel the voice in the mask." Clearly it's not only forward placement that leads to balanced resonance and volume. Both Eric Owens and Christine Goerke speak of diverse sensations *including* resonance in the mask. Goerke returns to the dual poles of "space" and "point," suggesting a dynamic between two extremes, which the singer adjusts constantly from moment to moment. An honest, receptive openness to the demands of different languages and dramatic expressions will bring "colors" to the voice. Most of the singers agree that altering the instrument or technique to create special effects leads to problems and, in Eric Owens's words, "ends up encumbering the sound and making your voice smaller than it is."

Talking about specific vocal registers—chest voice, *passaggio*, high voice, and the like—may seem bewildering to the reader who enjoys singing but neither sings nor has spent a lot of time in vocal studios.

Even though there's plenty of difference of opinion here, there's also lots of agreement, at least among those singers who recognize a specific technical hurdle as real enough to merit discussion. Joseph Calleja has clearly done a lot of thinking about technical matters as they apply to the tenor voice.

Singers will find the notes on warming up very useful—varied, yes, but all practical and jargon-free. Responses to demanding operatic stagings are also practical and refreshingly collaborative: Christine Goerke suggests trying even an implausible idea three times, then if it really interferes, begin the dialogue with the director with, "Can you help me?" Goerke also gives good advice in managing long roles: her "mental road map" is a good start for any singer. Questions about uniting singing with acting naturally take our interviewees in many directions. This question clearly has legs: the answers here could easily expand to fill a whole book.

All of our contributors seem to agree that the recital stage offers very different challenges and rewards than the opera stage. Even if, as Kaufmann asserts, "I use the exact same instrument and technique," clearly the repertoire and venues are wildly different. None of the singers interviewed here are primarily recitalists in the way that Ameling, Auger, or Bernac were. Those for whom recital is an important part of their artistic profile— Hampson and Keenlyside, for example—have valuable insights. Concern over the continued public for recitals is widespread, but there's hope in the resourcefulness of these singers. Programming for actual audiences rather than abstract ones is one tool. Stephanie Blythe has interesting ideas about connection with audiences which break down the barrier between stage and public. Ewa Podleś writes, "I like to make the audience happy," perhaps a far cry from the *Heilige Kunst* instilled in students but close to the impulses that inspired this marvelous repertoire.

The issue of vocal longevity is a perplexing one. Eric Owens sums it up succinctly when he admits that no one has all the answers. There's a lot of indisputable wisdom here: Ewa Podleś admits that she never sings 100 percent, only 90 percent, while Joyce DiDonato looks to athletes for tips on how to stay healthy over the long haul. Some of the veteran singers interviewed here work with voice teachers and some don't, but all show a humble respect for the ongoing challenge of maintaining a healthy technique as they confront the demands of the career. Stephanie Blythe offers some advice that resonates strongly with me: "Being a young artist means that you have to take it upon yourself to be your own mentor and your own teacher." Eric Owens continues this train of thought: "I know it's hard, but we are all responsible for our own vocal development." This book is a real inspiration to those who want to grapple with the invisible elephant: with so many curious seekers, we're bound to find the answers.

Brian Zeger
Artistic Director,
Ellen and James S. Marcus
Institute for Vocal Arts, Juilliard School
Executive Director,
Metropolitan Opera Lindemann
Young Artist Development Program

PREFACE

This book has been written by master singers, artists who have developed their voices with study, skill, and determination. The term comes from *Meistersinger*, a member of the German Renaissance guilds that established standards for the composition and performance of poetry and songs. Our master singers offer us a varied palette of ideas in artistry and performance. Using this palette, we wanted to create a book that offers practical advice on what must be done to perform on the major stages of the world. We also wanted to develop a format that could be used as a reference book, that is, a go-to book with answers that allow immediate comparison of each singer's perspective. The result is *Master Singers: Advice from the Stage*.

Master Singers is divided into six chapters, covering such topics as vocal technique; performance on the operatic, concert, and recital stages; vocal study; teaching; recording; and the business of opera. The last chapter, "Extras from the Experts," includes tips on vocal hygiene and performance anxiety and contains some final thoughts on succeeding in the business today. We created the questions with the college student, the studio teacher, the emerging artist, the professional singer, and the opera lover in mind. Each chapter is arranged in a question-and-answer format with the artists listed alphabetically; additionally, each answer is limited to approximately 150 words.

The twenty-one artists interviewed range from young professionals to international stars. Each of the artists was given the same questions. Several submitted written answers, while others preferred personal interviews. Our communications were done in a variety of ways, including through email, "snail mail," Facebook, and even texting. Some of the interviews were done via Skype or Skype chat, sometimes in different time zones with an ocean or a continent in between. Many of these busy singers were in a performance series or traveling to their next production. Jonas Kaufmann was interviewed at the Met cafeteria between performances of *Parsifal*. Alan Held was in Japan singing Hans Sachs. Doing her *Maria Stuarda* debut at the Met, Joyce DiDonato charmingly wrote she might be late with her answers. (She wasn't.) David Daniels was in Barcelona for a new production of Handel's *Agrippina*. Thomas Hampson was interviewed between flights in Switzerland and England, and Christine Goerke was heading off to London to sing *Elektra* at Covent Garden, to give a few examples. Some singers chose not to answer all the questions, while others answered each one. We edited the singers' words as minimally as possible, leaving their individual voices to speak for themselves.

What follows are the informative, educational, and thought-provoking words of some of today's most acclaimed singers. With this book, all who love classical singing, whether student, teacher, young professional, performing artist, or opera aficionado, will gain a broader understanding of this great art.

Donald George and Lucy Mauro

ACKNOWLEDGMENTS

There are several people to thank for their invaluable assistance with this book.

We thank Suzanne Ryan, executive editor at Oxford University Press, whose keen insight and advice helped us in so many ways, and Joellyn Ausanka, Adam Cohen, and Jessen O'Brien, also at OUP. Our thanks also go to Meggie George and Carleen Graham for their assistance with the interviews, and to Deborah Massell, Constantine Orbelian, Carol Rosenberger, Stephen Schmidt, Evelyn Smith-George, Robert Tannenbaum, Thomas Voigt, Melissa Wegner, and Stephen West, who gave us helpful suggestions on any number of issues and occasions. Special thanks also go to Sanna Myrttinen for the use of her painting "Backstage." Additionally, our thanks go to Plácido Domingo, Alvaro Domingo, Mirella Freni, Brian Zeger and to the friends, artists' managers, agents, and public relations people who helped to arrange the interviews and provided us with biographies and photos. Above all, our gratitude goes to the artists, who gave so generously of their time and advice.

Master Singers

CHAPTER 1

को

On the Craft of Singing

"When you control both energy of voice and color of resonance, you are one of the greatest singing artists." So said renowned teacher Giovanni Battista Lamperti, who further stated: "This depends on sensibility of the imagination and intensity of emotion... It is realized through poetical and musical stimulation and understanding, and balance between power of breath and energy of vibration. It is a long road. But it pays." This maxim sums up much of the craft of singing. The "long road" of developing both the voice and the imagination has its roots in building a sense of *bel canto* or beautiful singing, a critical ear, and a heightened awareness of feeling in the body and the emotions—what Eric Owens calls "the freedom of an unencumbered technique." Once that freedom is found, it's easy to understand why Joyce DiDonato states: "Your body is a Stradivarius and perfect as it is." This chapter, which Jonas Kaufmann and many of the other artists considered the most important, provides a variety of personal ideas about vocal technique, which especially highlights another famous maxim by Lamperti: that "each voice is a law unto itself."

1. WHAT IS YOUR APPROACH TO BREATHING?

STEPHANIE BLYTHE: "Breath release" is the term I would use. I breathe using the diaphragm, and I think of taking a deep, supported breath and then releasing it as needed. Think about it this way: You look across the room and decide that you want to go to the door. Do you stop and tell your feet, "Okay, left, right, left"? No. You visualize what you want, and your body does it. It is the same with breathing and singing. Know what you want, and get out of the way so your body can do it.

LAWRENCE BROWNLEE: I have a very simple approach to singing, very natural, with quiet breaths and relaxed breathing that's low. I envision a balloon that inflates, and I always think of a downward pressure. I never think of it as forced but rather as an engaged breath that is down and low— in the "bikinis," if you will. It's a natural thing. The breath gets going before the sound does, and then I go with the sound. Breathing in this way is the energy that gives my singing life, and I don't get overly technical about it.

NICOLE CABELL: I try to keep a good balance between support and re-laxation. Relying only on what feels "natural" is dangerous, as what feels natural is, many times, inherently flawed. If one has to sing a long phrase, it is appropriate to take a big, deep breath (keeping the ribs comfortably extended and avoiding collapse on exhalation), and measure out that breath in the way one does when slowly "hissing" it out. A slight resistance of the diaphragm can help. This avoids an overly breathy tone and unneces-sary loss of breath, and provides enough fuel to get through the phrase. When singing higher or louder, I may increase the resistance of the dia-phragm, which is usually felt in my abdominal muscles. It's paramount to relaxation to release most of my breath before completing a phrase. Other-wise, tension through stacking of the breath occurs.

JOSEPH CALLEJA: We are all *Homo sapiens* and we all breathe pretty much the same way. We singers should try to emulate the breathing of a newborn, who can cry for hours and not get tired. The baby's diaphragm is like a bellows—it goes in and out, and the chest area is almost not engaged at all. The way I visualize it is the diaphragm supports the air and pushes the air gently, and the vocal cords are a light plastic ball floating on a column of air. The minute the air is too little, the ball drops; the minute the air is too much, the ball shoots out of the picture. The technique is how to bal-ance, produce, and sustain airflow so it is right in the "Goldilocks zone," in that the column of air is constant and comfortable and produces the best sound with the least effect of tiredness on the voice.

DAVID DANIELS: I definitely think of it because it's something that corrects issues with diction or intonation. I think about this stuff at the beginning of the performance and I get on automatic pilot with it. If I start with a bad habit, it tends to haunt me for the night. It's really more about taking an open-throated /a/ (ah) breath noiselessly and about low breath support than it is about the diaphragm or the upper part just under the sternum. I don't think in terms of diaphragm, but in terms of depth in the body. I feel at times a sense of pushing down and out with my core, with my abdomen, and the lower muscles.

JOYCE DIDONATO: I tend not to use the word *support*. I prefer to talk about *freedom* of breath: the freer the mind, the freer the inhalation, the freer the vocal apparatus, the freer the musculature, the freer the breath, the freer the *voice*. When you take air in, it should be relatively silent as you allow it to "drop" like a weight 360 degrees around your midsection, from your tailbone all throughout your side ribs like an inner tube. If you are too aggressive with breath or take too much in, you will be forced to contain and restrict it somehow, which could cause jaw tension and base-of-the-tongue tension. I use octave chromatic scales in working on the breath so there is no chance for the breath to collapse. "Sirens" will also give seamless *legato* and passage through the range.

CHRISTINE GOERKE: I don't think about it. It's such a natural thing. I was a clarinet major before I was a singer, so I had already dealt with breath issues. I have a hard time talking about breath without talking about support, because the two are so connected to the muscles around the abdomen (which is the word I prefer to *diaphragm*). Once you have the breath in the abdomen, then you use your breath in the most efficient way that will give you the longest phrase and easiest sound. Everything has to work together, or it doesn't function. I judge my breathing and how I take breaths based on what the music requires.

DENYCE GRAVES: My very first voice teacher had me lie down on the floor on my back and observe my breathing. I watched my inhalation and the expansion in my back and lungs and observed how the diaphragm descends and the belly protrudes slightly, or gets fluffy, as I like to say. The supporting of the breath I liken to sustaining a hiss and allowing this gentle connection to emit without force. Because I have a fuller, darker instrument and I don't want to flood or overwhelm the tone with sound and body, I think of a slender approach when initiating the beginning of a phrase. While singing, I think of releasing breath or allowing breath to flow and spin as it nourishes the tone, but, above all, to enjoy and be present.

GREER GRIMSLEY: My philosophy is that breath is the root on which we base all the rest of our technique. It is one of the most important things in technique. It is, at its optimum, fully integrated into your singing, acting—indeed, your whole performance. It is not a separate thing. When I was a student and still trying to get it to be as second nature as possible, or when I'm working with young singers, I have to remind them it's about being low in the body. There has to be this grounded feeling. As you breathe in, there's a release that you feel in the lower abdomen. The muscles release as you breathe in, and as you sing, there is a metered resistance.

THOMAS HAMPSON: It all starts with understanding how your body functions, i.e., a question of engineering. Simply put: stand up straight, ears over shoulders, anchored strong in your core muscles of your body—strong abdomen, flexible chest, and above all a straight spine. When we sing, we hear the sound we are to make, the reason for the expression, the technical necessities of the musical sound, and we breathe exactly what we need to make that audible. Balancing the inhaling preparation with the exhaling effort physically keeps your ribs expanded and allows the diaphragm, lungs, and all organs of breathing to do their work. That preparedness to inhale while you are singing out is what the Italian school is implying with the idea of *inalare la voce* or drinking in the tone.

ALAN HELD: A breath needs to be taken in a relaxed manner with the feeling of "going up" before it heads down into the lungs. This way, placement is taken into consideration at the same time as inhalation. The larynx and tongue are *not* a part of breath support. Sadly, too often you find that singers use them as primary sources of support. Singing should be natural, and since we use both the nose and mouth in breathing, we should use them both in singing. As for the larynx, I do not attempt to lower it consciously. Trying to manipulate the larynx is asking for trouble. Also, one must remember that the air does not go lower than the lungs. The diaphragm, just below the lungs, is the lungs' primary support, and the muscles below the diaphragm help support it.

JONAS KAUFMANN: Some say to breathe only with the chest, and others say to breathe with the diaphragm or belly. I think it is both. I keep the diaphragm low for as long as the phrase goes. I think it is necessary that your intercostal muscles are not tight and stiff, in order to provide a constant exhalation flow. The vocal power is built down low in the abdomen. So if you sing only from the chest, the sound can never be as solid or as profound as when it comes from lower down. It is a physical fact that the lower the diaphragm is, the more the lungs are being stretched. So the sound that gets bounced back and forth actually does the most part of our amplification.

SIMON KEENLYSIDE: How many of us really do feel the breath low down and around the back in the kidney area? My feeling is that one shouldn't have a panic about this. Experiment is the name of the game! There are a few basics, and the rest, to my mind, is trial and error. For me, ideally, I would have my chest up, shoulders relaxed and down, and the breath well in advance of the upcoming phrase but not so soon as to be left holding it. It's important that the breath is taken low and without tension. In addition, where possible, I would take it through the nose, as that encourages the throat to stay open and the larynx down, both essential to good voice production. My advice to young singers would be to try it! See how you manage. As Fats Waller used to say, "One never knows, do one?" And, if it don't work, don't do it.

KATHLEEN KIM: Sometimes I think about the diaphragm and it helps to breathe better. Usually, when I practice, I think about it, but when I'm on the stage, I don't. It becomes muscle memory on the stage and goes automatically.

ANA MARÍA MARTÍNEZ: I want to be sure that neither the shoulders nor the chest are rising and I feel a filling out of the lower back and the lower abdominal area. I used to think of the ribs expanding, but I now feel that I breathe into the hips, that my thighs have walls, which open out and stay out so that the lower back feels completely filled and there's nothing high about the breath. The breath is flowing with a buoyancy and openness. By doing so, the throat area mirrors what happens in my thigh area. Society says we have to have a flat tummy, which is all incorrect for singing and also for peace of mind. The deeper the breath, the calmer you are.

LISETTE OROPESA: It's all about the breath: lift the ribs, expand from the bottom up, send the breath up through the top of the head. Breath + vowels = singing.

ERIC OWENS: It has to be a low, centered breath in the style of what is coming. You don't have to take a huge breath, but the breath should be part of the phrase and not a gasp (unless that's what's called for), but as a note itself in the phrase. I believe that the inhalation and exhalation of air should be one motion. When you breathe in, you don't hold on to it. I see a lot of young singers who hold the breath for an instant before singing, but the intake of air and the saying of the word have to be seamless, much like a violinist who may have to change the direction of the bow while sustaining the same note.

DIMITRI PITTAS: It's important that everything always starts from the breath, which sets up the beginning of the phrase. I get my mouth and tongue into a neutral position, a "cold air sip" or the /u/ vowel, something I like to call "couch tongue"—that position when you're sitting on your couch just watching TV where the tongue is relaxed, maybe lifting a little in back. Just take in air and go right over the tongue. You actually feel that the air will connect itself a little bit lower, somewhere between the bottom of the rib cage up to the bottom of the shoulder blades. It's just a little puff that happens back there. To keep that through the phrase is the sensation I get when I feel I am breathing properly and not wasting any air—not overtanking, just using the air that's necessary to sing that phrase.

EWA PODLEŚ: Generally, there are two reasons I won't respond to almost all of the questions regarding vocal technique: first, because they seem to be too personal, and second, because in my opinion, especially for young singers, such answers can be more harmful than useful. Questions regarding the technique of singing should be answered and discussed live, during a direct meeting, with a possibility of immediate demonstration. For instance, I consider you can describe or even draw sexual technique (as in the *Kama Sutra*), but not how to master the art of singing or even the technique of breathing. To truly explain a problem of breath necessary for singing, I need personal contact, where I can show everything. This process would be impossible to describe, especially in a few sentences, and could easily be misunderstood, or not understood at all.

JENNIFER ROWLEY: My approach is sort of a release or lean. I release from the oblique muscles of the abdomen and I feel the diaphragm drop down. Then I prepare the throat muscles for whatever word is coming up. I like to think about how things feel. It's like you're in a ski boot and you have the support of the ankle in the boot and can lean forward and backward and you're not going to fall. I have been skiing since I was ten, and this image reminds me of that sensation.

GERHARD SIEGEL: By studying the trumpet, I had the term *support* internalized, of course, long before voice lessons, so the conscious use of the diaphragm to hold the breath column was present from the beginning. During my early years of voice study, the main problem was to make this fixed support achieve a certain flexibility. In other words: release. In many difficult and/or high notes, in the soft dynamics, or in the high middle voice, I have to consciously think of that to this day.

2. WHAT DO YOU CONSIDER THE MOST IMPORTANT WAYS OF ACHIEVING EFFECTIVE DICTION?

STEPHANIE BLYTHE: You have to want to be understood. Full stop. If I ask you to explain something that is very important to you, then you will truly enunciate, use the clearest language possible, and speak to be heard. Why think any less of that when singing?

LAWRENCE BROWNLEE: For me, it is the statement *Si canta come si parla*. I think you should speak in your "place." You can really turn a word or a phrase because you are constantly speaking in that place.

NICOLE CABELL: There is an image in which vowels are the clothesline and the consonants are the pins. I'm in favor of this to a point, as the beautiful *bel canto* line is achieved through uniformity of vowels, consonants, and line. The tongue should never be depressed to the point of tension, and the tip of the tongue should usually remain forward, mostly touching the bottom teeth. In most languages, the vowels can be made when the tongue touches the middle or front of the hard palate and not the back of the hard palate or soft palate. I tend to round my lips a little bit when singing. When

I sing lighter music, I will favor a brighter mouth position, a more pronounced "inner smile," and a clarity of vowels more exaggerated than with classical music. Words are the priority in lighter music.

JOSEPH CALLEJA: The first step is to produce the same sounds on all the vowels (*a, e, i, o, u*), and the second step is not to let the consonants get in the way of the *legato*. In my case, I never really had to study diction because, being born in Malta, I am fluent in Italian, English and Maltese, and I learned French at a pretty early age. My teacher always told me to sing like you talk, and when you phonate keep your mind on the best position of the vowels. If you are fluent in the languages, then diction should come pretty much naturally. This is why I do not yet sing in German because, although I am studying it, I do not know it yet. I am sure that when I become more fluent, then I can start on German repertoire. Singing a language I do not understand perfectly would not be for me.

DAVID DANIELS: It's obviously one of the most important things we bring to the stage—you have to tell the story. For me, it's using the proper breath, singing through the word, and enunciating. I'm not fluent in any language—typical American. But I do work very hard with people who do speak the language. I'm very open to diction coaches. I never dismiss them in rehearsals, as others might do. I know a lot, but I don't know everything, and I never will.

Stephanie Blythe
A renowned opera singer and recitalist, mezzo-soprano Stephanie Blythe is considered one of the most highly respected and critically acclaimed artists of her generation. Her repertoire ranges from Handel to Wagner, German Lieder to contemporary and classic American song. Ms. Blythe has performed on many of the world's great stages, such as Carnegie Hall, the Metropolitan Opera, Covent Garden, the Opéra national de Paris, and the San Francisco, Chicago Lyric, and Seattle Operas. Ms. Blythe was named *Musical America*'s Vocalist of the Year in 2009, received an Opera News Award in 2007, and won the Tucker Award in 1999. She is a graduate of The Crane School of Music. Photo courtesy Stephanie Blythe.

JOYCE DIDONATO: Being expressive with text is not rocket science. What more melodramatic way to express how terribly you suffer than with expressive consonants, which are supported fully on the breath? A double *ff* in Italian, as in *soffrire* (suffer): quadruple the *ffff* on the breath stream. Where you want to paint with the voice and the text, give more consonant and emphasis. And if you are doing it the right way, not employing the throat apparatus but connecting using the lower breath just like you connect to the vowels, you'll achieve a wonderful, supported *legato* with the flow of expressive word-painting floating above.

CHRISTINE GOERKE: The basis of all good and healthy singing is *legato*. I plan vowel to vowel to make sure I have the line going. Consonants, obviously, are wildly important, but once you understand how to connect all the vowels to make a *legato* line, there is no way that you can insert the consonants, even with force, and interrupt that line. Then it's an issue of knowing your space, the acoustic, the score, and how much consonant you need. Also, if you don't know what's going on underneath you in the orchestra, you have no idea how explosive you need to be with your words. You have to combine all of these things together and find a way to keep your line and add as much consonant as you need to be clear.

DENYCE GRAVES: Ah, yes, in our efforts to crisply articulate, it is important that those efforts not impede or obstruct the beauty of the sound. Beautiful singing is based on a *legato* line, a seamless flow of spun air. Singing through the consonants is, of course, the biggest problem, as it can stop the air flow. I sing from vowel sound to vowel sound as long as possible and have the consonants be crisp and fast so as not to disrupt the *legato* line. For diphthongs or triphthongs, I sing into the first vowel sound longer and add the other sound at the very end, so that the first vowel sound is sustained longer. Singing isn't speaking, and the integrity of the melodic line is to be preserved and foremost, in my opinion. I'd rather be felt than understood, and my diction is pretty good!

GREER GRIMSLEY: Technique is important. When technique is really solid you are able to live on the vowels as long as possible, while making the consonants when they need to drop in. There are languages where the consonants are explosive, like English or German, and you have to learn how to do that without costing yourself. Also, there's music to every language. For example, with Richard Strauss, if you're having trouble fitting in a rhythm, just look at the text and say it, and the rhythm is so evident. Strauss was very good at notating that, as are all great composers. Understanding what you're singing is foremost in communication.

THOMAS HAMPSON: One of the fundamental differences between singing and speaking is that when we speak, we separate vowels with consonants.

When we sing, every vowel that is sung has every other vowel to be sung resonating in it, and we bind vowel to vowel in a consistency of resonance known as *legato*. This migration from vowel to vowel is facilitated by the consonants that are sung as well—even aspirated consonants, to some extent. I have enjoyed singing in some fourteen languages, quite fun and challenging, everything from old Turkish to Yiddish to Czech to Russian. I think it was my work in Russian that gave me real clarity about this process. I love consonants and have never met one I couldn't make friends with. This idea that we have to deal with consonants as if they interrupt our *legato* is a priori the wrong mind-set.

ALAN HELD: Approach all languages and diction from within your technique. Projecting diction means keeping the vocal production forward. The major problem is that we tend to let vowels and consonants fall too far back. This means that they become less easily understood, which actually decreases vocal projection. Both the lips and the throat are used to form vowels, but one cannot lose sight of the mask either. Don't let consonants explode at the beginning of a word (which throws the following vowel out of line) or anticipate them too much at the end of a word (which destroys the integrity of the vowel). Finish the word on a vowel, and then apply a consonant.

JONAS KAUFMANN: The vowel is the most important ingredient of every word. So you concentrate on the right sound of the vowels and place the consonants softly on top of them. In an interview, I heard Fritz Wunderlich talking about the so-called *Vokalausgleich* (vowel balance), how vowels should be formed more or less with the same mouth position and similar sound. This is the only way to sing real *legato*, since the flow isn't interrupted and no syllable sticks out. I personally also feel that /u/ is the most important vowel of all, as it lowers the larynx, and ideally all vowels should come out of /u/. So you leave the jaw in the same position, and the tongue, in a relaxed manner, should form the vowels in your mouth. If the tongue root gets stiff, it pulls up the larynx, but if you do it in a smooth and relaxed way, it works. It's fantastic!

SIMON KEENLYSIDE: Ideally, good diction is not about spitting gobbets of text into a room. Rather, one carries a line of sound into the hall: a really good *legato* onto which is pegged the text. How that is achieved is by practice, endless patience, and understanding how one note relates to the next, at times with an early consonant so as to leave a difficult passage less complicated to negotiate, and at other times a late consonant for the same effect. In extreme cases, I often find myself using an unphonated consonant—early or late—and then introducing the sound a fraction of a second later. It helps ensure that the word is heard where there may be too much "competition" for sound.

KATHLEEN KIM: Consonants are very important, but if you sing as you speak, that is best. However, I usually record myself so I can fix it if there are any words that are unclear or I have to add more consonants.

ANA MARÍA MARTÍNEZ: The whole purpose of diction is to exclaim the text. The vowels have to be true to the language, with the consonants giving the parameters of the words; otherwise, it is all just a long diphthong sound. You have to do very diligent work with your own imagination for the meaning and the picturesque qualities of those words. I do not think I form the sounds in the throat, but in the mouth cavity, with some soft and hard palate feeling. I love the /i/ sound because it is quite frontal and, for me, the anchor vowel. If I sing /a/ I first think the /i/ and put the other vowel around it like a cushion cover. If I think throat, it starts to get stuck and then I am not free. I like to think mask behind the eyes.

LISETTE OROPESA: Learn to speak the languages and get the grammar in your head. It's also important to get the text in your speaking voice by practicing the recits without singing them.

ERIC OWENS: Diction is a part of *legato* and the musical line. Clear consonants don't have to mean sacrificing *legato*. We singers have this luxury and responsibility of text, this extra communicative device that instrumentalists don't have, so we have to make it an integral part of our overall approach. Diction is achieved by way of the lips, teeth, and tongue, but the face doesn't need to go crazy with contortions in order to create different consonants and vowel sounds. The vowels *a, e, i, o, u* are very close together, so you don't need to have as much movement of the face muscles to go from one vowel to the next as one might think.

DIMITRI PITTAS: It has to do with communicating and being committed to what I'd like to get across. I think that diction takes care of itself. There are those moments where you need to think a little technically if it's a strange passage and goes through a weird part of the *passaggio* that's hard to tackle. Ultimately, I think that diction becomes most refined when there are the fewest amount of lines between point A and point B—point A being the thought and point B being what is being expressed vocally. The clearer that line is, the clearer the diction.

EWA PODLEŚ: One cannot just sing the notes perfectly. You have to give more to express the words and meaning. The text and clear diction are essential. Some might say I exaggerate, but I do what is required to deliver the text.

JENNIFER ROWLEY: For me, the people who have the best diction are those who have the best vocal techniques. The jaw and tongue are free and nothing is shaking or moving, so everything is far easier to understand even if you don't speak the language. If you don't speak the language, you have to do your homework and break out your Nico Castel and see which vowels are open and closed, etc. Good vocal technique will give you the dexterity to be able to have good diction.

GERHARD SIEGEL: From the very beginning, it was made clear to me by my voice teacher that singing without very good diction makes no sense. And it didn't matter in which language. That it sounds unnatural, often exaggerated, in the practice room is obvious. An excessively good pronunciation is essential. This distinctness is necessary in any language. To overemphasize *legato*, which is currently common practice, is not good. The understanding of the text must be from the beginning of the study as important as proper tones and healthy technique.

3. WHAT IS YOUR IDEAL PLACEMENT OF THE VOICE FOR RESONANCE AND THE MOST BEAUTIFUL TONE?

STEPHANIE BLYTHE: I do not need to think of that anymore, fortunately. However, you should feel where the sound originates, along with the mask, breath, and the support you are giving. You must work on this combination until it becomes natural or second nature.

LAWRENCE BROWNLEE: I remember a teacher saying to me that your sound should be so forward that you can look at it. I don't think the nose; I don't think nasal. I just think of my sound as very forward. Even when I go down to the chest, it is still with a placement that has to be heady. I can sing a low C, which for a tenor is not bad, but I also have to be able to access my high Cs. I know that if I put weight on the bottom, or if I sing fat in the middle, I won't be able to access the top. So I approach the natural voice in that I bring the head voice down. You are your sound, which is a unified sound from top to bottom.

NICOLE CABELL: I strive to sing with balanced forward placement. This means not pushing it in the nose or mask, not driving the sound forward, but thinking of the sound buzzing between my lips and forehead. This is step one, followed by the idea of looping the sound through the back of the head (again no lower than the upper jaw), up and around, and back toward those frontal resonators. In other words, while forward placement is very important, I cannot shut off back space, or a connection with the openness of the whole head. This balance is very tricky, so it's a high-wire balancing act of making sure to keep that forward buzz all of the time, while not veering toward a strident, overly exaggerated tone.

JOSEPH CALLEJA: This is all visualization because you can't place the vocal cords somewhere right or left or up or down. You have to aim the voice to the resonators—to your nose and head or to the cranial structure, which gives us our voice. Let the voice guide you to the most comfortable placement, because cranially speaking, we are all different—differently sized noses, mouths, sinuses. It all changes the sensation of vocal production, but to say you place the voice in the nose or sinus is ridiculous. Release the voice and let it find its best position. Depending on the repertoire, sing as high in the cranium as possible. Importantly, you have to sing with the base, and the base, for me, is the breath or the diaphragm. You have to release the jaw as much as possible. The more you try to engage the jaw or try to control the jaw, the worse it is.

DAVID DANIELS: Beautiful tone is not so much about placement as it is about *legato* and even tone through a phrase of music. It is that *bel canto* approach to singing, where you connect each word with a constant spinning of the air. I studied with my mother as a boy soprano, and she was very big on forward mask placement, which was ironic because her voice had a lot of ring but had a very warm sound. The most important aspect of having a beautiful sound is having a forward feel to it, but I don't know if you can really technically teach that. You can talk about it and you can demonstrate it, but how do you get someone to sing really forward? There are a hundred different aspects of the vocal mechanism to make it really a beautiful and present sound, and it's not just about singing in the mask and singing forward.

CHRISTINE GOERKE: That depends on what part of your voice you're in. The space that you make, or the placement that you use in your *passaggio*, isn't exactly the same space and placement you would use if you were in your lower *passaggio*, the middle of your voice or up very high. Also, I am that weird singer that never thinks about soft palate. If I think too much, I can't sing. I prefer the words *space* and *point* to *resonance* and *focus*. In the end you have to be really well acquainted with your instrument to know how much point versus how much space you need in order to make the most beautiful sound on any given note or vowel.

DENYCE GRAVES: Resonance. Yes, areas like the face, the cheekbones, the forehead, the chest, the hard palate, the pharynx, and the body itself are all vibrators. The vocal folds are the transmitters through which the air passes before the resonance actually happens. I have been taught a "high" placement, one that is not in line with the speaking voice. Most of my singing teachers taught me to sing into the "yawn space" along with training the ear to hear and feel the "center of the sound." Then I find vocal amplification and resonance. A lot can depend on imagery and imagination and the ear that brings the intention into focus. We must allow the instrument to seek its own vibrating surfaces.

GREER GRIMSLEY: I use that term judiciously because if someone gives us directions, there is a tendency to overcorrect. It's a sense of releasing the sound, which you want as forward as possible. I don't specifically say placement, but it's where you feel that sound on the bones in the front of your face. It's about releasing the control in your throat to allow the sound to flow freely through the resonators. As a visual aid, I will go in back of a singer and form a triangle with my fingers right in front of their nose, where you want to feel that sound. It's not a question of putting it there; it's a question of feeling it and releasing the sound to those resonators. An exercise to feel where to resonate is to aspirate an *h* and feel the warm air flow through the nostrils and on top of the hard palate at the same time.

THOMAS HAMPSON: I do not use the word *placement*, but if there is one "place" that is enlivened (my voice teacher used the word *impingement*), it is where the tone starts in our head. It is where the hard and soft palate join in the back of the mouth. I certainly feel my voice in my head before I feel it anywhere else in my body. I like the sensation of the ng or /ŋ / resonance that enlivens the nasopharynx and buccal pharynx at the same time. This starting of the tone encourages a supported and low larynx and actually informs the physical energy necessary to support its resonance.

ALAN HELD: Placement is the most important aspect of my singing. I try to have my inhalations start "in place," and my vocalization be exactly in the same place, in the mask. Without it, I couldn't produce a sound that resonates or carries two feet in front of my face, let alone over a Wagnerian or Straussian orchestra. A high soft palate helps in resonance, but let the airflow itself help raise the palate. I advocate a relaxed tongue, no matter where you place it. There are singers who raise the tip of their tongue, some who leave it flat, some who force it to always be touching the bottom front teeth, and some who mercilessly swallow it when singing. Obviously, I'm not a fan of the tongue swallowers. But I've found singers who do very well with the tongue doing various things.

JONAS KAUFMANN: I do not feel the voice in the mask. I know that it is a common idea of placing it there, but I believe the more you connect it to your body, the more you're relaxed and open. The goal should be not to "place" the voice anywhere, but release it so that it can unfold as it needs to. Five years ago, when I was singing *piano*, my lips would curl inward. I felt more secure in doing that. But then I decided to keep the mouth and lips open, more like a trumpet. But I would not call that placing the voice in a certain spot. I think if you do everything in your body right and the larynx is down and relaxed, it automatically falls into the right position.

SIMON KEENLYSIDE: I don't think I can answer this one. It's color that is of most interest to me. It's the thing that occupies me only slightly less than the words and notes.

KATHLEEN KIM: I honestly don't think about it. I don't try to place the sound. I just try to feel the sensation, which for me is more space in the back of my throat. I don't try to find a beautiful tone. I just use support and the right sensation. Then I don't feel like I'm singing, but the singing feels effortless.

ANA MARÍA MARTÍNEZ: Think of a living room where you are going to live but you can move around in that area. It is not a fixed place but an area. I feel an area behind the eyes and the nose and above the bridge of the nose. I think of that as resonance, not nasal sound. However, in the higher range I have abstract images and feel as if the nose detaches and the top of the head almost lifts off, or goes over my head. I also feel the hard palate in this resonance. I recently discovered the flageolet, the whistle, and with that I think of the soft palate, because the sound seems to come from there, but without controlling it.

LISETTE OROPESA: Yes, I focus on aiming toward French vowels more often than not. I do also think of a lift in the soft palate for ideal breath flow and a buoyant sound.

ERIC OWENS: I feel resonance and placement, mostly, in the front/mask area, but with an open sound. I'll add height to it from time to time, but I never feel that this space is in the back. If anything, I'll feel like the space is through the top of my head, in addition to the forward placement.

JENNIFER ROWLEY: If the voice is free from the bottom of the breath up to the placement in the mask area and you have an open throat and no tension in the face, you can put the voice wherever you want it to go. If you want to color something with straight tone or with *pianissimo* or chest voice, you can. As long as everything is open and free, you can do anything you want. Again, for me it's imagery. It's like placing a baseball if you're batting: you place your foot wherever you want in order to aim the ball, when you swing the bat to left or right field.

GERHARD SIEGEL: The term *mask* is well known to me, but I think singing can be reduced to five things that need to be pictured individually and differently for everyone. It should be noted I'm basically pragmatic, and I have learned: breathe deeply, support, mouth open, tongue down, tongue tip stays on the front incisors, and sing. I think it is not more than that.

4. WHAT DO YOU DO TO CREATE A VARIETY OF SOUND AND COLOR IN YOUR SINGING?

STEPHANIE BLYTHE: I always connect sound directly to the text, which dictates the variety of vocal color. Vocal color is pictorial for me. I think about how a particular word sounds, almost like vocal onomatopoeia. I once worked with Barbara Bonney on just a simple Brahms song. It was a private coaching on how to sing softly by thinking about the text and connecting to it. When I thought about what I wanted to say and what the text was saying, the dynamics and the color changed automatically. There is such infinite variety in text, so there is infinite variety in sound.

LAWRENCE BROWNLEE: The voice needs to sound the same from top to bottom. Having four or five different voices is not conducive to having a successful career. Some people, however, will have very different sounds. I have a great deal of respect for Ewa Podleś with her many different sounds, which is part of who she is as a singer. For me, though, I sing with the naturalness of what my voice is, which is to have a unified sound from the top to the bottom.

Lawrence Brownlee
One of the most sought-after artists internationally, Lawrence Brownlee has been featured at the Metropolitan Opera, Covent Garden, the Hamburg and Vienna State Operas, La Scala, and the Opéra national de Paris. He has worked with the New York Philharmonic, the Boston and Cleveland Symphonies, and the Berliner Philharmoniker, and performed with Cecilia Bartoli, Renée Fleming, Anna Netrebko, and Joyce DiDonato. Brownlee has appeared on numerous CDs and DVDs. His most recent album, *Virtuoso Rossini Arias*, was released in 2014 by Delos. Brownlee was named Seattle Opera's 2008 Artist of the Year and was the winner of both the 2006 Marian Anderson and Richard Tucker Awards. Photo courtesy Derek Blanks.

NICOLE CABELL: It is easy to achieve color simply by thinking of the meaning behind the words. A word like *sciagurato* (scoundrel) can be sung through gritted teeth, or making the word ugly by driving the sound. The darker tones usually can be produced by singing with a more rounded lip position, a little more space in the head resonators, or a darkened expression in the face. Happiness involves a smile upon the face, which spreads the mouth position just enough to brighten up the sound. Breathiness translates to breathlessness, and can be used for expressive purposes. The vast majority of the time the music is written with color and variety in it, and singing the music straight from the page, with keen attention paid to dynamics, tempo, and rhythm, can achieve an accurate interpretation.

JOSEPH CALLEJA: I have a distinctive voice and I had it from day one. I do not work on my sound or the distinctiveness that is there. That is my timbre, and, to be honest, I think it is very hard to alter one's own timbre. With regard to color and warmth and to different inflections, you need to study and reflect. It is 90 percent technique and 10 percent heart. As the old singers used to say, "Think the note before you sing it." To give the muscles time to form the note, that's again practice and trial and error and checking what colors work and don't work. There are no rules as such for this. What works for me is I try to think of the word, *la parola*, and I immerse myself in the character.

DAVID DANIELS: I sing with my technique and my voice that I developed as a boy with both my parents, who were my teachers. I developed my sound by listening to great singers as a child. So it's a most natural way of singing. I don't think about creating some sound. I think we all sing with the voice we are given and try to do the best with it that we can. I am a true believer in singing beautifully, and I can have color change within the palette of beauty. Beautiful singing is what we all strive to do, but many people would think that's boring. You need to have something ugly and edgy or else it's not interesting, but I think there can be beauty even with an edgy emotion. When it comes down to it, I want to make a beautiful sound.

JOYCE DIDONATO: When the voice is in a "good zone," I don't feel like I am singing at all. If anything, I feel like I am painting. It is the timbre of the vowels and consonants that is the pigment; the color and speed of breath becomes the brush stroke. It's not simply making "sound"; it's being completely at one with the character and emotion via the music and breath. I tend to also think very strongly about singing into the harmony and not simply concentrating on the vocal line. The vocal line cannot be disconnected from the harmony but should actually make the harmony happen, which is, I think, where the goose-bump moments come from, because we are then allowing the entire harmonic system to carry the sound, not just the isolated vocal line.

CHRISTINE GOERKE: I am huge on the text and the cool things that we get to do with our instruments. I am not afraid to make an ugly sound for an ugly word. I think that Americans have fallen into this "make beautiful sounds all the time" thing. But if we are only making beautiful sounds, we are only utilizing a quarter of our instruments. I talk about space-versus-point resonance (see question 3). I can go 100 percent point, and that will make quite a sound, or go way back with more space and make a very different sound. I can also go in between. So it becomes an issue of what space and what point I want and how much of each. The composer set the words in the way that he or she heard them, but then it's up to us to make decisions that change colors.

DENYCE GRAVES: One can do a lot with shaping the vowels themselves to create different colors, but it is absolutely imperative that one keep the fundamental center to the sound. I have a dark, velvety instrument and I have to constantly work to keep my voice slender to maintain its vocal presence and core, so that the overtones accompany the phonation. I've always been taught to work or tune for sensation and not for sound or volume. Once the singer has a handle on this technically, he or she can then play with the voice and experiment and enjoy creating different colors and have a wider range of expression. Technique is the basis for everything!

GREER GRIMSLEY: My first voice teacher told me to go off and play with my voice and bring things back, which is something I've kept with me all these years because there is some validity to it. Not that you go off and scream until you're hoarse, but see what your voice can do. Do not restrict yourself to superficial ideas of what can be. Explore what is possible. Let text feed your music making, and let the music feed your text.

THOMAS HAMPSON: I do not believe in coloring your voice. Our voices are colored because of our emotional and intellectual connection as to why it is we are saying a particular thing. I don't believe in an a priori color of German, or Russian or French or any damn thing. And I don't believe in, "Oh, I think I'll give it a pastel #4 with a splash of something on this vowel." All of these things—whether in a Schubertian or Mahlerian or Debussyian context, etc.—have to be what you determine to communicate. I was awakened to these possibilities in my singing when I worked with Elisabeth Schwarzkopf. They were all about the "why" information and about the musical language being sung.

ALAN HELD: Mastering the ability to change colors and provide healthy effects is important to anyone wanting to communicate strong emotion properly. It is something we all work on constantly. Again, this goes back to placement. If I have the voice in the mask, I can support the sound there at all volumes and in most of my range. It is important to be able to practice your singing at various volumes and on all of the vowels. Learning to keep the tone at the proper resonance is the secret of singing. As singers, our goal is to have the voice resonate freely and accurately from the bottom of the range to the top—with all vowels, at all volumes—and to have it happen evenly. Gee, that's not too hard now, is it?

JONAS KAUFMANN: You shouldn't do artificial coloring, darkening, or lightening. You just have to create real feelings according to text and situation, and immediately they are reflected in the sound. Of course, you must know the meaning of every word you sing so that your conscious and also unconscious combine to inspire different colors and shades. When I sing in French, Italian, English, or German, I know exactly what I'm talking about. Sometimes I find new layers, new interpretations, and new double meanings while I'm doing it, which changes the mood and the color. So again, colors come naturally once you have your technique and aren't distracted by technical issues. You just have to interpret, and the colors come automatically.

SIMON KEENLYSIDE: The dialogue that one can achieve by choosing the right color is enormous. Think of how our voices sound at times of great stress or high emotion. The color alone can affect us deeply. I see it as tinkering with the engine of the voice. If it's a wide variety of different music and styles that fires you up, then you will be forced to address all issues of color. A desire to be a good conduit for the story will give rise to a wide range of color. For me, it's almost a game. No singer will be able to do it all, but if we achieve even some of it all the time (or all, some of the time?), then we are not doing badly.

KATHLEEN KIM: I think if you are expressing the words, then you don't need different colors. It comes naturally with the words. It doesn't come artificially but in the context. If you want to say "I love you," then you sing it in a certain way, but if you express something angrily, you sing it differently.

ANA MARÍA MARTÍNEZ: For me it's picturesque imagination, which is very alive with different images. The colors and feelings are conjured up at those images.

LISETTE OROPESA: Breath pressure can be manipulated to create dynamics, which gives the listener a sense of variety and flow. It's also important to focus on the direction of the musical phrase. So, I ask myself: where is this phrase going? Then I sing it with that purpose in mind.

ERIC OWENS: This question is of great interest to me because many young singers are more interested in creating a color than going for clarity of sound. I'm not a fan of the idea of "creating" colors with young singers, as it may lead to the manipulation of the vocal production. If you start creating colors and tones, you start piling things up on your technique that are unnecessary, especially if you try to "manufacture" these sounds in your throat or around your neck area. It ends up encumbering the sound and making your voice smaller than it is. I think you should actually go for a free-flowing, uncomplicated sound, with the clarity of pitch being your primary concern. I find that trying to "make" an already beautiful voice beautiful ends up making the *singing* unnecessarily undesirable.

DIMITRI PITTAS: When you're first discovering how to create different sounds and colors, it's nice to be able to just play technically and discover what kinds of things work. Find those colors and connect the voice first just on a purely technical standpoint, and then see if they work with what it is you're communicating. If I'm saying something that requires a lot of depth, it helps to have that palette of colors to apply, and eventually it just becomes second nature. A lot of it has to do with where you place the sound: in your mouth, on your lips, etc. A romantic sound may have a lot more head voice in it, the sound of honesty and vulnerability may come from the chest.

JENNIFER ROWLEY: I like the idea of using diction to create color. You can use words, elongate consonants and darken vowels to create more colors. You can color with the different registers of the voice as well, for higher voices especially. I love when a more dramatic voice can color something by the use of chest or *voce di petto*. I also love the use of *pianissimi* for color, if you can create a nice spinning sound to make a magical moment. I also think about where the vowel is placed. You can gather up, close, or open the vowel for color or to create more darkness. You can also use your mouth, throat space, lips, and tongue to create colors, too.

5. HOW DO YOU MANAGE THE *PASSAGGIO* (TO THE HIGH REGISTER)?

STEPHANIE BLYTHE: The notion of passage can become a real stumbling block, and over the years I have sort of developed a personal technique that works for my voice but may not work for everyone. Suffice it to say that I try not to think of a separate place for high and low. I just know how it feels when I am doing it right: smack behind my teeth with a big dome over my head, supported through the entire range on the same breath.

LAWRENCE BROWNLEE: There is a "turnover" that happens. Every tenor has the break: some at E-flat, E, or F, but mine is a little bit higher. I always think slender in the *passaggio*. If I get thinner, the sound can get through the *passaggio* without any real interruption. It's tubular, if you will. I sing in my sound, but I make sure that I keep it in track in a way that goes through the *passaggio*, thinking slender so that I don't ever get too fat.

NICOLE CABELL: I tend to operate from the viewpoint of chest, head/ falsetto, and whistle voice. Exercises starting high and moving slowly and easily down the scale from *sol* to *do* on /a/ or /u/ exposes the problems that need work. If my transition is not smooth, it means my larynx is high and squeezed as opposed to the slight yawn position, or my nasal passage is open, which is solved by making sure my soft palate is closing off my nasal passage. My jaw naturally drops when I sing higher. The transition should match a vocal siren generally note for note. Gradually slowing down my sirens and transitioning into singing has helped me, and also establishes where my jaw naturally drops. Working on sirens and experimenting with the sensation of a slight drop in the jaw may help.

JOSEPH CALLEJA: There are two schools of thinking: one school is that the tenor voice has two different registers, while others think it has one. I believe the voice has two registers, but they have to become one. We should find the path of least resistance or, in this case, of *correct* resistance, because without resistance there is no singing. Subglottal pressure creates singing, but the more you force, the smaller and more constricted the sound is. So what I try to do is educate the sound. Pavarotti thought of the hourglass when approaching the *passaggio*, but I think of an inverted pyramid. So, a normal pyramid in the lower approach, then a thinning and an inverted pyramid over the *passaggio*. It is important to sing the right repertoire, so when you reach the top notes, you can sing them and not be so tired. You get a little tired in every performance no matter how good your technique is.

DAVID DANIELS: The countertenor voice is not like a soprano or even a mezzo, but I do have a *passaggio*. The lower one is between B-flat and B-natural, and there's a real obvious one between the E-flat and E in the top space. That's very "baritonal" because that's where their *passaggio* begins. I do think of covering, and if I were to work with baritones or tenors, I would speak of covering or the narrowing of the sound in a much more specific way than I do with my singing. There is a modification that happens in that area, a narrowing of the sound that has to happen in order to launch up into the top voice in a healthy way. The appearance of covering is much more apparent in the male voices than in a countertenor. A lot of people shy away from the word *cover* because they equate that word with *woofy*. I don't. There's a difference to me.

CHRISTINE GOERKE: When I started singing I absolutely believed that I only had the *passaggio* to the top. Mine was F to A. The older I've gotten and the bigger my voice has gotten, my *passaggio* has dropped to D to F-sharp. It wasn't that I was singing differently; it was that I had to pay more attention to support, breath control, and the color that I was making. However, what's dangerous for a singer is that we want to grab hold of everything and make it exactly right and control it. This is going to sound crazy, but sometimes not controlling it is the best thing we could possibly do. The more we grab at things, the worse we make it for ourselves. I also have a *passaggio* at the bottom where I need to make decisions about mixing for chest. That has moved up. So my *passaggi* have moved closer together.

DENYCE GRAVES: There can be lots of controversy when it comes to managing the passage through the different registers in a singer's voice. I start as low and relaxed as is comfortable and sing an /o/vowel sound beginning at the very bottom of the register and *glissando* to as high as I comfortably can go. Doing this, you notice these subtle divisions and where they occur naturally; some people call them "breaks." I always work to bring a homogeneity to the entire voice. I vocalize chromatic scales through the *passaggi* on a variety of vowel sounds and adjust by blending those sounds. I work in both directions, from the lowest note to the top, and then from the top to the bottom. It exposes weaknesses in the technique like breath and support, which are vital when working through the *passaggi*. The goal is to make it sound like one voice from bottom to top.

GREER GRIMSLEY: I am of the belief that the voice will do what it should do naturally if you stay on your support. There is not a lot of vowel modification. I'm not talking wide open to progress to those upper notes, but I do feel a narrowing in that area. The *passaggio* or transition point works naturally, along with a redoubling of the support and giving a little more energy as you pass through that area of your voice.

THOMAS HAMPSON: So much of this issue of the *passaggio* is thinking about a gear you've got to deal with. I prefer Oren Brown's idea of light and heavy adjustment. That idea allows me elasticity for a heavier adjustment in a higher range, or I can lighten it up, making sure it's connected to the rest of my resonance, but in a lighter way. But I don't like the idea that you get to a certain part of your voice, which for a baritone is around D-sharp, and all of a sudden you have this no-man's-land you have to deal with to release the G and A-flat. I do not see how putting it in gears and places helps that process. I want to remain elastic in that process. In fact, the word *register* is better thought of for pipe organs.

ALAN HELD: Every singer's *passaggio* is going to be different. You can't jump over it or skirt under it. One should not only look at the voice getting higher in working through the *passaggio*, but also start above the *passaggio* and work down. I do a great amount of the "siren" exercise—trying to line up the voice and resonance from the top to the bottom. I find this more helpful than constantly approaching from the bottom. I drop my jaw as I sing higher, but not too much. Some space is added but should not be overdone. I think of the high notes in an upward as well as a frontal placement. It also is important to learn not to pressurize your singing through the *passaggio*. Primarily, I think of focus as I ascend to the high notes. Placement is the key.

JONAS KAUFMANN: For me, the most important thing is that you let the voice instinctively find the right way to the *passaggio* without trying to think where to go. There's a trick I found useful: sing while closing your ears or even covering your mouth in order to prevent you from influencing and manipulating the voice. It places itself automatically. It really works and is something that is extremely powerful. The only thing to think at the beginning is the soft palate: this gentle yawning, or the beginning of a yawn, or whatever you would call it. It's a very gentle thing and there is no forcing. So I think of a lift of the soft palate, a kind of covering, when I go into the high register through the *passaggio*.

SIMON KEENLYSIDE: Aha! One of the foundation issues for all singers. There is, of course, an "open" position beneath the *passaggio* and a "closed" one above it. There is also a closed-open position, and an open-closed one. And to my mind, therein lies the clue. The sound can then be better integrated to what has gone before, either descending or ascending from the preceding phrases. To have good effective high notes, reliable and over a career, one must take good care of the preceding phrases. The approaches, they are the springboards to the top. I always think of the region of the *passaggio* as being like the shape of an hourglass. One has to "waist" the sound, taking the foot slightly off the gas (as one passes through the neck of the glass) before allowing it to blossom again above and in the bony resonances of the head.

KATHLEEN KIM: Just one word: support. Actually, more support. Then after the *passaggio* I open the voice.

ANA MARÍA MARTÍNEZ: I recently discovered the flageolet (the whistle), and with that I do also think of the soft palate, because the sound seems to come from there. I think there are two *passaggi*, especially for sopranos. E at the top of the staff is one, but then there's another one at B-natural or so, and then you have to go into the flageolet space. For example, Antonia in *Tales of Hoffmann* has those high notes. In general Offenbach keeps the voice in the *passaggio*. So I use the flageolet, but always grounded. It's like a thick rope that you are pulling as you are sustaining; otherwise it's going to be too highly placed.

LISETTE OROPESA: In the simplest of terms, yes, I use the word *register*. Covering or focusing the sound through the *passaggio* is how to get through it. It's the bottleneck of the vocal range.

ERIC OWENS: Having been a woodwind player, I'm well acquainted with the idea of "breaks" in the scale of your instrument and having to spend much time smoothing them over. The same has to be done in singing. You're not going to sing open all the way to the top because it'll sound like yelling, not singing. There are a few "breaks" in my voice, but I cover the voice, usually around E-flat above middle C, which I can sing open or closed, depending on the style of the music or the drama of the particular phrase. For me, the upper break is best managed with a frontal placement, singing in a way that is truly *legato*, which helps to make the top actually sound like the continuation of your voice and not like someone else started singing. Ultimately, the answer lies with each individual singer.

DIMITRI PITTAS: It's good to find an /i/ vowel that's comfortable in the middle voice and maintain the structure of that vowel through the *passaggio*. The structure changes from /i/ to an /œ/ but always traveling through the /i/ vowel. The vibration of pitch is what actually changes; hence, adjusting the airflow while maintaining the /i/ structure is what helps you through the *passaggio*.

JENNIFER ROWLEY: *Passaggio* is most easily managed if you think economically. I like to say "singing on the interest" of the voice and not blowing too much air nor taking too much sound up through that area. Then you can let the sound bloom. It is an issue for young singers because you can hear it in your head and feel it in your throat. It can be scary because some singers say that they hear air going through the *passaggio*. So they hear air and grab at it to try to push through the *passaggio*, which is the worst thing you could do. If the vowels are too open and you're carrying weighted heft up through the *passaggio*, oftentimes the top will cut off. Sometimes singers will crack because they are carrying too much weight up to the top.

GERHARD SIEGEL: The break is the problem area for all. There are exercises like the vocal balance that need to be carried through the registers and must be practiced. The danger to sing with three different voices (that is, that the voice sounds different in the low, medium and high "registers") is very great. Very often, one can observe onstage that the voice is deliberately darkened, for example, in the low and mid-central position to achieve a baritone color, and then, in the high position, the voice is suddenly shining like a tenor. (That is only an example of the tenors.) Another phenomenon is the sudden excessive darkening of the voice from the break. That the voice must be "covered" is not to be taken lightly, but the voice should and must, in my opinion, have the same sound through top and bottom in all three registers. The voice in the lower register carries the best, if one uses the "think bright" idea.

6. WHAT DO YOU CONSIDER THE MOST DIFFICULT PART OF VOCAL TECHNIQUE, AND HOW DID YOU MASTER IT?

STEPHANIE BLYTHE: *Coloratura* was not natural for my voice. I worked with my teacher Patricia Misslin at The Crane School of Music on different scales and exercises. With practice and through her help, I not only learned to sing fluidly, but also understood that through a focused, spinning vowel, I would have more power and equally be able to sing softly, which was very exciting.

LAWRENCE BROWNLEE: I always think about how I breathe and how I get going. Then I continue in that process of spinning the breath and the voice. However, it is always based on the standpoint that I know the things that can get in my way, namely, vocal production, freedom, and breath. As a young singer I had the sound very far back. So, in my approach, to make sure the sound is always forward, I purse my lips slightly. That reminds me to make sure my sound is forward so that it will hopefully travel to the back of the theater.

NICOLE CABELL: If my breath is slightly off and I'm breathing a little too shallow, I get tension that can manifest itself in my jaw or tongue. When my tongue is slightly gripped at the base, or depressed, this affects my larynx, and I develop tension in my body stemming from the muscles in my throat, which can result in troublesome breath. Muscle memory is key, and if I concentrate enough on my breath, it will eventually become natural. I must maintain a deep, almost thought-less physical understanding of the singing process without having to fret about my larynx.

JOSEPH CALLEJA: The one thing that is most difficult for an opera singer to achieve is consistency. Keeping the voice in the right place at the right time and right color. That takes years to achieve. Let there be no mistake, we are not just talking about the vocal cords, which are made of ligament, etc., and are affected by humidity level, hormones, emotions, lack of sleep, worry, whatever. The trick is to use technique to overcome those problems. A tenor is pushing the limit all the time. The bass baritone is the natural voice for a man, just like the soprano is the natural voice for a woman. Those of us born tenors are freaks of nature in a way, and we are pushing our limits all the time much more than other singers.

DAVID DANIELS: I would say the fast *fioritura* singing was never the most natural for me. It was something that always scared me and continues to. As I get older, it is not getting any easier. So I have made it part of my practice and warm-up routine, even if I'm doing a role that does not have it, because I think it's healthy for the voice. It keeps the flexibility that needs to be there even if you're not singing fast notes. (Considering that I'm a Handel singer, it's probably not the thing to tell you.) I have found, though, it is much better to have a moderate, clean tempo with *fioritura* then ultrafast, where you have to take thirty-five thousand breaths and have to be sloppy. It sounds much faster to be clean in the moderate tempo than fast and sloppy.

JOYCE DIDONATO: *All of it!* I've struggled with massive tongue tension, poor posture, and a right elbow, of all things, that apparently loves to hold copious amounts of tension. Learning to trust the breath has been the key to overcoming these challenges. My aim is to have a technique that allows me to make any musical choice I wish in the moment—and the key has always been the breath. However, not to be underestimated: we also must keep our minds free from the very destructive "inner voice" that is trying constantly to undermine us. These destructive mental hurdles may actually, in the end, be the most challenging for singers.

CHRISTINE GOERKE: When I was thirty-three everything started falling apart, so I began studying with Diana Soviero. The first thing she said was that I had disconnected from my low support. I thought I *was* low, and she said, "You're not low. You've got to support from your *vagina!*" It's weird, because you are wondering how you are supposed to do that in the

Nicole Cabell
Nicole Cabell attended the Eastman School of Music and the Ryan Opera Center before winning the 2005 BBC Cardiff Singer of the World competition. She has recorded solo and ensemble albums with Decca, Deutsche Grammophon, Delos, Opera Rara, and Blue Griffin. Ms. Cabell has appeared with many of the world's leading opera companies, including the Metropolitan Opera, Deutsche Oper Berlin, the Lyric Opera of Chicago, the Royal Opera House, Covent Garden, and the San Francisco Opera. Her symphonic engagements include the New York Philharmonic, the Cleveland Orchestra, Rome's Accademia Nazionale di Santa Cecilia, the Bavarian Radio Symphony Orchestra, and the Los Angeles Philharmonic. Photo courtesy Devon Cass.

lower pelvic region. What she also said was that if I don't feel like I have to pee, I'm not supporting low enough. My big thing was really understanding how far down I had to stretch, to connect, and to open. I think of support as low and as wide as possible at the bottom, like a triangle. I can't go up without going down and wide. But, in fact, the first time you connect, all of a sudden you're like, "Oh, that's it? Duh." There are so many "duh" moments. They're my favorite.

DENYCE GRAVES: It's a difficult answer, as it can change from performance to performance, depending on how the voice is that day. Some days the voice can be clear and easy and speak without effort, and there are other days that it can be veiled and stubborn. What I find maddening is that we have to sometimes be the servant to the instrument itself, and that is what vocal technique is about. The day that you're "in voice," sometimes, is the day you're at home doing the laundry! I work daily to master it, but discipline is *the* key!

GREER GRIMSLEY: I had never been trained classically nor had music training until I started college. I was very interested in musical theater. However, I never took that turn because when I got into opera, it was a love affair. I was so enthralled, so entranced, that I had two lessons a week with my teacher, and I paid for an extra lesson. I think the hardest part is trusting that your body knows that you don't have to drive so much, and also having the patience until your technique is second nature. I've seen colleagues on the road who are miserable because they are still trying to figure things out, simply because they have to think about technique.

THOMAS HAMPSON: Mastering the essence of every tone containing every other tone, which sounds like such a profoundly simple statement but which is the alpha and omega of vocal technique and goes back to the old Italian school. This is the concept of *messa di voce*: a voice swelling and receding on the same pitch as a function of expression. Remember that *messa di voce* is going to be different in the middle of your voice or in the top or bottom. A pithy word of advice: if you can't sing it quietly, you probably shouldn't sing it loudly. I believe that the voice is best trained from the lighter adjustment into the heavier adjustment and not the other way around. It is definitely going to be a lighter kind of sound, a constant vibration that remains even and balanced and connects all of your range.

ALAN HELD: Relaxation of the vocal apparatus is the most important part of vocal technique. This includes singing in the most natural procedural way. I constantly work on this and find, when I'm singing as naturally as possible, I can then do pretty much anything on a dramatic level. If I don't have natural singing going on, I'm too tied up to do anything but stand and sing, which is an anathema to me.

JONAS KAUFMANN: I would say that the most difficult part is to find your instrument, your unique sound given by nature. This is the ingredient that only you can bring. Everything else (breathing, etc.) they can explain to you, but finding your sound is something only you can know, following your instincts about what feels healthy and right, doesn't feel artificial, and lets you sing long without getting tired. It's really crucial to have an instrument that's comfortable and reliable. While finding your voice, you also have to be willing to really let it go, really free it. The idea that you can build your voice with Mozart is, in my view, entirely wrong. If you do not have first an open throat and deep breathing, Mozart can tie any singer into a thousand knots. It's also like this when you construct a building. You cannot begin with the delicate details and nuances. First the structure has to stand.

SIMON KEENLYSIDE: Every day I try to manage technical issues better. Some days one door shuts, and another door shuts! Other days, things go more according to plan. Actually, I say this with good reason. Why practice at all, if not to increase the chances that the voice will work well on any given occasion, in any given piece, in different weather or time zones, after plane journeys, and in dubious health or state of mind? Practicing technical things has always helped me in this respect. It keeps nerves at bay, and I enjoy it, too. I find the puzzle of any given song or opera an interesting pastime. Everything about technique is of equal importance, isn't it? All interconnected and the instrument, one holistic thing. Sometimes it's better to practice well for twenty minutes than sing for an hour, doing gentle, disciplined, and thoughtful work, addressing weaknesses and not just strengths.

KATHLEEN KIM: The most basic thing: breathing. When I was a student, I didn't know how to breathe properly. But when the breathing was fixed, most of the problems got solved.

ANA MARÍA MARTÍNEZ: Having the confidence for the top. It's funny— in the past year I started jogging (I come from a whole family of runners). I tried it, and the stamina and the mental peace of mind is tremendous. This parallels how I felt about my high notes. When I was eighteen, I thought I was more of an alto, because my nature is more introverted, and the high notes were just so flashy, which felt very uncomfortable. So, face your fear and you can go through it. It's the courage to sing all of those high notes, which are in almost every role I do. Now I don't feel self-conscious about it anymore.

LISETTE OROPESA: Evenness of tone—mastered through constant attention to breath flow and vowel modification.

ERIC OWENS: I haven't mastered anything—by a long shot! Students ask me when did I stop studying and start feeling comfortable, and I say that day has not arrived. I will be a voice student until the very end. I will say that one of the most difficult things as a performer (after all the practicing and relentless work on diction, technique, *legato*, etc.) is to simply let go. And when that happens in a performance, it's unbelievably special.

JENNIFER ROWLEY: Using technique on the stage and applying it. It's one thing to stand in a voice lesson with your teacher, and it's another thing to be on autopilot and think about staging and emotion and looking at the conductor. In other words, implementing it—getting into a performance and singing with technique. I know a lot of young singers who are great in a practice room and then they get onstage for a recital or performance and the technique goes out the window! I suggest practicing and singing in low-pressure programs and situations, so that you can concentrate on certain aspects of vocal and stage technique.

GERHARD SIEGEL: I had the great fortune to have a God-given natural "forward resonance." The most difficult part of technique is to bring the vocal placement as forward as possible so that the voice and the brilliance and metal are viable. The danger of staying throaty and back and singing on the "material" is enormous. This is one of the most difficult things in singing, especially because you have to also respond individually to students in explaining and to be sure to look for more than just two different images to explain what that means.

7A. FOR WOMEN: PLEASE EXPRESS SOME IDEAS ABOUT EITHER THE LOWEST OR HIGHEST PARTS OF THE VOICE (THE CHEST VOICE OR THE FLAGEOLET).

STEPHANIE BLYTHE: Chest voice can be an incredibly sexy tool to employ when it is done right. I try to never drive into the chest voice, but instead allow a healthy mix of head into it to allow for greater color opportunities. Allowing head voice also provides more spin, and the sound will travel *much* farther. It is very important to remember that the best way to develop the chest voice is through developing the middle voice. A healthy middle ensures *one* voice, not three.

NICOLE CABELL: Chest voice used to be an untouchable thing but can be a problem if ignored. In fact, I didn't have secure high notes until I understood how to sing low notes. For a woman, the majority of her music is written in head voice, and she may be used to dragging up the chest voice past her natural register, creating a myriad of problems. When I choose to sing jazz, musical theater, or any variation of modern music, the *tessitura* usually lies lower, and this is primarily how I learned to sing in chest voice. I have now been able to incorporate chest voice into my operatic repertoire.

JOYCE DIDONATO: I approach the chest voice as an extension of my natural speaking voice. I'll never force it, but simply allow it to "speak" and resonate. And then, in performance, I'll just go for it, because it's one of my favorite things to do as a singer—to plunge right down into the depths! I don't allow myself to indulge in that too often, but I definitely want to keep it as part of my vocal choices, because I think the communicative affect can be extremely powerful.

CHRISTINE GOERKE: I use it a lot. I love it. It makes me giggle when I do it. I am preparing The Dyer's Wife (*Die Frau ohne Schatten*) for the Met and there's a sustained low F. I'm like, rock on! My full-out chest voice— I call it my "man sound"—is not a pretty sound. That's okay, because some-times it shouldn't be a pretty sound. But sometimes it *is* meant to be a pretty sound. So how do you do that? I make sure that my vowels are rounded, and I use as much of that space in the back as I can. You should be able to make your chest voice sound much like the color of the rest of your voice, so you can make departures from there. If you can't make it sound somewhat like the rest of your voice, perhaps use it sparingly.

DENYCE GRAVES: I am one of those mezzos who believes in "blending" down into the chest voice as much as possible by bringing the head voice into the chest resonance—like a hum. Rarely do I "slam-dunk" down there, and I know plenty of mezzos who do. I realize that slam-dunking into the chest voice is impressive for the audience and can also feel good for the singer, plus it's fun. It feels as if you have super powers, but I try to keep a mix until it is no longer possible, and then I allow the chest voice to fall and find its natural vibration. There is a certain type of freedom that one feels when in chest voice. Feeling that rumble and power can be fascinating, but it should not be substituted for ongoing good technique.

KATHLEEN KIM: Some people use that term, *whistle tone*, but I don't use that expression. I don't use whistle tone. I think some people have nat-ural whistle tone, but I do not; I just use full voice. When I breathe in, I feel the tone going past the uvula. I breathe in and it goes far back. If I have to sing, for example, the high D in Zerbinetta, then I have to sing a small high D, but then for the high notes in Madame Mao I use full voice.

ANA MARÍA MARTÍNEZ: My teacher at Juilliard, Marlena Malas, had this exercise where we started on a pretty low pitch and opened the base to the chest and sang a tone mixed with high voice and chest, just allowing the voice to go there, not pushing it, but not afraid of it. A lot of the repertory I sing uses chest voice. Butterfly uses it, and Mimi is also quite low. I think in these cases, Puccini wants the text exclaimed clearly. The old saying applies: what goes up must come down, and what goes down must come up. The stronger you feel your lower register, the more it actually helps to open up the higher register. Don't fear it. Embrace it. Also be aware that if it hurts, you're not doing it right. There has to be a blend.

LISETTE OROPESA: Up high, it all comes with a lift of the soft palate and a supported breath flow. I suggest looking at the floor, which helps to lengthen the back of the neck and gets the sound going up through the crown of the head. When I sing down low, I open the mouth and I am not afraid of using chest voice. I like to say you can visit but not build a condo down there in the chest. Learning to mix the registers is always safest.

EWA PODLEŚ: I am a real contralto and typically use my chest register, which is a natural part of my kind of voice. People often say my chest notes are too heavy, more like a man's, but it is how I sing. It is my voice and it is impossible for it to be the same from top to bottom.

JENNIFER ROWLEY: I love to hear chest voice used in a dramatic fashion and for color. If Tosca does not use chest voice when she stabs Scarpia, I would have a problem with that. People do stay clear of chest voice, but with good supported technique, there shouldn't be any change going into the chest voice. There's no change in technique; there's a change in registration. I think a lot of people get scared because it sounds like there's a change of pressure in the voice. If your technique is serving you, there shouldn't be any pressure.

7B. FOR MEN: PLEASE EXPRESS SOME IDEAS ABOUT HIGH VOICE.

LAWRENCE BROWNLEE: I do something that I call "timbre matching." I don't want to say tricks or gimmicks, but if I have to sing an /u/ vowel, I think /o/ instead of /u/ (because /u/ is a vowel that is more closed than /o/), then that works for me. So, how do I find this /u/ vowel? I find the vowel that really works for me and I make it sound like an /u/. In other words, you have to find the vowel sound that helps you produce the vowels that are on the page.

JOSEPH CALLEJA: The smaller you imagine the sound of your high notes, the bigger they'll come out. It is a conundrum. I used to make a mistake when I was younger, to make a big high note. Now I start them from a small *piano* note and then expand them. The metaphor is that no one should hand you a heavy weight, but you should lift it yourself, because your body is not prepared for the weight you are given. Singing is exactly the same way. You float the note and then you expand it. If you look at the greatest coloraturas and the greatest singers, you hear this. Listen to Edita Gruberova—every high note she sings she starts *piano* and then she expands. I think Gruberova knows one or two things about high notes!

DAVID DANIELS: I don't use the term *high voice* as a countertenor. I use the term *head voice.* The chest voice is very important, although some of my colleagues refuse to use it. For me, chest voice adds one more color to the palette that I have. And for some things that are just too low, it adds some power to fill the house. But the important thing in the use of chest voice is that it stays blended with my head voice. I've yet to meet a countertenor that can go smoothly between head and chest without a blip. So I have to choose the places that are really going to work where I can blend it so it doesn't sound like I am changing registers, and that's usually with a consonant. But I do it in a way that nobody would know. And it's all thought through way before I walk out on the stage.

Joseph Calleja
Blessed with a golden-age voice that routinely inspires comparisons to "legendary singers from earlier eras: Jussi Björling, Beniamino Gigli, even Enrico Caruso" (AP), Joseph Calleja is one of the most acclaimed tenors of his generation. Born in Malta in 1978, he has already sung an impressive twenty-eight principal roles. His frequent appearances on the world's leading opera and concert stages have prompted him to be hailed as "arguably today's finest lyric tenor" (NPR) and led to his being voted *Gramophone* magazine's 2012 Artist of the Year. Calleja is a Grammy-nominated recording artist for Decca Classics, and his discography includes five solo albums. Photo courtesy Simon Fowler.

GREER GRIMSLEY: I stay connected to my support. Here is something to think about: take a look at the music on the page because the way the music is printed is totally incorrect as to how we produce notes. You look at the music and you think you have to follow the notes, but our voices work on the horizontal plane until the very high top. So instead of reaching for high notes and dropping for low notes, it's an easy horizontal stretch.

THOMAS HAMPSON: For high notes, I think of that upside-down hat IPA symbol, /Ω/. If you think the vowel and you sing in the resonance of the /Ω/, everybody's going to go home happy. If at the top of any voice you try to sing pure closed vowels, you're going to have a lot of trouble. Vowel modification sounds like some sort of trickery, but it is acoustics, pure and simple. Every voice has a particular resonance that will let the voice "work" as it needs to at the top. This is a release in unparalleled dimensions, and yet we still hear in that releasing resonance very defined vowels. I have helped a lot of young singers work out the top of their voice by working with this /Ω/ space. The word may be *questo* up there, but sing /kw Ω sto/ and think *questo*. We'll hear *questo*, and everyone's happy.

ALAN HELD: The high register is simply a part of my registers. The entire voice is connected from bottom to top. The registers must be produced in a manner where each is completely connected and in line with all others. I do use falsetto in vocal exercises. It helps me to find the placement for the rest of my voice. I don't use /u/ too much in my vocal exercises. If I do, it is in relation to the /i/ vowel, which is the king of vowels to me. In the /i/ vowel, we have the most proper placement and the most "open" throat. All vowels derive from the /i/ vowels. Every other vowel should have its properties. In the high register, I am always moving toward /i/. In fact all vowels are related and are grandfathered by /i/.

JONAS KAUFMANN: When I met my teacher Michael Rhodes, an American baritone from Brooklyn, he was in his seventies. At our first lesson he sang some high Bs with ease. I said to myself, "He's old, he's a, baritone and he can do that just like it's nothing, and I'm young, I'm a tenor, and I can't do it without effort?" That's what I need to learn! He taught me not to think about changing anything when going up and to keep the larynx in a low position. The gear change is where you cause yourself unnecessary problems. So when I sing from a low to a high note, I don't do anything except for lifting up the soft palate. The space you need for the high note should already be there for the low one. Rhodes also encouraged me to sing with my whole body. When people heard me doing this, they were all convinced I would lose my voice right away. Instead, it is this technique which has brought me to where I am.

SIMON KEENLYSIDE: I believe that the key to reliable high notes is in the middle register. That is the springboard that precedes those top notes. The position for me is almost a nondescript /ã/ nasal vowel, or /a/ placing. That catches the bony resonances of the head, but with an open throat. It encourages the larynx to stay low and the throat open. Hopefully, then the sound feeds back downward. If one uses, for example, an out-and-out /æ/ vowel up high, the sound might be in danger of being too horizontal, with the soft palate not sufficiently open so as to catch the head resonances. Sometimes, on an /i/ vowel up high, I will not incorporate any /a/ sound in the vowel, but use an acute and more horizontal vowel.

ERIC OWENS: Singing both bass and baritone rep, I approach the high notes slightly differently. For bass roles, notes are more cylindrical, and with baritone, it's a bit more open and bright. In baritone roles, I might not cover as quickly and would definitely leave the E-flat uncovered. Finding my way around the upper part of my voice has been a long process, which is still ongoing. But, the key to my progress has been frontal placement, simplicity of sound, and support, support, support!

GERHARD SIEGEL: In my mind, a healthy high register is easier if healthy and solid low notes are available. Actually, individual notes with full support and good technique are not the problem. Continuous singing in the break (*passaggio*) and above that is the problem area. Pay attention that the lower jaw is not held and that the mouth is opened properly. I have observed that is when the most mistakes occur. In this placement/register, I have to concentrate constantly and pay attention. *Support!*

CHAPTER 2

❧

On the Operatic Stage

Mezzo-soprano Janet Baker once said, "Our business is emotion and sensitivity—to be the sensors of the human race." Perhaps nowhere is that more evident than in the opera, the stage where the complete blending of voices, words, and instrumental music provides a window on the human experience like no other. For the singer, achieving his or her part in this *Gesamtkunstwerk* (to borrow Wagner's term) requires skilled preparation and the ability to manage multiple challenges. The singer must learn how to work with costumes, lights, staging, acoustics, and ensemble, besides the voice, music, style, language, and emotion. As Alan Held says, "When I have nothing left to learn concerning singing, then I will stop singing." The emphasis on stage direction also causes some commentary; Jennifer Rowley makes the case that "the crazier the production and the more difficult the staging, the better I tend to sing." Even practical advice on warming up or memorizing and learning a new role is given, so that, as Lawrence Brownlee reminds us, when "we get on the stage, we are our own selves."

1. HOW DO YOU LEARN A NEW ROLE?

STEPHANIE BLYTHE: I read the text—all of it—getting the words into my mouth and brain. Then I go to the notes. The composer wrote text first, so why shouldn't we learn in the same direction?

LAWRENCE BROWNLEE: I always encourage people to listen to a recording, to go to YouTube to get an idea of the style or tips for the pace or the traditions. However, anytime we get on the stage, we are our own selves. I can't be another Alfredo Kraus. I have to be me. In addition, listening to a performance will get me in the mind-set by taking it into my body. Sometimes I go running and take a piece and listen to it to feel the rhythm in my body. I always go to the piano by myself and make sure that an eighth note is an eighth note, so it is always perfect. I also take it to my teacher or my coach so I can be comfortable with the piece and have it inside my bones.

NICOLE CABELL: I have a pretty reliable routine to learn a new role. I will listen to three or four recordings, not to copy anything, but to listen to how the voice fits in. After translating the libretto, I make sure I have the correct notes and rhythm on the piano. I will speak through it to match words and diction with text, and flesh it out with an understanding of exactly what I'm saying and how it fits in with the music. I have to figure out where I'm going to put emphasis, where I'm going to rest my voice, and where I need to give 100 percent. Coaches come into play after I've prepared all of the above, and we will work to find the subtleties. Historical research into the opera and time period is helpful. This has to be flexible, as a director has the final say as to what you might want to bring to the role, but I try to come into a project with as much personal input as possible.

JOSEPH CALLEJA: I first listen to as many versions of the piece as possible. Not doing that is like being a leaf on a tree and not knowing which tree you are on. It helps you vocally and tires you even less if you know some of it before rehearsing. Then I go with a *répétiteur* through the role, learn it, make sure the notes are good, and then with my teacher I go through it. I record myself as much as possible, sing in front of a mirror to see the expressions and how I approach the notes, and preferably debut it in a smaller theater to get the feel of the role.

DAVID DANIELS: I am not big on research. For example, I did the premiere of *Oscar* at Santa Fe. I knew about Oscar Wilde and his life, but I didn't read every autobiography and every piece of material out there. I read *The Ballad of Reading Gaol* and *De Profundis*, but other than that it wasn't a huge seven years of research, because I don't really believe that the emotional content and heart that I bring to the stage to tell this tragic story are going to be influenced and enhanced by reading a hundred books. I actually got into the rehearsal period for that piece and found it more interesting to read about him after the rehearsal period. That's what piqued my interest. I don't think my reading eight hundred biographies of Julius Caesar will make my singing of that role any better.

JOYCE DIDONATO: In general, I will highlight the text and then go back with a red pencil and mark every single articulation and dynamic marking so I see them clearly at the start (*crescendi, staccati, portamenti,* etc.). The translation of every word must happen very early in the process, marking open vowels, closed vowels, and double consonants, but also to know right from the start what the emotional journey of the character will be. I then sit at the piano and learn the score myself, just "conversing" with the composer and what he has written. Then I will begin to listen to recordings to hear the different interpretations to pique my musical curiosity; however, I want the first impression to be mine and not from a recording. Then it's a matter of putting the role into the voice—which takes careful study, a *lot* of patience, and a lot of productive repetition.

CHRISTINE GOERKE: For me, the music goes in like wildfire. The text takes longer. I like to read through and learn as much as I can at the piano. Then I get a blank journal for every new role because they are $4.99, and I am a fan of that. I write all of the text out by hand, which is a gigantic pain in the ass, but there is something for me about putting pen to paper that puts the thing in my head. I memorize terribly to CDs, but if I put the DVD on, somehow seeing movement associated with the text, it goes into my head faster. Also, I add the subtitles in the language I am learning, so I can put away my score.

DENYCE GRAVES: First of all, I get the score and look through it, but this is, of course, after having some idea of the role and if it suits my voice and temperament. Then I begin highlighting my part. Then I translate and write out beats, if necessary. If there's a novel or literature about the story itself, I will at some point read it. I might organize sessions with a pianist to hear the entire work. I will then begin woodshedding and going measure by measure, sitting at the piano alone, learning the notes, singing lightly. Once I've learned the notes, I begin singing through passages until it's learned. Then I take it to a coach and/or simultaneously to voice lessons. I sometimes listen to a recording, but not often. Then I start singing it over and over until it's memorized and in my muscles.

GREER GRIMSLEY: I like to investigate my roles, but I have to put a limit to my investigation because I get carried away. I think it's fascinating. Will you use all the information? No, but it makes your performance that much more vivid when you come at it with a greater understanding.

THOMAS HAMPSON: I learn very quickly. I play piano well enough to explore a piece, even in twentieth- and twenty-first-century music. However, I enjoy also that process with coaches, and I have a handful that I regularly go to. I learn a lot of music every year and sing a lot of modern music. First, if it is a foreign language, it has to be translated in absolutely excruciating detail because, for me, it is almost impossible to memorize a piece if I don't know what it means. My goal with everything I do is to inhabit, in some humble way, some part of the process the composer went through making this glorious piece. Learning starts for me rhythmically and with the nuts and bolts of how the piece has been assembled, trying to understand the engineering of the house before I become terribly involved with the architecture.

ALAN HELD: I generally start by going through a score, checking out the *tessitura* and the range, and looking for the real pitfalls. I also give great concern as to whether the role actually interests me and if I think I can really bring anything to it. Now, I play a lot of evil characters on top of the few good guys I play. How refreshing it becomes to play a very human and warm person such as Hans Sachs after playing all of the bad guys or gods. I will often listen to a recording to hear the orchestration and the colors—the composition as it was written. I will then work out how this fits into my voice. I check out all aspects (vocal production, diction, etc.), as it all has to be incorporated at some point—it had better be there from the beginning.

JONAS KAUFMANN: I am thankful that I am a quick learner. In two or three days I could memorize a part, but it is much healthier to do it over a longer time. The best way for me is that I go to a coach and sing through the part two or three times. Then I let it sit or sink in for about two weeks, and when I come back to it, it feels and sounds familiar. I do not do it 125 times. I do it. I wait. I do it again, and then when I come back the third time, it is most probably done. I find that the brain can't stop repeating the music wherever I am, and by looking up the gaps in my memory that I find, I memorize the part automatically.

SIMON KEENLYSIDE: I wish there were shortcuts to learning a new role. I don't think there are any. For me, it will take around two to three months to learn a new role or a recital program. During this period, I would have endless sessions with a pianist as well. Also, I make my own recording, which becomes a soundtrack to my daily life. After the piece is committed to memory, then the more interesting business of molding it to something more alive happens. That would be in the rehearsal studios and for the weeks preceding the first night. One thing I would say is, don't copy. Once it is committed to memory, well, only then is it a good idea to dip into tradition, convention, and the approaches that great singers of the past may have taken.

KATHLEEN KIM: I translate the text and I listen to CDs to get a sense of the whole opera or how the role is. Then I learn the notes. Once I'm comfortable, I sing with a pianist or with my coach, and then I take it to my teacher.

ANA MARÍA MARTÍNEZ: I first want to know the story of the character, because my imagination works a lot in fantasy. I love to take a recording with my favorite singer of all time, Mirella Freni. I listen to this once or twice with the score. If necessary, for the language, I do an IPA. Then I start dissecting it. I use different colored pencils for that. Then I'll take it to a coach. I learn things really quickly. Usually the first coaching is how I'll sing it and perform it.

LISETTE OROPESA: Text first. I translate the entire score, using my own interpretation as much as possible. Use a dictionary when necessary, but the more of the language you have under your belt, the easier it is. Dirty work comes first: text, rhythms, and dramatic intent. Then I listen to one or two great recordings for tempo and phrasing ideas, but I don't use them to learn the role. I hit the practice room.

ERIC OWENS: First, I read the original source material. Then I will read through the libretto. This is new with me, as I used to start with the music, but now I start from the drama. If I'm doing some wild modern piece, then I do start musically. I also listen to several recordings just to get an idea orchestrally of what's going on, not vocally. Then I will sing the role just on an /a/ vowel to make sure that the voice is free, then I add the real vowels with the openness of /a/, without consonants, and then finally adding the consonants, with focus on *legato* diction (a blended concept). I don't work with a coach or voice teacher on this, as I'm usually learning roles on the road. The only time I find myself using coaches is when I have to do Russian or Czech, for the diction.

DIMITRI PITTAS: The translation is absolutely the first step, which also involves learning the plot, your character, and how you can relate to the emotions. I take a list of emotions, and when I'm reading a passage, I pare it down to the simplest emotion and write that word on a Post-it in my music. I don't take it away until my mind is able to convey the same emotion. I tend to listen to recordings mid-learning. Importantly, when you're learning something, you shouldn't just be sitting on a couch or slouched in a dark room. You should be in a singing position, able to breathe properly. Once I've learned it, and it's in my head, I go to a coach and/or teacher. At that point, it's about the music and the communication.

EWA PODLEŚ: Obviously I study the score, both the music and the text. I learn a new role alone and with a coach. I do not use recordings, nor do I listen to other artists. As to the choice of roles, I am careful that I do not accept a role beyond my natural possibilities.

JENNIFER ROWLEY: I learn every role the same way. First, YouTube. I want to hear what singers who have come before me have done with this role. Second, I do research and read source material about the piece. Third, I translate it, because I want to know what I'm saying from moment one. Then I start learning the notes down an octave. I take it to my teacher to learn the difficult passages or the famous aria. Then I go to a coach for musical, stylistic, and diction help. I go back to my teacher, and we marry the two ideas together: style and technique. After that, I start memorizing, and before rehearsals I try to sing the whole thing with other people.

GERHARD SIEGEL: I read the role in the piano score and try to sight-read. I find it very important that studying the notes must also include the emotional side immediately, which means that the role is already alive, without being performed on the stage. Thus, learning the role is much faster for me, and I avoid having to do interpretation rehearsals.

2. HOW DO YOU WARM UP BEFORE A PERFORMANCE?

STEPHANIE BLYTHE: It all depends on how much singing I have been doing during the day or even the week. If I have had a very hectic rehearsal schedule, I stay warm most of the time. Here is what I have learned (sometimes very painfully) *not* to do as a warm-up: do not sing every high note to make sure that they are there. My good friend, the great Paul Plishka, once told me: "You have only so many of those notes a day. Don't waste them in the dressing room."

LAWRENCE BROWNLEE: It was Jussi Björling or someone else who said, "I don't warm up, because I spend the whole day speaking in that place." If you begin to sing from where you speak, then a clear voice can happen, especially if you have a good supported breath. Again, the statement *Si canta come si parla* holds true.

NICOLE CABELL: I will do exercises that bring my voice forward and out of my throat, like scales with my tongue out, pinching my nose with my fingers and singing on an /e/ vowel, and eventually sirens. I sing scales on /u/, beginning on the lower note, jumping an octave (trying to match larynx and tongue position), and descending to the original note. Different repertoire requires slightly different warm-ups as well. I sing a lot of Mozart, so I warm up with exercises that focus on long lines and smoothness of tone. Runs in Mozart are very even, and there is very little to no stylistic scooping or *portamenti*, so I focus on these aspects in my warm-up. When I'm preparing Donizetti or Verdi, I try to bring a little more *squillo* into my voice, and practice *staccati*, fast scales, and breathing exercises that support a fuller sound.

JOSEPH CALLEJA: I start with humming because it is almost impossible to hum in a bad way, and the humming gets the muscles in the correct position. I gargle with salt water to remove phlegm and drink a lot. Then I start slow vocalizations from middle C. This process doesn't take more than twenty minutes. You should not overly warm up your voice, and it should be done in stages. When you go running, you don't start at a sprint. You start by two minutes of walking, then a light jog, and you increase as the circulation is heightened; so I also do exercises to warm up my diaphragm. It might be a fast walk or jogging on the spot just to get the diaphragm working and the blood circulating. Remember, the vocal cords are just part of the instrument, so you have to have the whole body tuned and ready.

DAVID DANIELS: I have a routine which has evolved over the twenty years of my career. It involves waiting as long as I can before I warm up because I'm one of those singers that feels there's no voice all day long. I'm not going to be able to sing until I warm up, and if everything is there, then I relax and everything is fine. I eat a big meal about three hours before, then I warm up, then I go to the theater. I used to eat carbohydrates, but it

David Daniels
David Daniels is known for his superlative artistry, magnetic stage presence, and a voice of singular warmth and surpassing beauty, which have helped him redefine his voice category for the modern public. The American countertenor has appeared with the world's major opera companies and on its main concert and recital stages. The *Chicago Tribune* has called Daniels "today's gold standard among countertenors." An exclusive Virgin Classics recording artist with several critically acclaimed and best-selling albums, David Daniels has been the recipient of two of classical music's most significant awards: *Musical America*'s Vocalist of the Year for 1999 and the 1997 Richard Tucker Award. Photo courtesy Robert Recker.

caused too many reflux problems. Now I stick to protein. My routine is about twenty to thirty minutes at home before I go to the theater, and I warm up in the steam of the shower. Then I get out of the shower, and I will sing maybe a section of an aria, so I know the voice is there, and then I leave it alone until I get to the theater.

JOYCE DIDONATO: I have a twenty-minute routine of vocalizes that I've been doing for roughly eighteen years which has changed only slightly over that time. It is all about making sure the voice is "speaking," completely moving on the air and free, and then stretching the voice on each end of the scale to be sure it's flexible and moving. I know that at the end of those twenty minutes, even considering the normal daily fluctuations in the body and voice, that I will be fully and properly warmed up. It's great medicine against nerves, because unless I'm ill, I know that the routine will put me in the place I need to be for the show. It's become bankable for me, and I think that is the goal of a solid technique.

CHRISTINE GOERKE: It depends on the role that I am singing. Some roles start in the basement, and I don't have to warm up that much. But for a role like The Dyer's Wife in *Die Frau ohne Schatten*, which starts on a B-flat above the staff, you have to warm up high. I know right away how warm I am if I sing for ten minutes and everything is functioning. There are some days I really need a good solid thirty to forty-five minutes to really get ready. But for a role like Elektra, which is nonstop singing, if I warm up too long, I am exhausted. I try to judge what each role needs, and then I base my warm-ups on that.

DENYCE GRAVES: Well, I most definitely do warm up before every performance of any kind. I try not to be rushed through this important process because I believe how you warm up and how your voice sets is how it will perform that evening. I allow one hour alone, uninterrupted, to warm up the voice. I do not like or appreciate the constant barrage of people coming into the dressing room before a performance. I just hate it. Most of my family and friends know this, but there is always the artistic administration of the theater, who believes it's good practice. Afterward, however, is another story. I'm the girl you want at your event! I'm happy to meet with donors and supporters and attend receptions and dinner parties, but not before.

GREER GRIMSLEY: I try to keep the day of the performance as normal as possible instead of overemphasizing it, but also keep clear what my intentions are. It's about focusing the energies that you're going to use. I will sing only a little bit because usually I will have been singing in rehearsals. It's just to see how things are feeling, since the voice and body are different every day. I just want to connect to how my voice is on that day. I also am mindful of my food. When I started doing *Ring* cycles, I had to think even more about what my diet was going to be because the *Ring* is about endurance. I eat early enough so I won't feel so stuffed, usually about two or three hours before I leave for the theater. In the longer ones, I lean more heavily on protein, and I do take snacks during the *Ring*. I take a sandwich, which I can eat in the break, or a banana or a PowerBar. You use a lot more energy than you think you do.

THOMAS HAMPSON: I warm up every day, even if I am not singing. It is part of my daily yoga routine. When I start to warm up, I check regions. So I'll do some /ŋ / (ng), which kind of gets the breastbone or the lower resonances going, and then I'll do some /n/s in the middle and then scales of two-plus octaves up and down, going to /m/ on the top. I just want to know that the cords are vibrating their edges with each other, and it's all balanced on my breath. This happens every day. If I have a performance, I like to warm up early in the day and then let it simmer like a good stew. I don't like to wait until the last minute.

ALAN HELD: How I warm up for a performance is pretty much the same how I would warm up on an off day. Many of my pieces start out with needing vocal impact from the very first note—there isn't much time to warm up during the show. If I have a night that requires hours of singing, however, I try not to overdo the singing during the day. I primarily try to get the voice buzzing in placement and the body loosened up so that the muscles are loose and the breathing is natural. Singing is very athletic, and we must learn to warm up the entire body in much the same way. *And* it is important to "warm down" the body and voice at the end of the night as well. Do not leave your voice in a "shocked" state of being.

JONAS KAUFMANN: First of all, you should warm up your body to be able to support your voice from the first note; otherwise, your body wakes up while you are singing. But I'm sure you are more interested in warming up the voice, so.... Once I was sharing a dressing room with four colleagues and I wanted to warm up, so I sang with my palm covering my mouth. I found that so beneficial that I now warm up like that. You immediately realize if you have a jaw thrust going on. You feel the support, how much you are exhaling, and you have something to lean against with your breath. Also, you have to have a certain amount of pressure to keep the air flowing between your palm and your mouth. You have control and you learn to have a continuous flow. And, last but not least, you don't hear how you sound, only the pitch. Therefore, you can't manipulate your voice when it's still cold to how it sounds when you are warmed up.

SIMON KEENLYSIDE: Warming up is a very personal thing. Two days before the show, I will have a full sing in order to stretch the voice, but gently. The day before the show, I wouldn't sing. That day of rest gives the voice time to relax and regain elasticity. It's not necessary for me to have total silence, just rest and quiet. On the day of an opera performance, I would just make sure that I am upright around five hours before the show. The warm-up itself might only then be ten to fifteen minutes, depending upon the role. I would also remain in the lower and middle register for most of that fifteen-minute warm-up, working the flexibility up to, around, and over the *passaggio*, just enough to know that it is working and elastic.

KATHLEEN KIM: I don't warm up much because most of the roles I'm singing require very high notes. Too many high notes and my voice can get tired before the evening starts. I think I have a different approach than other people. I just do some lip trills, two or three scales, and that's about it. With a role like Zerbinetta, I have a long night to go, so I warm up just enough to be able to start the opera. Then, by the second act, I am fully warmed up.

ANA MARÍA MARTÍNEZ: I wake up in the morning, have a glass of water and coffee, then I hum and do some sighs going up and down without a break and see if I have an easy access to my flageolet. I will also do some exercises to be sure my body is awake. Then I live a normal day. A lot of productions today are so physical. I have had to do things with dancers or do back flips, so I want to be sure that I am limber. I do have a dancer background, so maybe that's the reason that I want to feel physically strong. Before I go onstage, I will do jumping jacks or something to get the blood flowing and the circulation pumping. As far as eating, I love spaghetti with extra-virgin olive oil and sea salt, and I eat a huge portion about two hours before curtain.

LISETTE OROPESA: The voice needs to be rested for the ideal performance. I sleep as late as possible, warm up the body, then warm up the voice. I do yoga or light running (do any exercise that gets you feeling good but not worn out) and have a healthy meal. I take a hot shower, prepare a light snack if necessary for midafternoon, and mentally review the staging. I hydrate and warm up the voice gently and think positive thoughts.

ERIC OWENS: It depends on the role or type of performance. For baritone roles, I'll probably come to the theater in the early afternoon and warm up for forty-five minutes, go away, come back two hours before curtain, and warm up for another forty minutes, just to have my voice sitting as high as possible from the very beginning. For a recital, I often sing through the entire program in the space with the pianist on the day of the performance. Then at the start of the performance I feel ready for business. There were times when I would reach the end of a recital thinking, "This is where my voice should've been sitting at the beginning." So, when possible, I make sure that my voice is in that place at the beginning of recitals.

DIMITRI PITTAS: Warming up before the show is about making sure that my body is alive and energized and my mind is focused. Every time I warm up, I'm trying to accomplish something, a task. Performing is my fun time. In between performances is when I do my vocal work. When I'm getting ready to go out onstage, I try not to stress myself out if my voice isn't working properly. I've done the work, the rehearsals, the setting up of my voice many times before, and I'm aware of the hoops I have to jump through that night.

EWA PODLEŚ: Usually I warm up twenty to twenty-five minutes, regardless of the performance. And, even if I am not in great shape, my vocal routine remains the same. On the day of a performance, I eat lightly and I have no rehearsals, nor do I give interviews. I also plan my schedule so that I would not have extremes of performance obligations, such as a Mozart opera following a Verdi.

JENNIFER ROWLEY: I start early in the day and warm up the voice and the body. I have to do forty-five minutes of cardio before the performance, every day. It gets your breath and your body going and gets you loose. I always stretch afterward to get everything open. Sometimes onstage it is very athletic, especially as a young singer. They want to throw you into all the crazy things. I go to the theater and chill out. I put my headphones in and go to makeup. I don't talk to many people. Then I go to my dressing room about forty-five minutes before start time. I warm up again, maybe ten to fifteen minutes. I might sing more difficult areas of the first act, for example, but I feel if you warm up the body first, then the voice comes with it.

GERHARD SIEGEL: I take a walk before the performance and hum something to warm up the vocal cords. Mostly I test it in the morning to see if I have "voice"; it is usually enough to sing three or four notes. It is important that the vocal cords are warmed up, which you can do with humming. I don't have a formal procedure for the day of the show. There may be times that I need to sleep, but it also often happens that I am still renovating the house or fixing a wall or cutting firewood.

3. THE EMPHASIS ON STAGE DIRECTION CAN OFTEN INVOLVE DIFFICULT SINGING POSITIONS, ABSTRACT IDEAS, DIRECTOR-ORIENTED STAGING, OR REINTERPRETATION OF THE LIBRETTO. WHAT ADVICE WOULD YOU GIVE TO YOUNG SINGERS FOR MANAGING THESE DEMANDS?

STEPHANIE BLYTHE: Make sure that no matter what body position you take, you must have a clear column for breath. If the position you are asked to do limits a supported breath, then find a way to diplomatically change the staging. Do not just flat-out say no. Offer some alternatives to show that you want to be part of the process.

LAWRENCE BROWNLEE: Honestly, this is my honest, honest, honest response: I always put myself at the stage director's demands. I always try everything, and if it doesn't work, I think the director will know that it doesn't work. Yes, there are stage directors who are more demanding. I think it is good. We don't need the static opera that we are used to having, and I think people with video and cinema and YouTube are more demanding to see things that are engaging visually. Now, if the stage director sees something in me that I can do, and that magic happens that is the brilliance and specialness of live theater and performance, then I always open myself to say, "Okay, I'll try it."

NICOLE CABELL: Knowing one's technique is key to surviving staging that requires us to twist our bodies up like a pretzel, roll on the ground, and sing on our backs. It's really a matter of paying a little more attention to your technique while you're rehearsing, and singing out during difficult rehearsals so you can get used to what it feels like to truly sing while doing something physically crazy. The best emotional advice I can give is to lighten up. We can take ourselves far too seriously. Learn to be savvy in bringing forth your ideas and disagreements, or simply lighten up and laugh a little, because it's a small price to pay for being privileged enough to sing for money. Try it, because you might end up liking it.

JOSEPH CALLEJA: It is not the place of the singer to judge stage directors. My business is to lend my voice and my body to the stage for the direction and trust him or her to do a complete portrayal. Remember, when we are rehearsing, we are not seeing the whole picture. What temporarily might not make sense to us might make sense in the whole. You always learn something new no matter how bad the director is. You should go with an open mind and try to do your best to bear the fruition of his or her efforts because that's why you were contracted. If not, just stick to concerts. I am sure that the people working in offices and hospitals don't agree with their bosses on each and every issue, so suck it up and do your best. Excluding extreme gestures and if my singing isn't compromised, then I'll do it.

DAVID DANIELS: I will try anything, but if it gets to a place where it's affecting my breathing and my music making, then we have to come to some sort of compromise about the movement. If you're a young singer, you're trying to make everybody happy and to create your career; it's very difficult to fight against that. I don't know if that's possible, and it might not be at age twenty-four.

JOYCE DIDONATO: Try it and see what happens. I was a part of a magnificent cast of *The Barber of Seville* at the Royal Opera House, Covent Garden, and we rehearsed it as if it were a play. We knew it inside and out, and yet we were there reading it, discovering all kinds of nuances that we had never noticed before. As a result, routine scenes became completely new. And when I fell on opening night, breaking my leg, and had to finish the rest of the run in a wheelchair, we were able to improvise a completely new staging because of the depth we had gone into during the rehearsals. I think the emphasis on acting will only make us better performers—as long as we never sacrifice the vocal aspect, for we are singers first.

CHRISTINE GOERKE: Try everything three times. You have shown goodwill and made an effort. Then if it doesn't work, don't go angrily, just go and say, "Look, I am trying so hard to make this work. Can you help me?" The "Can you help me?" thing is always great, not "Your idea sucks." That never goes over well. Then you can hit them with your ideas. Politeness goes a long way. Even if someone is barking at you, kill 'em with kindness. In the end, not only do you come out on top, but you also show that you're

Joyce DiDonato
Joyce DiDonato has soared to international prominence in operas by Rossini, Handel, and Mozart, as well as in high-profile world premieres. Her signature parts include Rossini's *La cenerentola* and *Il barbiere di Siviglia*—she was called "the best Rosina around" by London's *Sunday Times* for the portrayal. She has been described as "perhaps the most potent female singer of her generation" by the *New Yorker*. Her awards include the 2012 Grammy, 2010 *Gramophone* Artist of the Year, the Beverly Sills Award from the Metropolitan Opera, the Royal Philharmonic Society's 2005 Singer of the Year, and the Richard Tucker Award. Photo courtesy Simon Pauly.

a great colleague to the folks at the theater, your colleagues, and the music staff. There are crazy things that happen (I had to wear a crocodile head as Kundry). Try it. You may not get it, but you're not directing it.

DENYCE GRAVES: Any young singer embarking on a career will learn right out of the starting gate that the art of diplomacy is a necessary skill. You will, at some point in your career, be asked to "sell" an idea or action or concept from a director that you don't agree with, or that is physically difficult to do and compromises the singing. The advice I would give is to do it to the best of your ability or tolerance and then schedule a meeting with the director to share your position and try to work toward a compromise. Most directors want the singer to be comfortable and happy. The bottom line is the work itself and to serve the music, but you can certainly bump up against tremendous egos.

GREER GRIMSLEY: You have to decide how much you personally can deal with if it is really crazy. I've been in situations where they ask you to do crazy stuff and I am of the mind that I can try it once. I try to see the value in what they're asking. Then, after trying it, I can come back and say that this is not working. It's a much more respectful and less histrionic way to deal with it. In order to be true to the composer and to the music, you can get through the craziest of things. That said, I have not been asked to do the Planet of the Apes *Rigoletto*, which was done in Munich. But I did a *Dutchman* where the original idea was that I had been abducted by aliens; however, cooler heads prevailed, and we ended up with a saner production.

THOMAS HAMPSON: Good luck! We do live in a world where pieces are being reinterpreted, manipulated, or loosely based on the original context and turned into something that they were never intended to be, all in the effort that it will mean something more in a contemporary way. If the director wants you to do something that is physically not possible, just say you can't do it and why ("My spine has to do this, and my ribs need to do that"). You know, hunkering or thundering about is not going to get you anywhere, but a lot of the producers that I have worked with, given a chance, will take the journey of trial with you. My biggest advice, quite frankly, to any singer is to know everything you can about the production before you sign the contract.

ALAN HELD: Always keep the body in line. No matter what position you're being asked to sing in, you must keep the breathing apparatus free and able to produce your tones as naturally as possible. This comes with great practice and application. Do not sacrifice your singing for a visual effect.

JONAS KAUFMANN: Well, that's a tough question. I'm lucky in that I can sing in pretty much every position. But, if you don't feel comfortable, you should just say it. I think directors have to understand that the audience doesn't actually come because the director invented something, but because the composer has written some beautiful melodies. There are singers who are capable of singing in an awkward position and others that just can't, so you just have to tell the director. There are friendly and unfriendly ways to say that. Propose an interesting alternative, and the director most likely will buy it.

SIMON KEENLYSIDE: This is a very difficult topic on which to advise anyone. In addition to our differing vocal abilities, we also have different temperaments and demeanors. The trick is to stay calm and cooperative. Ask a conductor before a rehearsal begins if such-and-such is possible. Speak with a difficult director, or one who is asking too much, and see if another way is possible. They will usually like the contact and the fact that you're showing interest. Confrontation brings nothing but trouble and isn't necessary. In the end, it's only a job. The music will still be beautiful, and the sun will rise as usual, once the uncomfortable period of work is over. To take poor direction, or none at all, is not the end of the world. A grumbling singer, however silly the production, is not a thing of beauty.

KATHLEEN KIM: If you have a sound technique, you should be able to sing in any position. So get your techniques solid. If it's really a position that you can't possibly do, then just talk to the director and try to change it.

ANA MARÍA MARTÍNEZ: Let your mind grow and be stretched, especially if directors ask you to do something you know is not going to work. Try, because it shows you're a good team player and you're respecting the person in charge. You're still part of this process. If you really can't make it work, then privately go to the director and say you're uncomfortable and have some other suggestions. It's all about diplomacy. We all want to feel that we are working toward the same common goal no matter what field.

LISETTE OROPESA: Most directors are accommodating to our needs. At the very least, try to keep the breath free by keeping the spine long and the ribs lifted. If you're in a position that compromises this, have a heart-to-heart with the director to find what works for you. It's your performance, after all!

ERIC OWENS: Unless something is absolutely physically impossible, my advice is to try to give the director what he or she wants, and not dismiss something without even trying—and, trying does not mean doing it once, finding it uncomfortable, and saying no. What feels uncomfortable on day one might feel like second nature on day ten. Also, a performance shouldn't necessarily be about your comfort; it's about inhabiting the world of the piece, via the director's vision, and finding the authenticity of each moment. Now, if after really trying to make something work, it's inhibiting you from inhabiting the character with authenticity (knowing that singing is the principal means by which this is achieved, and staying true to the composer *is* staying true to the drama), then it's time to ask if you could assist in finding an option that works for both singer and director and which still tells the story.

DIMITRI PITTAS: I think art is art. A director has something he or she wants to say, and you owe it to art to at least give it a try. If it's a new production and the director is trying to create something for the first time, I think you owe it to your job and your career to be able to stretch yourself. You'd be surprised at the inspiration that comes out of those moments when you are thinking that this just isn't going to work but you try it anyway.

EWA PODLEŚ: As far as the new demands of modern staging, I believe that a common understanding with the stage director is of primary concern. If there are difficulties, then compromise seems to be also one of the most desired positions in such situations.

JENNIFER ROWLEY: I've done a lot of crazy things already. I sang Donna Anna, who went crazy and cut off all of her hair. I also had to sing with my legs wrapped around a tenor's neck! How do you sing with your legs in the air? Well, you breathe. I find that the crazier the production and the more difficult the staging, the better I tend to sing. So I try to make sure that everything is open and free, and I do what I'm asked. Being in shape and working out helps a lot, and I am able to do things that other people cannot. When you're young try everything, and if it doesn't work, then talk to the director. Also, I think that young audiences want to see the same things they see in musical theater.

GERHARD SIEGEL: I believe that it is especially important not to say no and not to say, "I do not do that." If you try it and it's good, then it is fine; but when it's not so good, you should try a variation, and then, when it finally makes no sense, just say so and explain it. It must also make sense. I was never forced, in all of the many productions, into positions that make singing impossible. I believe that happens relatively rarely.

4. HOW DO YOU PACE YOURSELF IN A LONG OR VOCALLY DIFFICULT OPERA? ARE THERE ANY SUGGESTIONS YOU CAN MAKE, FOR EXAMPLE, IN PREPARING FOR A WAGNER ROLE OR FOR A LONG OPERA SUCH AS *DER ROSENKAVALIER*?

STEPHANIE BLYTHE: The most important step is to sing in the rehearsals. You don't have to sing every day full out, but you must *sing* at some point. I have been in far too many shows where my colleagues never learned how to pace themselves because they were saving it for the performance. Rehearsal is where we learn not only the blocking but also how we feel as we are doing staging. That really affects the ability to pace.

LAWRENCE BROWNLEE: One of my teachers said you have to sing on the interest and not on the principal. If you sing on the principal, your career will be two years; if you sing on the interest, of course you can sing and sing. As the voice and the body mature, it is not necessarily about the overwhelming amount of sound, but the color of voice and how you produce it that will allow you to expand your repertoire. I will be doing *I Puritani* at the Met. I've done it twice, and I feel that it is a role that is appropriate for my voice, so I will approach it my way. There's definitely a difference in the way Corelli sang things, with a more heroic sound, so you need to be sure that you are not singing beyond who you are.

NICOLE CABELL: To get through a very difficult opera, I believe the repertoire has to be right for your voice. With a role like Juliette (Gounod), for instance, it's a long role, but there is, at no moment, a time when the *tessitura* gets too high to manage. I can make it through if I adhere to my technique and several important tricks. If I'm singing with the chorus at any point, I don't have to sing full out, and I can occasionally drop out, because I have to sing the next night and the next, and I must conserve where I may. I usually will not do a lot of speaking the day before a long performance, so my voice remains healthy and fresh, and I will do minimum warm-ups. Long roles require more concentration on technique, particularly the aspects that eliminate tension.

JOSEPH CALLEJA: The honest answer that everyone should say is "experience." There is an element of pacing no matter what anyone says, even on a subconscious level. I have never heard a great singer going all out constantly throughout the performance. They all hold back before certain climaxes, etc. You know why? Because that is what you are supposed to do. The singers who don't pace themselves are the ones that have five-year careers. If you don't pace yourself, it is dangerous. Opera is all about pacing—the way you pace your career, the way you plan your roles. Pacing is one of the major factors in a career. Giuseppe di Stefano comes to mind. If he had been more careful with his voice, and his private life as well, we would have had twenty more years of one of the most absolutely gorgeous voices of all time. (Magda Olivero, in comparing him to Björling, Pavarotti, and Caruso, said that she could not compare di Stefano with anyone. For me, only the young Carreras came close to giving us what di Stefano really was.)

DAVID DANIELS: In the rehearsals, yes, but every role is different. I'm still trying to figure out how much to rehearse, sing out, keep in shape vocally, and how much to rest. When it comes to the performance, I don't ever think about saving myself or starting slowly. In fact, I'm probably too warmed up when I walk out onstage. I have a feeling that some of my colleagues warm up much less than I do, so they warm up during the performance. There are times when the voice isn't working as I would want. We are humans. It's just different every day. But if an audience is there, I would never give them a show of Mr. Daniels pacing himself. I remember attending *Winterreise* in college and watching this person pace himself through this enormous piece and I thought, "I don't ever want to do that." The audience comes there for a performance, and I want them to hear it from the beginning.

CHRISTINE GOERKE: I have to have a road map of where the really big places are and where I can lay off. Without fail in a Verdi opera, there's going to be an ensemble where you don't necessarily need to be giving 150 percent. So lay back. Save it for the aria or for the big duet. It's all give and take. So make your mental road map and decide where you need your big moments and where you don't. You should do that planning before you start each show because our physical state is different, so you might put a couple more little rest moments in. I take a few seconds to think through everything before I do it—where I'm really going to give and where I am not.

DENYCE GRAVES: Each singer will certainly find his or her own survival system. How I would pace myself would of course depend on the role itself. The first time I sang Amneris I found it very difficult to sustain my energy during Act Three, when the character is used very little, and then come out of the gate for Act Four and immediately deliver. I would hum and sing and walk around and stay quiet on my own. I know some singers like to eat in between acts to strengthen their bodies; some others exercise. The bottom line is that the role has to be sung through and through, over and over again, to build up the stamina needed, and that informs your learning and frame of reference on how you function and your voice functions. I know some singers that won't drink or have salt or even speak days before a heavy role.

GREER GRIMSLEY: I keep on my support and keep my voice as clean and supple as possible. I learned *bel canto* technique, and what I took away from it was that you were as streamlined as possible and that you get the most sound for the least amount of effort. I have approached my roles with that in mind, which has stood me in good stead. I've been blessed with good genetics and good stamina, and that enters into it as well. I, for example, very rarely mark unless I'm feeling under the weather. And I actually find new things by not marking. It's actually easier to just sing it!

THOMAS HAMPSON: Is there pacing? Yes. There are some roles you are going to be singing nonstop for three hours. Doing Busoni's Faust, or Mandryka in *Arabella*, I hit the stage and I don't know what happened until two hours later, and it's everything, soup to nuts. A role like Iago is a good example: you've got a "Brindisi" within five minutes after walking onstage and you'd better have all the pipes at your disposal. *The Barber of Seville*, the same thing. You must be mindful of where the heart of the role lies, both in vocal demands and ultimately endurance.

ALAN HELD: Stay hydrated. Stay hydrated. Stay hydrated. How many times have you heard singers come off the stage or out of a jury or audition and say, "Man, it was dry"? During a performance, especially a long one, I am constantly aware of not letting the voice dry out. I drink when I can and focus on placement all the more. Having a high placement is not only proper vocal technique but also is useful in helping the vocal folds not dry out so easily. It is also important, in my long Wagner roles, to keep the posture as steady and most productive as possible. This is why it is wise not to take on Wagnerian and other heavy roles too early in one's career. One needs time to learn and let things soak into the vocal apparatus and the entire body (which are inseparable).

JONAS KAUFMANN: I don't think about pacing myself. Sometimes if you try to save energy, it backfires because what actually happens is the opposite. You're tiring your instrument by not supporting it for every single phrase. This physical support might be tiring for the body, as I sometimes have problems with the abdominal muscles and the back, but if I marked through without body support, I couldn't do it. Just go for it, because if you have the right technique, you can do it from beginning to end. Trust your instrument and trust the amount of volume that you have naturally. It will be enough, and then you can sing all night without having to calculate how much voice is still left.

SIMON KEENLYSIDE: I think the process of practicing the piece, molding it, and performing it reveals the moments when the foot can come up off the gas and when it must go down. Performance itself is a great teacher, and to be honest, there's not much substitute for those "racing" conditions. Paying heed to the score will also help. No score will dictate *forte* all the time, and the elasticity brought about by steering the voice throughout the evening will keep it alive and responsive. For me, too, half the secret of pacing is in the preparation during the preceding days: enough stretching and resting, in turn, so that the voice is ready at the show to jump when the occasion demands.

KATHLEEN KIM: Just warm up enough so you can sing the role. There are always some parts where you can save your voice in the opera, so you just find those places and save your voice a little bit. I love rehearsing because that's when you know how you can do the role and pace yourself for the role. So you should sing in the rehearsals and find where you can save your voice and where you can sing full out.

ANA MARÍA MARTÍNEZ: It is similar to gymnasts. When they're looking at a routine, they stop before they do their next move. Most of the composers (but not all) thought about how to pace in the opera. You just have to start doing the role to know how to pace it. You discover that you gave more in this section than you really need to, because you're running out of steam for this next section, which might not be happening vocally but because of all the stage business. So pace yourself through repetition, so that you build muscle memory. If you're going to do a long role, for example, Susanna in *Le nozze di Figaro*, be sure the production has a certain amount of rehearsal time. Jumping into an existing production with only two or three days of rehearsal is not the best way to debut that role.

LISETTE OROPESA: The key is being rested, hydrated, and well prepared. This means plenty of sleep and plenty of fluids. Most important is having sung the role through. You can test your limits in rehearsal. I mark very little in order to mock the performance day for myself.

ERIC OWENS: The freedom of an unencumbered technique will help with stamina. Hopefully, what ends up getting fatigued will be the abdominal area, but sometimes you'll be in situations where you are not well or the acoustics are fighting you, and you'll find your voice getting tired. At that point is where a certain trust has to come into play: trust that even though you may not be hearing what you are used to hearing, you need to refrain from singing in a way that forces your voice to *have* you hear what you're used to hearing. On the flip side of this, I've shared performances with ill singers who were trying to sing gently, who, *unknowingly*, sounded better than when they were well, while bemoaning how terrible they thought they were sounding, when, in fact, they were singing how they should be singing all the time.

DIMITRI PITTAS: The longest show I've sung so far is *Don Carlo*. You have to stay focused for four hours. You open the show, you end the show, and you're there the whole time. I found that during the moments when I thought I could relax during the chorus scenes, particularly the *auto-da-fé*, it actually tired me out more than to sing it. If you're singing properly and you're taking time in rehearsal to set it up, by the time you're in those performances you're playing and having fun and adjusting in the moment. You're not worried about anything and you can just focus on what it is that you're communicating.

EWA PODLEŚ: I take care never to sing over 100 percent, but I sing rather less, like 90 percent.

JENNIFER ROWLEY: That starts when you begin preparation. If you have time to start preparing six months to a year in advance, you will have all the stamina you need. If it's an engagement that happens really quickly, you need to sing in rehearsals. If you mark through rehearsals, you're never going to gain the stamina you need. The mind will hurt you more than the voice will, so tell yourself you can get through this. The other thing I like to do, especially if the role is fairly long, is go through the whole score and pick ten places I'm going to use full voice. Those places would be really full, exciting places and the rest I will be singing on interest. You have to think about how you're going to get to the end.

GERHARD SIEGEL: A long opera requires a certain kind of stamina. But what I do not think is right is to start more or less just marking so that you are certain to have a voice at the end. I tend to the view of singing honestly from the beginning, in order to present the role 100 percent and know that you can make it to the end. Likewise, I am of the absolute opinion that the role and the acting are much more important than whether one or another note is not perfect at the end.

5. HOW DO YOU INTEGRATE YOUR SINGING WITH ACTING, THAT IS, COMBINING THE EMOTIONAL CONTENT OF AN ARIA OR ROLE WITH THE TECHNIQUE OF SINGING? DO YOU HAVE SPECIAL TECHNIQUES YOU USE TO CONNECT WITH THE CHARACTERIZATION OR THE EMOTION OF THE ARIA OR ROLE?

STEPHANIE BLYTHE: You can learn so much about characterization on-stage from others on the job. For example, I remember debuting Azucena in *Trovatore* at Covent Garden with Nicola Luisotti, who taught me everything I know about that piece. (He is a marvelous singer's conductor and a fantastic singer himself.) In addition, he taught me a different way of looking at recitative in any kind of opera; above all, a way of looking at language in a more expressive way. In other words, using the language of the character to shape the role.

LAWRENCE BROWNLEE: If the stage director asks for something, I try to do it. I was in Hamburg doing back flips. I thought it was fun. The general director came and said that nobody else will be able to do this role like I did. I've ridden bikes onstage. I've lifted things or people, and I once sang an aria while carrying someone around onstage. When you look at people like Plácido Domingo, who have been in this career for many years, you can look at them as constantly learning, constantly informing a character, or building on a character. If my Count Almaviva (in *The Barber of Seville*) is the same as twelve years ago, I don't think that's good.

NICOLE CABELL: A lot of acting through a role is libretto study. Our challenge is dealing with a director who may ask us to go against something instinctual for us. If I find myself challenging the director at every step, I eventually look into myself and realize I'm being closed-minded. A basic acting technique I use is to be inside my character's head moments before I come onstage. I must think about where she's just come from, what her emotional state is based on the things she's been doing that day, who she's spoken to, and, most importantly, why is she there singing that music? Another idea I try is to challenge my first instinct. If my character is saying something blatantly joyful, I try approaching it with melancholy, maybe doubt, something that adds another texture to the statement.

JOSEPH CALLEJA: My acting onstage was a bit of an interesting factor. I started very young. I was pretty slim and nobody commented negatively on my acting. On the contrary, they used to praise it. Then I had some problems in my personal life, and my weight exploded. I became obese. Then my acting became an issue. Then I realized that acting is 50 percent looking the part. I mean, how can you take a bus on a Formula 1 race? In the bus it would be difficult to make the turns gracefully, even if you are Michael Schumacher. It's knowing the role, the story, looking the part, and experience. Now that I have lost a lot of that extra weight again, people have stopped being negative about my acting. The last three years since the weight loss have been positive because I look the role more.

DAVID DANIELS: For me, it's more about an acting physicality than a vocal physicality. It's about the words and what I'm saying and what really brings out the character. I would never change my voice for a particular role. I want my voice to be the same in everything.

JOYCE DIDONATO: If a composer is completely specific in what he or she wants, do it. This is where we get all the intended information about color and characterizations of the text and music. Punctuation gives you a treasure trove of information—it's the key to most phrasings and, therefore, the internal expression of the character. If there's an exclamation point at the end, be like Victor Borge (see YouTube) and sing the exclamation point. Physical gestures often do not mean anything when they are disconnected from the text or unmotivated and are often the scourge of the opera singer, because it's usually an automatic attempt to find expression. As an exercise, restrict your hands so you cannot gesture, and you'll find that the only recourse is to put the expression into the voice. Then any gesture that follows organically will be much more motivated.

CHRISTINE GOERKE: I'm the colleague onstage that you never know what you're going to get because I never do the same thing twice. I think of the characters as human beings, and human emotions can change on a dime. In fact, my problem is going too far with the emotion so that it affects my singing. So I am adamant that I use my rehearsal time for that reason. For instance, the first time I sang Ellen Orford's "Embroidery Aria" in *Peter Grimes*, all of a sudden I burst into tears and couldn't stop for twenty minutes. I thought, "Right, that can't happen again. Good that it happened in rehearsal." Our job is to go right up to that line. So I use the rehearsal period to find out where the line is for me.

DENYCE GRAVES: If you listen to some of the older recordings of great artists, you can hear clearly how they acted with their voices. I believe that they go hand in hand and can strengthen each other. I have been celebrated in our business as someone who is a good actress onstage and with the voice, but depending on the role and style, I usually will choose the voice first. I believe that if you're honest, if you're really singing, and by that I mean you understand intimately every word and sing every word and phrase and communicate that with your heart, to sing the feeling of every

Christine Goerke
Soprano Christine Goerke has appeared in the major opera houses and concert venues of the world, including the Metropolitan Opera, the operas of Chicago and San Francisco, Covent Garden, the Paris Opera, La Scala, Deutsche Oper Berlin, Maggio Musicale Fiorentino, and the Saito Kinen Festival. She now sings the heroines of the dramatic Strauss and Wagner repertoire, including title roles in *Ariadne auf Naxos* and *Elektra*, as well as Brünnhilde, Ortrud, Leonore, Eboli, Ellen Orford, Alice Ford, and Madame Lidoine. A two-time Grammy Award winner, she is also a proud mother of two beautiful girls and is ever juggling motherhood and a career! Photo courtesy Arielle Doneson.

word and approach it with authenticity, it will be felt. I think that the truth is loud and the stage is a magnifying glass; you cannot hide honesty. I think that you can make anything work as long as *you* believe in it, and that, in fact, is our job: to make the director's or conductor's ideas as our own.

GREER GRIMSLEY: When technique is second nature, a singer is free to explore dramatic content without compromising the musical intentions. I don't separate singing and acting. I allow them to grow together.

THOMAS HAMPSON: To me, it's all about why. Why are you saying that? Why are you going left? Why are you looking? Why are you afraid? Why, why, why? The *why* informs the *when* and the *what*, and the *how* comes out of that. Whether that's a ninety-minute *Winterreise* or a second-act *Onegin*, it has different contexts and answers, but it's still the *why* of the character. The *why* can also be a cultural question, or what kind of person you are, what kind of clothes you wear, or the historical context. For me, it's not rocket science. It is certainly in my desire as an artist to live in the moment of that musical language of the character, the poem, or the context that I am singing.

ALAN HELD: Do not let vocal emotion come from the throat—it has to come from the mask. Do not let physical emotion come from tension— it has to come through natural muscle movement. Emotion is natural and organic; it can't be forced and be effective. The singing has to come from within your natural instrument in your natural moving body. The muscle features on the front of your face show emotion, as does how you raise an arm, move a leg, wiggle a finger, or any other part of your body. Posture shows emotion. But the most important expression comes via the eyes. Through them, we can show the entire realm of emotion with a single blink. Acting with one's voice can be dangerous, and I don't like to describe it that way. However, learning how to color the voice, place it differently, change vowels, etc. to create effects is fine—and, when applied alongside eye expression or bodily awareness, great things can then come through.

In the end, singing and acting have to be organic and natural.

JONAS KAUFMANN: When I sing a role, even if I've done it many times, I always start from scratch. So I do my forty-fifth performance of *Tosca*, and I don't start it and say, "I am going to do it the typical way." No. I start by slipping into that character, by understanding what mood he is in. In the very beginning, he is so much in love with that girl, he can't wait for her to come back, but there's this other one—she wasn't bad either—and immediately all the colors are there. Also, importantly, while not actually crying on the stage, you have to convince the audience that you have totally lost your mind, that you're completely nuts, and you are this other person.

Herbert von Karajan called this "controlled ecstasy." That's what we are all looking for.

SIMON KEENLYSIDE: I think what I do is pay attention to the demands of the composer, the librettist, the director, the costume and time period, the conductor, my colleagues, and my own thoughts and ideas (if any) such that, in the end, I have a frame of reference for delineating the character. So long as one is in the right place at the right time for one's colleagues on-stage (the director, designer, and lighting?), well, then there are endless possibilities for nuance, characterization, and inflection. That's what I like best. It's a kind of rehearsed spontaneity, which means that one doesn't get cramped into endless repetition. One is open for play and to the happen-stance of one's own thought process, of opportunity, and of other singers' presentations. That way, all performances are really alive. If the homework is done, there will always be a way out of a car crash of one's own making.

KATHLEEN KIM: When I am onstage, I cannot think about technique at all. I just think about the words and the moment I am in and I think it will carry. Onstage I cannot think about how am I going to breathe or how am I going to sound. If you are really connected to the role and you know what you're saying, it will come automatically.

ANA MARÍA MARTÍNEZ: Some of the experiences the characters have are not going to be experiences we lived nor that we want to live, but we have to find that common emotional connection or even our own fears. My first *Butterfly* took place during a difficult period of my life when my son was about the same age as Butterfly's child, and I have to say it was very cathartic and liberating at that time.

LISETTE OROPESA: It is almost always very clear in the text or the music. For a sensitive musician (which most singers naturally are), this comes without trouble. It's learning how not to overindulge that is the challenge!

DIMITRI PITTAS: One of the techniques I use is to imagine a word to put me in a situation, or perhaps a picture, like a freeze-frame of that situation. It's got to be something that speaks to you, something personal to you, that makes you truly feel something. One may relate this method to Harry Potter and a Patronus Charm. You've got to think of the greatest emotion in the world, and that's really going to create the emotional con-tent. Once you find that image or that emotion, it's a matter of how close you want to get to that picture before it starts affecting your voice. Ideally, it's about getting as close to that picture while keeping your composure.

JENNIFER ROWLEY: When you're musically well prepared, you can go on autopilot with your technique. Then you can really focus on what you're saying and who you're saying it to and listening to what those people are saying to you. You can only do that if you turn your brain off what you're physically doing and start focusing on the piece as a whole. As far as acting techniques, I love to use Uta Hagen's ten questions from her book for actors, *Respect for Acting*. I answer these ten questions for every scene that I do because it's important to get these motivations. Also, it is important to read the source material: read the play, the short story, or the letters.

GERHARD SIEGEL: The vocal and the role characterization should not stand in the way of each other, or vice versa—an adequate emotional representation must not be influenced by thinking of vocal technique or the other way around. A special technique to combine the two does not exist. If you can sing technically clean, the characterization of the role will never interfere. Sometimes you might get carried away; however, always be careful. But an occasional section of off-the-voice singing must be in there, too.

6. THE ROLE OF THE CONDUCTOR IS OF GREAT IMPORTANCE IN OPERA. SOME CONDUCTORS HAVE MORE AFFINITY FOR THE VOICE THAN OTHERS. WHAT ADVICE DO YOU HAVE FOR WORKING WITH CONDUCTORS? HAVE YOU HAD ESPECIALLY GOOD EXPERIENCES (OR OTHERWISE) WITH CONDUCTORS HELPING YOU TO SING A ROLE FOR THE FIRST TIME?

STEPHANIE BLYTHE: I have worked with an equal number of conductors who were exceptionally good at conducting singers and others who were exceptionally bad. An opera conductor has to be a multitasker, knowing and anticipating what is happening on the stage both vocally and physically. Conductors have to know not only what we are singing, but also where we are. In large ensemble numbers such as in *Falstaff*, where you have different characters onstage declaiming different ideas, you need a savvy opera conductor who is connected with the orchestra and with the stage at the same time. The conductor must realize that with singers anything can happen, and I am not talking about mistakes, but rather that many singers are extemporaneous onstage and are creating in the moment. It is like creating a recital, not with a piano but with an orchestra.

LAWRENCE BROWNLEE: A conductor might offer ideas making what I do better or more mature or more thoughtful in that production. For example, I was just doing a show in Vienna, and the conductor was asking for some things I had never done before. I thought that he was asking me to sing non-*legato*, and I thought, "When do I get to *sing*?" But I tried it, and we really worked on getting away from my usual manner of singing. Yes, I still sang *legato*, but I sang it in the way he wanted me to, and it was quite effective from the reviews we received.

NICOLE CABELL: To find a conductor who works as your colleague and not your boss is incredibly satisfying. A good conductor will breathe with you, will watch you as much as you watch him or her, and will display inspirational body language from the pit. In my opinion, a bad conductor will make you feel small, and worse, will make you sound awful. If a young singer happens to encounter a difficult conductor, the only option is to react with grace and maturity and try to put aside his or her own ego. When I get along with a conductor and am inspired by this person, nothing is more satisfying than preparing a new role with him or her.

JOSEPH CALLEJA: There is a joke that sex is so much safer with a condom but so much more fun without—so it is with a conductor! The one thing a singer has to have is humility in working with a conductor. Whether it is Zubin Mehta, James Levine, Antonio Pappano, or a young conductor making a name for himself, when they see that you are open to new ideas and to working with them, they will like you and they will try to make your life as uncomplicated as possible. If, on the other hand, they think you are being arrogant—you go to rehearsal with a know-it-all attitude (you never know it all, never)—it can get off on the wrong foot. Domingo gave me one of the best lessons an opera singer could ever give. He was singing *Otello* a couple of years ago in Los Angeles. At the conclusion, he jumped in a jet and flew to London. Directly from the airport to the rehearsal room, he came bouncing in like he was twenty-three, and he was asking the maestro how he wanted it and was humble. After fifty-one years of singing, he is incredible and still wants to learn.

DAVID DANIELS: Certainly the conductor that's been most influential for me is Harry Bicket. We have a trust between the two of us. It is just so nice, when you're singing and so vulnerable up there, to know that you've got somebody with your best interests at heart down in the pit. He conducts every show being aware of what's happening that night. He's not simply conducting a loop of what the show should be. He adapts to what's happening. That's a great comfort. That doesn't happen often.

JOYCE DIDONATO: Know the score as well as, or even better than, the conductor does. Then you will have the foundation and knowledge to make constructive comments to try and plead your case, should the circumstances call for it. Plus, it will simply make you a greater musician along the way. I would like opera singers to also be seen as musicians!

CHRISTINE GOERKE: They're all different. The best conductors are the ones who are willing to work with the singer so that we are making art. With the ones that want to be dictators, you put your seatbelt on and go for the ride. That's when it becomes our job to try to make little modifications without disturbing what they want. You will know right off the bat what sort of conductor you have because if you ask politely for a modification and you get a "that's the way it is," then don't bother wasting your breath on other conversations. Just go figure out what you need. And you have to also know the conductors who want you to lead. They are the ones who want to accompany you. Our game is just to decide which flavor we are working with on the first day and go from there.

DENYCE GRAVES: I have had very good experiences working with conductors and I am grateful. I have also had unpleasant experiences with conductors who insist on imposing their ideas alone and who can sabotage you in the pit. I would always suggest to any singer to find some way to communicate directly with the conductor apart from the working environment. This could be in a coaching, or by telephone or email to share your thoughts or areas where you could use support, or just to solidify a collaborative relationship that is vital. It's always wonderful to feel and know that you have a friend in the pit, someone who's on your side.

GREER GRIMSLEY: I start by giving respect and expecting respect back. As with raising children, you choose your battles. If a conductor has an idea about a certain phrase and how it goes, I will try it. Lots of times you find new ways of doing things. It's just staying open to suggestions. But that's not always the case. For me, a conductor like Jeffrey Tate is one from whom I learned so much. I got to work with him after having done my first *Ring* cycle. I had put in a lot of work on that, having done three (four if you count the dress rehearsal) before I got to him. I felt like such a newbie when I came to him, he having done many, many *Rings*, and anything he was going to tell me was going to be pure gold. So, long story short, stay open.

THOMAS HAMPSON: I have had some of the most miraculous conducting experiences in my life as a young singer cradled between Jimmy Levine, Nikolaus Harnoncourt, and Wolfgang Sawallisch. I have learned a great deal from great conductors. They are superlative musicians, with sensibilities and hearing that are extraordinary. I heard once that Sawallisch was going to work with a young conductor I knew, and said, *"Herr Professor Sawallisch, bring ihm bei, wie man atmet"*—"Professor Sawallisch, teach him how one breathes." Sawallisch looked at me and said, "Ach, he doesn't breathe?" I said, "I am sure he does, but not vocally!" Everything we singers do is centered on the breath, whether you want to metaphorically call that your soul or your resonance, and if a conductor conducts from his head and his hands and is not breathing the musical phrase, then you're going to have trouble, and it won't be as musical as both of you want it.

ALAN HELD: A great conductor can make all the difference in how you sing a role. I don't like to sing a new role unless I know that the conductor has conducted the piece before. I need a conductor who will breathe with me. I want one that understands, at least to some extent, my voice and what I can bring to the role. We both need to understand that not all the music occurs during the actual aural experience; it also occurs during the rests. I believe that we all have to be open to each other and to each other's artistry. I have had wonderful collaborations with conductors at most times.

JONAS KAUFMANN: You have to have an agreement on the interpretation not only with directors but also with conductors. It doesn't mean that you have to stick with your opinion. It also doesn't mean that you have to follow 100 percent what the conductor wants. The conductor wants to work in the interests of the total opera, but he or she might not be a singer or know enough about the voice. You have to tell conductors when you have to breathe, etc. It's always a compromise.

SIMON KEENLYSIDE: To be a good conductor is an all but impossible job: to hear and structure the soundscape and to understand and appreciate the inexact art that is singing. A good conductor is also part psychologist, making the musicians and singers, almost by force of will, realize what he or she wants. What I would say about conductors is what I would say about all colleagues: cooperation is the order of the day. It behooves singers just to keep their mouths shut and do their jobs. If we do that well, then most conductors will notice, and then life goes on happily. I think it's fair to cut them a little extra slack and give them every chance to express what they want. Keep an eye on them, and show them (but don't tell them) that you know what you are doing.

KATHLEEN KIM: I've been very lucky and have had no problems with conductors. Some conductors I work with have been very helpful.

ANA MARÍA MARTÍNEZ: Patrick Summers was conducting my first Butterfly in Houston. I was nervous and I looked at Patrick, and he was beaming ear to ear and gave a beautiful, positive energy. It was lovely. Also, I worked with the wonderful Gustavo Dudamel, who is such a breath of fresh air. If he is doing something the first time, he says, "You have done this before. Tell me how it goes." (Of course he knows how it goes!) This attitude is so disarming, and you all work as a team. And of course the wonderful Plácido Domingo, who comes in being the great, incredible singer-legend and now a conductor, who's singing with us as he conducts. Remember it's not about you or somebody else. It's about the piece, the process, and the experience. We are there to serve and find common ground.

LISETTE OROPESA: I get key breath marks and tempos clear and go over them with the conductor if I feel that there is a lack of synchronicity. If your breaths are in line with his or her musical ideas, you can collaborate and go from there. If the conductor is asking for something that doesn't work, have a talk, but in private.

ERIC OWENS: Within the first five minutes, you know if someone's a singer's conductor—someone who's there with you, and you're dancing. Sometimes a conductor will ask what tempo I would like in an aria or a particular passage, and I'll say, "Let's just dance and see what happens." The conductors who smile get it. With these conductors, you don't know who is leading, and that is awesome! I hate the idea that a conductor is waiting for me, because then it gets bogged down. I love conductors who get a performance out of you that you couldn't have done without them. The best ones make it an exchange and a great partnership. (Reciprocity!) I always come with that spirit of flexibility. Other times it can be a nightmare. Being heard over the orchestra, for example, is not the singer's responsibility. It's the responsibility of the conductor.

DIMITRI PITTAS: I've had experiences where during the entire rehearsal process the conductor is just totally connected with me, and we're making music and there's a lot of play and give and take. Then you get in front of a machine of 80 to 120 instruments and that changes things. I tend to give conductors the benefit of the doubt. They're trying to create something. Unfortunately, sometimes people are on different pages where a tempo is that night. Sometimes you need to go a little bit quicker, but they're thinking they are going to stretch it out. Those are the nights you have to work harder. But if you have that bond with the conductor through the rehearsal process, where he or she knows what it is that you're feeling, then that makes it easier.

EWA PODLEŚ: For my personal use, I make a distinction of putting all conductors into two categories: walking/marching and singing. I hate to work with the first. I love to work with the second. The first seem never to have heard about phrasing, timing, drama, narration, space. They usually are possesed by a false rhythm. Unfortunately, singing conductors are a minority.

JENNIFER ROWLEY: As a young singer on the international scene for only three or four years, I can say you're going to come across conductors who love the voice. Will Crutchfield is an example of one of those. He wants to work with you and have the biggest success you could possibly have. Then there are other conductors who want you to do it their way. So you have to take inventory of the situation about which kind of conductor you have, and then prepare yourself accordingly. I certainly have had conductors who want it to be their way or the highway. You are going to run into conductors who are going to give you a hard time. Even stars have that problem.

GERHARD SIEGEL: Conductors, who are onstage with us, give entrances and breathe with us, and carry a singer in and through a performance and make singing easier, are special. It's like a kind of magic carpet because it feels safe and secure. That said, a prompter can also "conduct" so that the conductor can concentrate on the orchestra and the music. Often, one can also observe that a conductor does not really like a singer. That is a torment, and the performance becomes vocally and musically demanding, and it may go to the limits of the possible. It is important to say, diplomatically but determinedly, what you want and need. Anything you criticize should be based on knowledge. For my first big roles, I had a conductor who really liked me. Singing everything was like playing a game (Siegfried, Siegmund, Parsifal, and Stolzing). For my last big role, Tristan, I had a wonderful conductor who carried me note for note through the performance, which is to say the same for the many other wonderful great and grand conductors whom I may meet again.

7. WHAT IMAGES OR TECHNIQUES HELP YOU TO PROJECT IN A LARGE HALL OVER THE ORCHESTRA AND STILL MAINTAIN THE EXPRESSION AND DYNAMIC QUALITY OF THE MUSIC?

STEPHANIE BLYTHE: The only technique I use is a desire to get to the truth of the character and be understood.

LAWRENCE BROWNLEE: I don't have a gargantuan, huge voice like some others who can fill a football stadium, so I make sure that my sound is always present and forward and that it can hopefully travel to the farthest distance of the theater.

NICOLE CABELL: Breath, resonance, and diction are the main factors in helping a singer project in a large hall. Carefully measured out, low breathing gives body to the voice. Equally important is *squillo*, or properly placed tone utilizing the frontal head resonators, which enables a voice to sail over whatever sounds (choral, orchestral, piano, etc.) happen to be supporting it. Diction is the other key in projection; using sharp consonants and clear, pure vowels help clarify your sound. I find in certain houses I am singing between 70 percent and 90 percent much of the time, even using *squillo*, which may be adjusted if you have a sensitive conductor. In recital with piano, I use a broader range of vocal dynamics, perhaps 30 percent to 90 percent. I only use 100 percent of my vocal dynamics on a few select notes and only for expressive purposes, because I believe this reservation keeps a singer healthy.

JOSEPH CALLEJA: You cannot change your vocal technique or production according to where you are. That is ridiculous. We need the assurance that what we are putting out and what is coming back to us, and what we hear, is actually being heard in the hall. I concentrate on having my voice in a high placement, similar to what I do in a practice room. The worst thing you can do when you don't hear yourself is push, because then you overcompensate and unbalance the whole muscle structure.

DAVID DANIELS: It's important as a singer, no matter what voice type you are, to sing with the same voice and the same technique and weight of voice, no matter where you are. At times, the largeness of the house or, most importantly, the dryness of the house can really mess with your head and your ears with what you're hearing back. So at times it's very difficult not to push and drive the voice to try to make it bigger. When one pushes the voice, no matter what voice type, the sound gets smaller. When one sings with normal technique and normal weight, with the breath going through this sound in a lyric manner, then the voice sounds huge and very present. I do fight with that at times, but I certainly don't try to make more sound when I am in a big hall.

JOYCE DIDONATO: It's not a question of imagery—it simply comes down to the breath. Breath is the only thing that can help project the voice into any hall, regardless of size. If the voice is lined up completely on the breath, it will be directed into the perfect resonance space so that the softest to the loudest sounds will all be heard. (Think of the piccolo—the piccolo is never drowned out!) A resonant, concentrated sound that is produced entirely on the breath will always carry. Apart from that, to quote the great Soile Isokoski, my first glorious Marschallin, who said the following to me in bed as the curtain rose on my very first Octavian and I was freaking about the volume of the orchestra: "Balance is not our problem."

CHRISTINE GOERKE: I absolutely don't think of that. Once I was in Japan doing something with Barbara Bonney. She was being swallowed up by the orchestra. It was a young orchestra, and they really weren't quite listening to her. She turned around, faced them, and sang probably a dynamic underneath what was written. Magically, they were listening. I thought this was so brilliant. I have stolen that from Barbara. (Thank you, Barbara.) Occasionally I have sung a little underneath where the thing is, saying I'm giving everything I have (batting my eyelashes). And then magically the dynamic will go down a bit.

DENYCE GRAVES: As far as projecting in a large hall or over an orchestra, my technique is the same. Sing into the core resonance of my sound with focus. Period.

If a voice is focused and is lean, it will carry and project. I know that some singers under-sing rehearsals on purpose to get the conductor to bring the orchestra down and for the orchestra to get used to playing lighter, and then they sing full out during the performance. Well, that's another way, but the bottom line is to be consistent with your own technique. I feel that I have enough to be concerned with on my own than to worry about others, but it certainly can be said that orchestras can and often do cover singers, and the ultimate responsibility of this lies with the conductor.

GREER GRIMSLEY: I just sing and I try not to adjust to the size of the hall. If you are singing correctly, there shouldn't be a problem, and you don't have to adjust at all. There is a Zen proverb: "The more you try to do something, the further away you get from it."

THOMAS HAMPSON: If you think you have to put out more sound, then *projection* is the wrong image. Bullets and broomsticks can be projectiles;

Denyce Graves
Recognized worldwide as one of the most exciting vocal stars before the public, Denyce Graves continues to gather unparalleled popular and critical acclaim in performances on four continents. Her career has taken her to the world's great opera houses and concert halls. Ms. Graves is particularly well known to operatic audiences for her portrayals of the title roles in *Carmen* and *Samson et Dalila*. A native of Washington, D.C., Ms. Graves attended the Duke Ellington School for the Performing Arts and continued her education at Oberlin College Conservatory of Music and the New England Conservatory. She has on several occasions performed in recital at the White House and provides many benefit performances for various causes special to her throughout each season. Photo courtesy Devon Cass.

voices resonate. The idea that we inhale and smatter a sound against the auditorium's back wall is just nonsense. I said recently in a class that we do not project our voices, we resonate our souls. That is a very sweet sentence, but also essentially true. A better metaphor is: I keep the bow firmly on the string. I am not going to bounce around, no random movement in my *legato*, and I concentrate on the binding of consonant and vowel. If you want to have your voice carry more, concentrate on the inside of the word and the implosion of the consonant versus thinking you have to explode the voice into a hall. That is always a bad idea for a singer.

ALAN HELD: You can only sing with your voice, whether it be in a large hall or small space. You shouldn't compromise the instrument because of the orchestration or size of the theater. If what you have is not enough to sing over large orchestras or in large halls, perhaps you shouldn't be singing in that situation. However, it is also important that the conductor respects your instrument and capabilities and that his assistants help him to get the right balance. They need to be honest with each other and have the music served and the singer not compromised.

JONAS KAUFMANN: Nothing. Whether it is a small hall or a large hall, I don't do anything differently. On the contrary, if you think you need to make your instrument bigger, as do a lot of singers here at the Met because it's the Met, the result is the opposite. They over-sing and they are too stiff. A relaxed, natural sound or relaxed speaking will go to the last row even in a big hall. The less relaxed, the more problems you will have because the tone doesn't grow. Don't think about big. Think about having fun.

SIMON KEENLYSIDE: Part of the answer to this depends upon the nature of the stage and the set. If directors and set builders continue to cover the stages with material better suited for soft furnishings, then it will always be a nightmare. It's not just a question of being heard, but of having the right to color the sound without incessantly having to fight the acoustics. It is a fundament of operatic singing to identify the *squillo* and overtones which will cut through the orchestral textures without the singer using undue heft; at the same time, not to sound like a chain saw.

KATHLEEN KIM: I don't think about it. There's nothing you can do about it either. You use your own voice and you use what you have. You can't force it because it's a big house. It's not going to project more.

ANA MARÍA MARTÍNEZ: The idea to grab, hold, and drive is bad. You do need some muscle involvement and, of course, the airflow. We know if there's more air, it'll be breathy and not carry. If it's muscular, it's not going to carry, so there has to be the perfect harmony between muscle involvement and airflow. If you think you have to focus or tunnel it too much, it's just not going to work.

LISETTE OROPESA: *Squillo* comes from ideal placement of the voice, which comes from finding an efficient vowel placement for each note. Breath!

ERIC OWENS: A free-flowing ease of production, coupled with clear diction. But, what is most important is that you not try to push your voice past its limits in order to be heard. There have been very few voices that could win an audibility contest against more than eighty people with "machines" in their hands. It's the responsibility of the conductor and the wonderful musicians of the orchestra. If you're in an orchestra rehearsal and you've been singing in full voice and the infamous "they" ask you if you can give more, the answer is, pretty much always, *"No!"* (Drops hidden microphone!)

DIMITRI PITTAS: I have a pretty resonant voice, but in a smaller house I tend to feel a little bit more comfortable. I don't have to work so hard for the *forte.* When you get into a bigger house, you do have to adjust. Your *mezzo piano,* which might work really nicely in a 1,000-seat house, doesn't work so well in a 3,000-seat house, so that adjustment needs to be there. Your *mezzo piano* isn't always going to be the same, and your *mezzo forte* isn't always going to be the same. At the end of the day, as long as you're being true to the colors of your voice and to what you're capable of, the size of the house shouldn't really matter.

EWA PODLEŚ: Techniques for projecting in a large hall are not a problem, but conductors are. They forget that, usually, the leading element of a composition with a voice belongs to the singer. *Forte* in the orchestra along with a voice is not the same as *forte* with an orchestra alone. Richard Strauss wanted his orchestra to sound like Mendelssohn. He also said that a conductor must always hear a singer and create dynamics in the context of both.

JENNIFER ROWLEY: I always think about the people in the back row of the balcony, whether they're going to see and hear it, because they paid for a ticket too. If you have a conductor who loves the voice, he will bring the orchestra down to accommodate what you want to do vocally. You can only sing with your voice; if you try to push over an orchestra, you are going to get in trouble. I like to think about soaring over the orchestra to get to that last row of the balcony.

GERHARD SIEGEL: I have no picture or a special technique for this. A voice carries or does not carry. I trust my technique and carrying power, so I do not worry because of acoustics or large halls.

CHAPTER 3

✒

On the Recital and Concert Stage

In contrast to the grandness of opera, the recital features the intimacy of the art song, a blending of poetry and music in a kind of microcosm of each composer's style. Finding the right pianist and repertoire and creating a special artistic collaboration allow the singer to communicate with the audience in a more personal way, whether it be by adding narration and projected images or by reading the texts. Stephanie Blythe so effectively sings with the lights up because she believes that "an audience that is aware of each other and their surroundings makes a very interesting energy in the room." Nicole Cabell is enthusiastic that recitals offer her an opportunity "to really play, to bring more colors, dynamics, rhythmic variety and styles to my singing than opera." Tenor Gerhard Siegel insists upon using the music, while Greer Grimsley likes to incorporate crossover pieces or musical theater selections as well as talk to the audience. In addition, today's programs done for video and TV require the singer's awareness of such issues as performing arias out of the context of the opera or singing with the camera in mind. As Ana María Martínez said of the "flashy" stadium concerts she has done with Plácido Domingo and Gustavo Dudamel: "I think I let that Latina side out more."

1. COMPARED TO OPERA, WHAT ARE SOME OF THE DIFFERENT DEMANDS OF THE RECITAL STAGE? WHAT ARE SOME OF THE REQUIREMENTS FOR SUCCESSFUL RECITAL PERFORMANCE? ARE THERE THINGS YOU DO DIFFERENTLY EITHER VOCALLY OR INTERPRETIVELY?

STEPHANIE BLYTHE: I do not think of them as being so different. Recital is exciting in that it is so totally text-driven. In opera you have so many other ingredients making the experience for the performers and the audience. In a recital everything is incumbent upon you to make it come alive for the audience. When you are doing a recital, it's all you and the pianist, the composer, and the poet. The other difference is the inherent intimacy created in a recital—a visceral, active connection between the artists and the audience that contributes to the way we make music in that close-up venue.

LAWRENCE BROWNLEE: I've been doing recitals for some years now, but that first one is always a little bit bumpy and is a lot of preparation. I listen to recordings of Gérard Souzay, Elly Ameling, and others. I always encourage people to do that, but then you go and take it to the practice room. Also, going from opera mode to recital mode is quite a transition. I think it takes a great deal of concentration. You get better with age and experience.

NICOLE CABELL: Recitals offer me an opportunity to really play, to bring more colors, dynamics, rhythmic variety and styles to my singing than opera. I usually have the freedom of choosing exactly what I want to sing, and am not straitjacketed by exhaustive tradition and comparisons to other singers. The downside, of course, is I have to be very flexible, switching between styles and languages in an almost schizophrenic fashion. It's easy to become my character singing opera, as I only have one character, style, and language throughout the evening. I've known many singers who simply won't sing recitals, as it exposes too many flaws in their singing, while an equal amount of my colleagues prefer recitals to opera, as it can be incredibly personal and gratifying.

JOSEPH CALLEJA: When it is a concert performance of an opera the difference is minimal—pretty much everything is the same. There is even minimal acting in a concert performance nowadays. Also, you are at the front of the stage, so you do not have to worry about your position in some corner of the stage. Recitals—when you have different programs and different songs—that is a challenge, in that you have to try to inhabit the role and the character of each excerpt and do it justice. A smart singer will prepare a program that will help him or her do that. If you are singing about love and happiness, it is very difficult to then sing about death and sadness right in the next aria. The transition period between the arias or excerpts will help you to get into the role. So it is all about experience, proper programming, and the ability to give the right mood to each piece.

DAVID DANIELS: It is a different night of performing. There's no question about it. Although the technique of the voice doesn't change, I cannot go from a Handel opera that goes from middle C to D on the staff and sing a recital two days later. The recital repertory has a larger range both dynamically and *tessitura*-wise, so it does take me a while to get it back in my voice. You're naked in Baroque opera because Handel is just so difficult, with the sheer length of the operas, although you're not covered up by French horns and trombones. But you're emotionally naked in a recital. You feel vulnerable because you're not playing one character on the stage; you're playing a character for each song, and some songs might have three characters. It's tough with different languages and styles, yet I love it. I think it might be my favorite medium.

CHRISTINE GOERKE: Recitals terrify me. When I am on an opera stage, I am a character, but in recitals, people see your soul. That's why recitals can be so unbelievably great or so unbelievably boring. I will talk to people in between (because I don't feel nervous that way) and tell little stories about the first time I sang the songs. If people giggle at a song, I like that too. That's my way to do a recital. As far as orchestral stuff, the hardest part is sitting at the front of the stage not moving around and dragging attention away from everybody else and wondering if your voice is still there. I hate it when they ask me to sit there for the whole Beethoven Ninth.

DENYCE GRAVES: I don't have a "favorite" anything; however, if I had to choose between the operatic stage and the recital stage, I would choose the recital stage! This kind of intimacy and exposure is a thrill to me and makes the challenge and responsibility greater. A recital is much more refined and subtle and in many ways is the opposite of operatic singing in terms of delivery. While the excellence for good, healthy fundamental technique is always required no matter the genre or style, operatic singing tends to be "bigger" and can employ a certain vibratory pattern. One doesn't always hear that many nuances and so much "leanness" of the voice in an operatic setting as would be exposed in a recital, where it is much more intimate, up close, and personal.

GREER GRIMSLEY: I love the intimacy of a recital and connecting with people. I like Stephanie Blythe's idea of talking to the people and keeping the lights on, and I told her I intend to do that as well. Then you can feel the connection. You allow people to read the translation if it's in another language when you have lights on. Also, I like to put things together that are interesting to me and to share with the audience.

THOMAS HAMPSON: On the recital stage, you are the conduit of thoughts and emotions. I feel myself a doorway to the listener's own imagination. So I don't come out on the stage and sing to people, but sing *for* people. The recital is a walk or *Spaziergang* through various landscapes of soulful and intellectual experiences. In many ways, it is a diary of who we are as human beings. You're there to make echoes of the human experience.

ALAN HELD: In a recital, you are basically in charge of so much more than you are in an opera performance. As far as changing my style, I may, because the style itself is different. But if I can't sing the items with my own technique, I shouldn't be singing it. You can bend and interpret a lot more easily dealing with a single pianist than you can with a conductor who is

Greer Grimsley
Bass-baritone Greer Grimsley is internationally recognized as an outstanding singing actor and one of the most prominent Wagnerian singers of our day. He is a leading interpreter of Wotan in Wagner's *Ring* cycle, Scarpia in *Tosca*, Jochanaan in *Salome*, the title role in *The Flying Dutchman*, the title role in *Macbeth*, Mephistopheles in *Faust*, and the Four Villains in *Les contes d'Hoffmann*. He has performed these roles to international acclaim with the Metropolitan Opera, San Francisco Opera, Los Angeles Opera, Royal Danish Opera, Teatre del Liceu Barcelona, Lyric Opera of Chicago, Teatro la Fenice, Santa Fe Opera, and Tokyo's Nikikai Opera, among numerous others. Photo courtesy Kobie van Rensburg.

leading the charge and over a large orchestra. In recital, I am freer to color the voice and use more vocal effects than I am in an operatic performance. This puts more of the emphasis on expression—and allows you the chance to do more. You also just have more liberty to do your own thing—nothing wrong with that.

JONAS KAUFMANN: No, I don't think so. I am using the exact same instrument and technique. I may change slightly depending on the style. You can't do a Bach cantata as you would Wagner or an art song. I mean all the *smorzando* and the *portamenti*—you shouldn't use that, as they are inappropriate. It is true, many times in a Lied recital you can use sounds that are soft, sounds that you are not able to use in opera because there is an orchestra under you, but when you look here at the *Parsifal* we are doing now [at the Met], there are moments I am singing as softly as I can imagine, and it still carries.

SIMON KEENLYSIDE: In the recital hall, I would try to take away a lot of the iron in the sound. By not singing quite so forcefully for the preceding week or more, I would encourage gentler sounds, half tones, and *mezza voce*. The palette of colors possible in a recital hall can be wider. There are no competing forces for the sound space, and the story is held only by voice and piano. It would behoove any singer to "speak," as it were, with as many colors as he or she thinks the story requires. In the opera the same is true, of course. Also, perforce, the size of the halls requires a singer to introduce and develop the *squillo*, that iron in the sound that can cut through the orchestral textures and fill the room without the need for undue vocal heft.

KATHLEEN KIM: In a recital, you don't have costumes or acting onstage. It's all about the singing. It's you and the pianist and the music. You are naked. I think it's very hard because all the attention is on you. You have to be able to express and to do more. You don't have any help!

ANA MARÍA MARTÍNEZ: There is a classic recital concept and also the big arena concerts where you're doing a lot of the show arias. Although those are flashy, it's still you. I let that Latina side out more in some of these big concerts, with bling, makeup, and dress. But the song recital is so intimate. I love every audience, and since I can see their faces, it's about storytelling. I actually think of my child and his eyes and how he wants to think what's next. On the recital stage, it's more you, as opposed to the opera stage, where it's the character you represent.

LISETTE OROPESA: Recitals are all about an intimate space in which to deliver a fabulous text. I make a story out of the song recital, collaborate with the pianist for a mutual sentiment, and deliver it with 100 percent commitment.

ERIC OWENS: The recital is the hardest performing I do. It's the most challenging and takes the most energy. In fact, I am more tired after a recital than after a five-hour opera. There is nothing like this paring down, this intimacy, in a recital. It's easier to shout out to a group of ten people than to just talk to one or two people, with words coming out that have so much meaning. The ideal recitals take place in smaller venues, which take away the barrier of distance, and everything becomes quite concentrated, which requires more energy. What takes a lot of energy is dealing with many intense, emotional subjects, which, when coupled with a limited physical outlet, can be, oddly enough, physically draining.

DIMITRI PITTAS: There's always something you can learn on the small stage that you can bring to the big stage and vice versa. You are an artist communicating an emotion and taking the reins of hundreds of people at the same time. You are able to take them on a journey. In recital, there's a vulnerability and the ability for you to show who you are. It's important to round you off as a musician to be able to do opera and recital successfully. I'm not going to sing *mélodie* the same way that I would sing a piece that was written two years ago by a modern-day composer, but I don't necessarily change the way that I sing based on the stage.

EWA PODLEŚ: In fact, I believe that the recital is, above all, the real actor's theater. The assistance of a real pianist-partner (not an accompanist!) is necessary.

JENNIFER ROWLEY: For a solo recital, you have to carry the whole night with the pianist. Pick pieces you have a connection to because if you lose connection during the recital for a minute, the audience will lose connection with you. Vocally, the recital uses a simpler vocal technique, mixed with full operatic singing. So it's never just "Here is my full operatic sound." There's a differentiation that takes place.

GERHARD SIEGEL: In the opera, we compensate for vocal difficulties by acting, using the scenery, among many other options. At the recital, we are naked. However—and I stand by this statement—I tell the stories in the song just as vividly in performance (vocally interpretive) and play a character. Many may say that's not a Lied, but I would say it is. Also, a *Winterreise* has a statement. Or take Wolf—all wonderful, exciting, enigmatic, and funny stories which must be told and must not be only beautiful songs. I also insist that recitals must not be sung by heart. With the security of the music in front of me, I have a much greater freedom of interpretation. If you are clever, then no one will notice. I have often inquired, and again and again most listeners' replies were: "You used the music?" In recital I do nothing different than on the opera stage. Maybe I'm a bit stiffer because I move less.

2. WORKING WITH A PIANIST IN RECITAL OFFERS A DIFFERENT OPPORTUNITY FOR ARTISTIC EXPRESSION AND COLLABORATION THAN OPERA. HAVE YOU ANY TIPS FOR SELECTING A COLLABORATIVE PIANIST? HOW DO YOU APPROACH REHEARSALS AND COLLABORATING, IN GENERAL, WITH YOUR PIANIST?

STEPHANIE BLYTHE: Collaboration involves mutual understanding, especially in planning a recital. I will say what my collaborative artist Warren Jones says to me about artistic expression: I sing a song best when I feel my life depends on it. The music and the text really have to touch me and make me want to say something about it. It doesn't matter if it's funny or if it's serious. It has to be real and something that I can associate with. If a piece doesn't race my motor, then I will never be able to sell it to an audience. I always picked music, along with Warren, that was exciting for me. If something is sold to you, then you can sell it to somebody else.

NICOLE CABELL: A pianist should be a very similar artist to you, one that feels where you would breathe, where you might improvise a little bit, where your interpretive tendencies tend to lie. I work with concert pianists as much as possible, as they're used to performing and not simply coaching. Working with a coach is very important as well, even if you're just preparing the recital with him or her, and it's especially nice if you can work with a coach, prepare and perform it, if the coach happens to be a seasoned performer. Ultimately, the most important aspect of working with a pianist for a recital is that you understand and read one another. Any kind of dissent can be read very easily in that kind of intimate performance.

JOSEPH CALLEJA: A singer has always to prepare a role as if it is with piano. Why? Because with a piano, you can't hide. Every single blemish or intonation problem is going to be immediately apparent. There is a difference in style, of course. If you are preparing Lieder or songs, it is a difference in style but not a difference in technique or approach. Mozart has a style; Verdi has a style. You sing with your voice but change the style, inflections, and nuances. As to pianists, the greatest ones are those who make the piano sound like an orchestra and who breathe with you. This breathing is what makes a great pianist/collaborator. Then again, it is all about chemistry as well. Like love, there is chemistry between two people, and that is also imperative for a pianist/collaboration.

DAVID DANIELS: I've worked with the same pianist for seventeen years now, and that's Martin Katz. I have a connection with him. He and I are colleagues, but I'll always be a student of his, because he has such a vast knowledge of rep, and such a creative mind, and he's such a wonderful player. He's one of those that are equally a genius at teaching as they are at playing. So I take a backseat to him because I learn so much from him. I love my pianist to be aggressive and to be percussive with his touch, and Martin is all of those things. He's a big orchestra. I need that support; I need that push and pull. And it makes for a wonderful night of recital.

DENYCE GRAVES: When I choose a pianist to collaborate with, it's about the chemistry I have with that individual and how that individual feels and expresses the music, and if we are in harmony together energetically. For someone with whom I've had a long-standing working relationship, like Warren Jones, he and I can just meet before the engagement, once we know the material, and something magical always happens. I love his touch of the keys and his relationship with them. There are times when I forget that I have to sing as I sit back (energetically) and luxuriate in his touch and expression.

GREER GRIMSLEY: You never know how well you work with someone until you actually collaborate with him or her. If I connect well with someone, I tend to continue working with that person.

THOMAS HAMPSON: You have to share the same level of musical wonder. Clearly the pianist must be as interested in text and language as the singer, and the singer has to be as appreciative as the pianist is of musical architecture. Of course the alpha and omega for a pianist is to breathe as we do. My great mentor in song literature was Gwendolyn Koldofsky at the University of Southern California. She always had such wonderful simple sentences, such as "Essentially, the pianist is either beginning the musical phrase to which the singer joins, or is ending the musical phrase in which the singer has exploited the expression." That relatively simple but profound commentary to musical conversation is the essence of it. It's not brain surgery; it's open-heart surgery.

ALAN HELD: Obviously, you must choose a pianist whom you have complete confidence in. In addition, your personalities have to meld in a way that you are creating the desired impact. I observe pianists, listen to them play, hear their expression, watch how they actively listen and communicate with the singer, and try to decide if that could work for me as well. I like having a pianist who I feel "has my back" and that I can show my support to as well. And I think it is *very* important to always remember that this is a total collaborative effort between two people with distinct and absolute talents. I always offer my pianist the opportunity to show his or her individual talent via solo numbers during a recital. This is only fair and right, in my opinion.

JONAS KAUFMANN: I think it is very good to have someone that you like and is sensitive. It is very important because you're exposed much more to the audience than when you have an orchestra, a set, costumes, colleagues, and the lights. The great thing about Lieder is that you can be spontaneous. It's actually a duo—it's not a singer and somebody accompanying, but equal partners. You can only do that with someone you really trust. A pianist can kill you in recital if he chooses the wrong *tempi* or the wrong dynamics. You must be partners.

SIMON KEENLYSIDE: Choose someone who is fun to make music with. There's no money in recitals, and you will likely be doing all that legwork for many years and for very little financial return. I think it's also good to work with someone who is of the same situation: starting out and who also wants to make their way in the world of chamber music. That helps to foster a good partnership and also brings along the next generation of accompanists.

KATHLEEN KIM: I think communication is always important in a recital. It's cooperation. In songs the accompaniment is very important, so you have to choose someone who you can work well with and discuss things with—someone you are comfortable with.

Thomas Hampson
Thomas Hampson enjoys a singular international career as an opera singer, recording artist, and ambassador of American song, and maintains an active interest in research, education, musical outreach, and technology. The American baritone has performed in all the world's most important concert halls and opera houses with many renowned singers, pianists, conductors, and orchestras. He has won worldwide recognition for his thoughtfully researched and creatively constructed programs. Recently honored as a Metropolitan Opera Guild "Met Mastersinger" and inducted into both the American Academy of Arts and Sciences and *Gramophone*'s 2013 Hall of Fame, Hampson is one of the most respected, innovative, and sought-after soloists performing today. Photo courtesy Kristin Hoebermann.

ANA MARÍA MARTÍNEZ: Chemistry is so important with your pianist and understanding how you both think. Spend time together whenever possible, just to chitchat, maybe over coffee, so that the bond is there. Then when you look at each other, there's no need for words. You have that sort of communication. It's a collaboration that's musically and emotionally intimate.

LISETTE OROPESA: I like people who are sensitive to what I give out but who also have something to say musically when they sit down to play a piece. If it's just notes and technical prowess, we have a long way to go.

ERIC OWENS: I see it very much as collaboration, and I try as much as possible to have input from the pianist, especially if it's something he or she is just dying to do. This helps me along in the decision-making process. You should choose a pianist who sings and creates poetry with his or her playing. Also, you should collaborate with someone who is or could be a great friend. For most, these are the only performance opportunities where you get to be the Director of Artistic Planning, so, I urge you not to plan for a crappy experience. Choose repertoire and people that are inspiring, and whose company you enjoy! And, for goodness sake, don't treat them like they're the hired help. You're presenting a recital *together*.

DIMITRI PITTAS: I think it needs to be somebody that you get along with, that you would sit down with for dinner and have a flowing conversation without any awkwardness. It should be somebody that you need to connect with. Musicians aren't always happy-go-lucky, easy, approachable people. I choose to find people that I can get along with well because I know that they'll be able to understand who I am. No matter what it is that I'm feeling, they'll be able to connect to it and follow along. In the same way, I can also feel what it is that they're doing and trying to say. I think the more comfortable the relationship you have with that person, the better you are at serving the music and saying something with it.

EWA PODLEŚ: I don't like and I don't accept so-called accompanists. A real pianist, with whom the collaboration is based on a true partnership, is a performer I am looking for.

GERHARD SIEGEL: The chemistry between singer and pianist has to be right. I have two pianists, my father-in-law and Gabriel Dobner. Somehow, the chemistry was right so that almost no rehearsal is actually, strictly speaking, necessary. An example: you create a song interpretation and repeat it five to ten times. It comes to the recital, and I often have a sudden inspiration, other emotional idea, or completely different things which my pianist had not rehearsed, yet the pianist goes along. The other way around as well—it's a give-and-take in tenths of seconds. Again, the chemistry has to be right.

3. REGARDING THE VOCAL RECITAL FOR THE TWENTY-FIRST CENTURY: HOW DO YOU CREATE A PROGRAM AND SELECT REPERTOIRE THAT ATTRACTS AUDIENCES?

STEPHANIE BLYTHE: I sing with the lights up because I think an audience that is aware of each other and their surroundings makes a very interesting energy in the room. I make sure that there is no text in the program. I want them to have this experience not through the lens of reading it in a program book. What I do a lot now is I recite the poetry before it is actually sung. I will read the translations if it is in other languages. I do that so the audience has a connection to the poetry outside of the music. Then they have the added experience of how the composer reacted to the poetry. That makes an active audience.

LAWRENCE BROWNLEE: I think more than anything it's knowing your audience. I think the music should be accessible. Some things can be progressive, but a recital should not be completely above the heads of the listening public. I always consider the audience when we program the recitals, in the hopes that everybody in the audience can take something away with them.

NICOLE CABELL: Recitals are always going to attract a very sophisticated audience, and I don't believe they need to be entirely revamped to appeal to the masses. Some may say this will result in the death of an ever-declining art form, but because of the very nature of the recital, I don't think it can be changed too much without compromising integrity. A classical recital draws upon a wealth of classically composed repertoire, and if one adds too much modern music or visual stimulation, it ceases to be a classical recital. I've always been fond of the Great American Songbook, and will sometimes add selections by Cole Porter, George Gershwin, and their contemporaries, but I'll do so judiciously.

JOSEPH CALLEJA: A recital has to be entertaining and educational at the same time, giving the audience both something that they want to know and something that is new. I think if you have the usual warhorses that people know, then it will be a bit boring. Audiences are *Homo sapiens* and fascinated by discovery and propelled forward by curiosity. Doing stuff they do not know is a part of the planning.

DAVID DANIELS: First of all, you have to find someplace that's interested in doing a recital. These days, that's a bigger issue than what to program if you're lucky enough to have someone present you in recital. I've sung a lot of recitals in New York City and I've never repeated a set and have never used a music stand. I always want to have a new program when I repeat in cities. I know in the old days, artists often sang the same things.

That worked for them, but I think it's great to learn new things. It pushes me because I don't have a centuries-wide opera rep to sing from. It allows me to sing from centuries I wouldn't have an opportunity for on the opera stage.

CHRISTINE GOERKE: Know your audience and what they expect from you. That's the first thing. The second thing I like is to include some things that are fun. I don't get to do any fun roles, as mine are a little on the depressing side. So I try to find some things that are fun and that get the audience enjoying themselves. I can sing the soprano song rep, the mezzo-soprano, and the alto rep. So I have an opportunity to really stretch things. I try to do a couple of different styles and languages. But always, the most important thing for me is having something in there that's a little lighter because I feel like the ear and the soul need a break.

DENYCE GRAVES: I program first and foremost material that I love, that speaks to me. Then I look at what would challenge me and what would be an introduction for the audience. I choose material that they may not be familiar with, then material that they *would* know or that's familiar—the chestnuts. I'd look at different languages and styles and build the program so that it arcs and peaks. Sometimes I do this chronologically and other times not. I often program fun or unexpected material to finish the program, with a return to standard repertoire for encores, sprinkled with humor and charm.

GREER GRIMSLEY: I would include some classics and some of the newer things. It's been my observation that the less formal presentation is an effective way to reach people. Early in my career I did Affiliate Artists,* where you would do informal performances. You would put together music and would intertwine your personal story and add information about the music and process. I would do these performances in schools, in corporate lunchrooms, or in a women's prison. Inevitably you would have a full house because the people's interest was piqued. If I had the funds, for example winning the lottery, I would reinstate the program.

THOMAS HAMPSON: This is a very interesting point because some of the old rules and regulations do not apply, but I don't think we need to throw the baby out with the bathwater. I think recitals are best with songs even if an opera singer is coming to town. If you have an aria, then sing it as an encore. Program big songs as well as intimate songs. I always have

---

* Affiliate Artists was a U.S. nonprofit performing arts organization that was active from 1965 to the 1990s. Instead of giving conventional prizes, Affiliate Artists offered the winners performance opportunities throughout the United States and helped to involve communities in the arts and arts education.

contact with the venue where I'm performing to ask what the audience expects and is interested in, and then I can take them on a journey from there. You might hear that the audience is not interested in esoteric Schubert (no problem) or that Mahler might be a little hard. Fine. The days of "Here's the program for this season" are over. Tailor your program to the audience you're going to perform for.

ALAN HELD: It is sad that we don't have as many opportunities outside of universities to present vocal recitals. However, it is important to know that recital halls and concert stages are not the only places to take your vocal talents. I still enjoy taking my gifts to residents in nursing homes or other places where folks don't always get the kind of musical entertainment we can bring. This is important for our art, for our vocal development, and for our souls. Not to mention it does some pretty great things for the folks you're singing for. Crossover music is fine in a recital as long as the center of the programming is your central repertoire for the evening. Save the crossover items for the encores or the end of the program.

JONAS KAUFMANN: Actually, recitals are more conservative now than they used to be. We're still doing *Winterreise* and *Dichterliebe*. However, we know that, for example, Richard Strauss would improvise in song recitals. He was famous for adding all of his opera themes in between the songs before he would go on to the next one. Other pianists did the same thing. Have you noticed that many songs of famous Lied composers don't have an introduction? They just start right away, because one would sing the song, and the pianist would continue something in between that led into the next song. It was a much more relaxed event than it is now, where a recital follows a set format and is rather serious. You could try to recreate recitals like they used to do, but I am not sure whether the audience would accept it.

SIMON KEENLYSIDE: Of course, new music must be performed, good new music especially. It might be best to stick to singing music that you love the most. Besides that, we accept that a Rembrandt painting is one of the high points in representational art. It doesn't need updating. So too are Schubert songs one of the peaks of Western art. When I looked up in the Wigmore Hall or Musikverein twenty years ago, I saw a sea of gray hair. I wondered what would happen when that audience died. I know now. There is another sea of gray heads, myself amongst them! What does that mean? I think it means that not every art form is for the young. It's not to say that young people do not like song recitals. All the same, it's a form that appears to require time for people to grow into and appreciate. Why not?

KATHLEEN KIM: It depends on the audience and the venue. If it's for a traditional audience, then I would go with very classic, traditional repertoire. If it's a venue where I can risk twenty-first-century music, then I would.

LISETTE OROPESA: If it's music that you love singing, the audience will sense it.

ERIC OWENS: Finding repertoire that will attract audiences is quite the mysterious prospect, especially in this subset of audiences for an art form that can barely afford to dice up this already small demographic. Also, recitals usually come in the form of some sort of multicity tour, and rep that may be popular in one city might not be in another.

Dare to be original, but not for its own sake, meaning that if you have something specific to say, find rep that lets you do that, or find a way (and there are many) to commission a work with original poetry as well as music. There exists no definitive formula for formulating a recital program. Do what you love, and seek out the unfamiliar, which could introduce you to the musical love of your life!

DIMITRI PITTAS: If you program a recital well, you will take an audience on a journey musically and emotionally and maybe even give them something that they've never heard before. A lot of people just want to hear the Brahms or Schubert hits. In Europe there is just a bigger audience and market for it. I think, at least in America, there should always be an English set because they can finally put the translation down and sit up and appreciate something. There's a lot of music out there that deserves to have more widespread attention.

EWA PODLEŚ: I love to make the audience happy. For a successful recital in the twenty-first century, everything depends on the quality of the music and the performance.

JENNIFER ROWLEY: When I program a solo recital, I like to tell a story with the whole recital. Whether it be illustrative of love or something, there has to be a through line. I also think you should have good program notes, even if it's just a small donor's concert. I like the last songs to be something more contemporary and the encore to be something the audience can hum as they are leaving, even musical theater—something that's fun and beautiful.

GERHARD SIEGEL: My affinity for singing songs has emerged only in recent years. I've not had much experience in this direction and I have to catch up with it. For my voice, the choice is generally a little heavier. I find it in Strauss, Korngold, Schreker, Schoenberg, and Grieg, but also there are Schubert opportunities. The song repertoire, which I prefer, is a repertoire that is rarely done.

4. WITH THE EMPHASIS ON GLOBAL BROADCASTING OF PERFORMANCE, BOTH FOR OPERA AND FOR CONCERTS, SINGERS MUST BE AWARE OF THE CAMERA. DO YOU HAVE ANY SUGGESTIONS FOR HOW TO LOOK GOOD FOR THE CAMERA CLOSE-UPS?

STEPHANIE BLYTHE: You know, I don't do anything any differently with those HD performances than I would do any other time. I really like the HD programming because it brings opera to different parts of the country and the world and to those who would not ordinarily have a chance to see those shows. I generally don't watch them and I don't watch myself. I just don't want to think about how I look when I'm performing, because *no one* looks good when they are singing. I think about the audience I am singing to and I just hope that the camera captures the intention behind the words.

    NICOLE CABELL: My advice in dealing with global broadcasting is not to change who you are, and simply keep doing what you're doing. If you happen to be physically appealing for broadcasting, or an exceptional actor, that makes you lucky, but I've witnessed far too many singers altering their appearance to the detriment of the music, and that will eventually catch up with them. Of course, there are extremes that aren't healthy, and a singer needs to take care of their body for optimum health and energy. If one happens to be "camera-ready," then there are certainly things to do to optimize the broadcasting product. More subtle acting in the face, angles of the body, and anything that might be evident through close-ups can be attended to, but this puts the audience in the theater at a disadvantage, so there are consequences.

    JOSEPH CALLEJA: One of the things that really makes me laugh is this microphone. It is the most ridiculous thing because it is not amplification; it is capturing the moment. What critics don't understand is that you have to find and sing where the microphone is. Think about it: we sing fifty-five nights out of sixty without mics and then for two or three nights we have them and all the sensations are toppled over and different. But there is absolutely no difference in preparation for HD broadcast. Why? Because we are still singing in a theater, in the same opera with the same conductor and orchestra.

    DAVID DANIELS: It's like a television station. It's amazing. The second one I did was less stressful than the first one. The first one was *Enchanted Island*, and I was not well, which did not help. It was very stressful. But *Julius Caesar* was much easier even though Caesar was a much harder role than *Enchanted Island*. It's something you have to do when you work at the

Metropolitan Opera. It's not just HD we're talking about. Almost every performance is recorded for Sirius satellite radio. You are never just singing for the house. It's not easy, because if you allow yourself to be aware of it, it can really eat at you.

JOYCE DIDONATO: I think we must only be concerned with always being more truthful as actors, singers, and communicators. There is no-where to hide on a mile-high movie screen, and anything that reads as false will be the death of you as a performer. But I think false also reads in a theater, so the good news is that if we are concentrating on being more truthful, then the audience watching it live that day will also get a more genuine, hopefully heart-wrenching performance. Bottom line for me is that if we are true in our performance, it will read either on-screen or in a theater. I don't alter my performance when there is a camera present.

CHRISTINE GOERKE: I can't even think about it. If I think about the fact that I am performing in front of a camera, then I am going to forget about the two thousand people in front of me I am actually working for. The camera is very important, but the people who come to see a live perfor-mance are my audience. Otherwise, I would be in a movie studio. It's never nice when you have a camera coming up close to you when you are singing a high note! Sometimes we look great. Sometimes we look like crap.

DENYCE GRAVES: The singer must first of all feel good and be comfort-able in his or her skin. It's valuable for singers and for everyone to do some kind of exercise. In terms of the camera itself, I am always concerned about the double chin, which I do have and think I will have (unless I discover some method that won't be dangerous for me to have), so I'm often angling my face downward or asking the cameraperson not to shoot from below. I also ask to be filmed from the side or on an angle to look leaner, but I re-frain from straight-on shots, and *always* stand tall with good posture, but the bottom line is to sing well. Period. And you will be forgiven for any self-defined "physical flaws."

GREER GRIMSLEY: When they say they're filming, I try to forget that. I try to stay in the moment and in the character as much as I can. In San Francisco, they have placed the cameras in the hall so you can't see them, and for me, I am able to stay more focused in the performances. HD can be a help to the opera format, but for me, opera means seeing and hearing it live. It's so much better being in your seat at the opera. Local opera, also— it doesn't have to be the Met. Invest in your community. Take pride in your communities. Raise them up as high as you can. Another thought: the beautiful thing that we do, and the orchestra, is that with our sound waves we are touching the audience, and you don't get that when you have elec-tronically reproduced sound. It's not the same feeling.

THOMAS HAMPSON: The good thing about these HD performances is that they can get what they want without disturbing us as much as they used to. All of these multimedia forms are only about enhancing a live art form. It's all about the smell of the theater when the curtain goes up and the transport of emotion through the phenomenon of a human being singing. This enlivens our sense of being alive by participation. Is that possible in HD? Without question. Is it better live? Without question. So let's all take a big breath and say we're very clever, we've got great things going with HD, but this is a live art form.

ALAN HELD: Nope. Much of this is out of our hands. We have to sing the way we sing. It is up to the video director to get the shot that best benefits the product and the singer as well. Sadly, I don't think this is always being done, nor is it always possible to get it done right. Singing isn't always pretty. Opera wasn't meant to be seen constantly at three to four feet or less. I think more time needs to be spent preparing some of these video presentations, and I think some camera shots from farther away from time

Alan Held
A highly recognized singing actor for more than twenty-five years, Alan Held has won high praise for his solid technique and vivid interpretations and has performed in nearly every important international opera house with the world's finest orchestras, conductors, and directors. He is a noted Wotan, Jochanaan, and Wozzeck as well as Scarpia and Gianni Schicchi. Originally from Washburn, Illinois, he studied at Millikin University and Wichita State University. He has won numerous awards, including the Birgit Nilsson Prize. He holds the position of Ann and Dennis Ross Faculty of Distinction in Opera at Wichita State University and regularly gives public master classes at Yale University. Photo courtesy Christian Steiner.

to time would be beneficial as well. The important thing for a singer is to avoid looking for a camera and just to sing their performance. Hopefully, as this is being recorded for posterity, the best possible replication of the performance, as it was intended, will come through.

JONAS KAUFMANN: No, I don't have any. I do what I need to do for making my sound. It would make sense to look better, but it doesn't work. I would also say that I don't even have to change the acting because I realized that even the small things read in the hall when they are felt in the right way.

SIMON KEENLYSIDE: Pah! We should worry only about the silly tendency of casting roles based on looks and not voice. That is the real insidious nonsense. I pay as little heed to these broadcasts and cameras as I possibly can. I'm aware that some of the HD relays, such as those made by the Met, are so well done. I'm delighted too that people seem to like them, and that the artistic input of the camera makes these broadcasts a different experience to the theater. However, for this baritone, I consider the cameras to be nothing more than voyeurs, sent there to capture what is their brief. The fun for me is only the old-fashioned art of live theater. The craft of singing, and all the attendant magic of controlling a hall without a microphone, is my chief joy.

KATHLEEN KIM: Yes, I do something differently. I try not to move my eyes and to be more focused, as if I am acting in a movie. If I have to look at the conductor when he or she is not in my field of vision, I try to use my whole body or head to have him or her in my sight so that it looks natural instead of looking sideways.

ANA MARÍA MARTÍNEZ: We are so visual nowadays. We don't look really pretty up close. I would ask that they not video us at high notes, as we do not look particularly attractive at that time, and nothing from underneath as well (they have that camera on the floor). You can forget the camera and all that during the performance, but you also want to feel that you're coming across at your best.

LISETTE OROPESA: Great skin, great wardrobe, great hair. Get an honest friend to help you find good clothes, and get a great haircut. Don't eat junk food.

ERIC OWENS: I have the perfect "diet" for this: *sing your ass off!* You ever meet someone who is just drop-dead gorgeous, and then they start to speak, and that perceived "beauty" starts to melt away? Or you meet someone who seems average visually, and you strike up a conversation, and what you hear becomes a chrysalis to that other sense? This idea of being svelte and "beautiful" on the opera stage is not the recent phenomenon that some would have you believe. Since the days of Peri and Monteverdi, there have been slim singers onstage, and there have been big singers onstage, which continues today. Opera, ultimately, is about quality singing, and sometimes the very best singing (and acting) comes in a body that isn't Hollywood approved. We know the names: Pavarotti, Caballé, Melchior, Traubel, Ponselle, Leontyne and Margaret Price, for the same reason.

DIMITRI PITTAS: When people go to the movie theater, I want them to feel like they're in an opera. My first HD was *Macbeth* from the Met, and when "O figli miei" began, the cameras zoomed in on me. After that scene Peter Gelb was waiting for me backstage. He said, "That was amazing, the way you did that." I said, "I'm not really sure what you're talking about." He said, "The tear. You were crying." I said, "Yes." He said, "Can you do it again?" I said, "I do it every night. I'm not doing anything different." I got so much feedback that the aria was so moving because I had this single tear rolling down my cheek. But the fact is, I cry every single time I sing that aria. There is nothing different about that HD broadcast compared to any other performance.

EWA PODLEŚ: Just be yourself.

GERHARD SIEGEL: This question does not arise for me, since in an HD broadcast of the stage I look the way the director and the art department want me to look. At concerts, I am what I am. What should I do?

CHAPTER 4

ev3

On Maintaining a Career

Perhaps one of the great ironies of achieving a professional operatic career is that a beautiful voice is not enough, and, in fact, is just the beginning. Acting skills, excellent diction, musicality, and a well-developed sense of phrasing and style, as well as drive and determination, are all essential. Also, as American dramatic soprano and pedagogue Margaret Harshaw said: "The real singer is the one who gives you something that you take home with you and it sets up a vibration going in you. It speaks to your heart or your soul." Or practically, as Denyce Graves said: "It's important to have a type of 'package' together." Once this "package" is achieved, maintaining a career and keeping the voice in shape require careful decisions about choosing roles, scheduling, and navigating the business side of the professional world. Soprano Christine Goerke admonishes: "Know your path and do not take on things too soon."

1. WHAT ARE THE MOST IMPORTANT ATTRIBUTES A SINGER MUST HAVE FOR A SUCCESSFUL OPERATIC CAREER TODAY?

STEPHANIE BLYTHE: Learn repertoire! One of the biggest problems that I have in listening to young singers is that they have become so incredibly myopic, especially when going into the professional field. You hear singers who sing five arias extraordinarily well and then when they go to do something else, they have no idea what they are doing. I've talked to countless young singers who, when I ask what their repertoire is, they'll tell me their five arias. What they are learning is how to audition to get a job. They are not learning how to sing. They are learning how to audition and how to be successful in ten minutes. The thing is that opera and an opera career are not ten minutes long. When you go to sing a role, there is so much more involved in it than just an aria.

LAWRENCE BROWNLEE: I think having a normal home life is very important. I probably have too many hobbies. I am a big fan of salsa dancing. I am a very serious hobbyist photographer. I play table tennis, and I'm a big sports fan. More than anything, you have to have a work ethic and a passion for music. It's not easy to be on the road more than two hundred days a year. If we come prepared and we do our work, hone our craft, and show who we are, that's what touches people. Be the best, and that will open the doors for you.

NICOLE CABELL: Besides an excellent natural voice, technique, and acting ability, the main attribute a singer must have is discipline: showing up on time to rehearsal and performances, knowing your music, not throwing diva fits, being a good colleague, and keeping your emotions in check when dealing with difficult personalities. It's obvious a singer needs to keep away from excessive smoking, drinking, and drugs to maintain longevity. Most singers, in the beginning, are selling a product. We are, as artists, dependent on the generosity of profitable businesses as well as personal donations. A huge factor in keeping one's individual career is making sure to do your part after a show, greeting donors, sponsors, and audience members. This is part of the job, but should also be naturally enjoyable, as music lovers are the reason we are able to do what we love.

JOSEPH CALLEJA: Health is very important. It is very hard to have an operatic career with health problems. The whole body is the instrument. If any part of the body is compromised, then the rest of the instrument will suffer. I would recommend not singing too much, not more than forty-five to fifty performances a year. It is also so important to have a good state of mental health and to have a partner who understands you. Singing hates fighting, hates turbulence. And perhaps the most important thing is to say no. A career is more defined by what you say no to than what you say yes to, if you have a great voice. Then you have to have the talent. You can't say you are going to be Calleja, Kaufmann, or Pape. You have to be born that way. No amount of technique and study will give you that.

DAVID DANIELS: Having a successful career in opera means dealing with social media and keeping an integrity of the arts while playing the social media game. This is a balance that's not easy to figure out, because times have so changed in that way. If we're talking about getting out of the day-to-day opera business and keeping some state of sanity, it's my friends, it's my partner, and certainly it's sports. In twenty minutes, I'm about to put on the Redskins game on my computer and sit there and watch my Washington Redskins lose again. Sports is my life. It's as big a passion for me as my music is.

JOYCE DIDONATO: Aside from this truth and purity of communication that I search for (all ideally served up via exquisite musicianship and vocality, of course!), your body is your instrument and is the key to your vocal and physical health. I think this means we need to understand how we move, how we can achieve more freedom with our instruments, but also how we mentally prepare and engage during a performance. I look to athletes quite often to understand how they function at such a highly skilled level. I think we singers can learn a lot about the kind of discipline they employ, but also to learn from the idea of sports psychology they've mastered. The mental conditioning we need as professional singers is every bit as demanding (if not more so) as for professional athletes, and I think it is an underdeveloped part of our profession.

CHRISTINE GOERKE: Drive. If you don't have the drive, then none of the other attributes will help you. These days the way that you look has become almost more important than the way you sing. There's so much that's involved with this that has nothing to do with actually performing. In the beginning you want to do it and it's awesome, and all of a sudden you realize the amount of money that goes out on lessons and taxes and travel and housing and your manager. It can get frustrating so fast. It's totally worth it, but there are so many obstacles that people really need to think about. Also, if you have that sparkle that makes people look at you onstage (which, by the way, is not really something you can teach), then that is also an important ingredient.

DENYCE GRAVES: You must be gifted with a voice that can be developed and shaped. You must be intelligent and able to integrate all of the coordination needed in order to sing. Excellence in singing requires time, dedication, love, instruction, and regular practice. You must have musical skills: a good ear is paramount! You must be tenacious and passionate about just making music itself and not be tied to a result.

It's important to have a type of "package" together—the way you look, dress, your weight, how comfortable you are onstage, how well you're able to manage the theatrical component with the music, how effectively you're able to communicate, how much joy and excitement you have while singing and are able to impart, how quick a study you are, and how consistent you are. These are a few career challenges that should be in play, I think.

GREER GRIMSLEY: My wife, Luretta Bybee, who is on the voice faculties at New England Conservatory and Loyola University in New Orleans, and I have discussed this. Having stamina and drive is a lot of it, besides wanting it, in addition to being resourceful and supple in your thinking and technique and staying that way. The moment you get rigid, then you're done for.

THOMAS HAMPSON: The dumb answer is voice, voice, voice, and then voice. You've got to have chops. Speaking as someone who has had a very successful career, and I say that with gratitude and not arrogance, it's always difficult to tell a young singer you have to be talented. But there must be apparent the instinctual drive to share your experiences through music. A singer must have that overwhelming belief that what he or she has come in contact with, and what he or she feels so strongly, is so beautiful, moving, or important that he or she must, above all else, share that through their talents with us.

ALAN HELD: Good technique, good health, good training, perseverance, determination, and a thick hide. It doesn't hurt to have a good business mind and a wonderful manager. For me, however, the most important attribute (if you call it that) is faith. And let's remember that being a singer is what I do—it is not who I am. Be humble or the business will humble you.

JONAS KAUFMANN: First, I would say a beautiful and reliable instrument that allows you to concentrate on interpretation and acting. Of course, the often mentioned "package" is important as well, but the ribbon and the wrapping can never be more important than the content! Also essential is a

Jonas Kaufmann
Jonas Kaufmann studied voice in his hometown, Munich; his stage career began in 1994 at the State Theater of Saarbrücken. After engagements in Hamburg, Stuttgart, and Milan, he was engaged at the Opera in Zurich, where he enjoyed great success in leading roles of the German, Italian, and French repertoire. After this began his international career, with productions at leading opera houses (La Scala, Covent Garden, Met, Vienna State Opera, Paris Opera) and at the festivals of Salzburg and Bayreuth. The tenor has worldwide success as a concert and Lieder singer. His artistic versatility is documented on numerous CDs and DVDs, many of which have won international awards. Photo courtesy Dietmar Scholz.

continuous study and development of your voice and technique. As the body and the mind change, you must be aware of the developments and work with your voice. Then you should have two or three people on whose ears you can be sure to rely, and that you remain open to criticism. Maintaining your health is essential for a successful career, and this demands a lot of self-discipline in the daily private life. Another important point is to find the right management, one where you are able to establish a relationship of trust and in which there is always room for ample discussion. Oh, and lots of luck!

SIMON KEENLYSIDE: Er, a good solid technique. Perhaps also not to take on a huge repertoire too soon, however talented the young singer is. Be happy with a mix of roles and music in a variety of decent houses and halls. I think that a flexible voice and a long-lasting voice is also likely to be a healthy one. It's hard for a young singer to contemplate sixty-five years of age. But that's the aim, more or less. An innings somewhere shy of forty years of interesting and varied singing, to my mind, would be a good thing to aim for.

KATHLEEN KIM: Nowadays it's different. A singer must have everything. It has to be the whole package for a career. You have to look good, you have to act well, and languages are very important. You have to have stage presence.

ANA MARÍA MARTÍNEZ: I would emphasize networking and social skills, which are very important. None of that is important, though, unless you have the mind-set that you're willing to live out of a suitcase, and you can balance one foot on the stage and the other foot in your home and reality. In my case I'm a mom and a career person. I can be a great mother and have a career, but it's very hard to do them all at the same time. So one day something will get more attention than other things. You have to have a very level-headed approach. If you don't have that, make sure that you surround yourself with people who do have that sense of level-headedness.

LISETTE OROPESA: A complete package. People want to see singers with more than just a fabulous voice (although this is and always should be the primary attribute). They want to see a committed actor, energy, communicative skill, confidence, charisma, and spirit. These are things that are often tested and may even dwindle in performers. We must remember our craft begins with putting on a show.

ERIC OWENS: The most important attribute for a successful career is to sing well. Also, one must have a love of constantly perfecting one's craft. There are many other things you should do, but these are the most important!

DIMITRI PITTAS: It's about being an artist and having something to say, but it's also about recognizing the fact that you are a self-employed individual. If you don't do the work, you don't get paid. And I don't mean specifically having a job and getting paid. I mean if you don't put hours into your career, whether it's networking, translating, listening, or going to a show. The better you are at those things, the better chance you have of the payoff. Those are things you need to have as an opera singer, whether you're doing two gigs a year or fifteen gigs a year. You still have to work for yourself.

EWA PODLEŚ: Aside from the usual ones, talent and professionalism, young singers must be wise in their decisions and not be afraid to turn down offers for fear of losing future ones. Singers must be very clever and make intelligent choices as they develop their careers.

JENNIFER ROWLEY: Best attributes are five thousand layers of really thick skin, because you can't fight city hall. City hall wants everyone to be thin and beautiful and look like a rock star, and if you want to get hired by city hall, you'd better do it. It's not rocket science, and it's the business. There are singer stars; Jonas Kaufmann was compared to Hugh Jackman in *Vogue*. Also in *Vogue*, Annie Leibovitz photographed Renée Fleming in dresses by Christian Lacroix, Karl Lagerfeld, and John Galliano. You have to look at yourself and say, "Okay, these are the things I need to do to increase my marketability in the business." Whether that may be to change your hair, get hair extensions, lose weight, or get fit, you need to do these things so that you can make it in the front door. It's a crazy business, so you have to go with it.

GERHARD SIEGEL: An interesting voice with good technique should be the most important attribute. Today, the fact that outward appearances are more important than the abovementioned is a thorn in my eye. Looks are just superficialities. A certain kind of humility should also be present—to have gratitude for being *permitted* to exercise this wonderful profession.

2. HOW HAVE YOU MAINTAINED LONGEVITY IN YOUR PERFORMING CAREER? CHOICE OF ROLES? SCHEDULING? REPERTOIRE?

STEPHANIE BLYTHE: I have sung nineteen years in big exposure with a variety of roles which were for my voice. I do not believe in *Fach*. I am not just a mezzo-soprano; in some repertoire I'm a contralto, and in some an alto or a soprano (a low one). I think that singing recitals and early music have helped to keep my voice healthy. I also think that singing music that moves helps to maintain the voice and ensure longevity. A fluid voice is one that is going to have a much longer career. I believe that with all my heart.

NICOLE CABELL: Singing the right repertoire at the right time is just as important as taking time for yourself to recover and not sing for short periods. I used to think I could sing as often as I wanted, as long as the repertoire was right for me. I soon realized that taking time off was one of the major factors in longevity. Repertoire has been a trickier process. I have a warm voice, so the temptation is to sing repertoire that demands a rich sound. However, despite always adhering to *squillo* and breath technique, my natural voice is sometimes incapable of carrying over the heaviest orchestration, so I've had to regrettably turn down certain roles that I would have loved to sing.

JOSEPH CALLEJA: Some of it is genetics, some is pacing and technique and saying no. Singing is like a great Bordeaux, like a great Saint-Émilion bottle of wine. You can take a great bottle of wine and emulate the right conditions for aging by putting it in a microwave. Is the end result the same? No.

DAVID DANIELS: I was fortunate in two ways: I got to sing eighteenth-century opera, which is amazing, and fortunate that I got to sing with the voice type that was the most natural for me and brought me a career. I never thought it would be with the countertenor voice! The longevity happens because you're determined. I love singing. It's what I always dreamed about doing. I never want to do anything other than this. But you know you have good times and bad times. Then you have something happen in your personal life that affects you; sometimes health affects your singing. It's figuring out what is the most important thing.

JOYCE DIDONATO: I think it's a mixture of all of these things. Health must be first and foremost, because without that, our instrument simply doesn't have a fighting chance—and that includes not only physical health but, perhaps more importantly, mental and emotional health. Role selection has been vital: I have always returned to my core composers (Handel, Mozart, Rossini) to maintain my natural "home base" vocally. Perhaps above all, I have always searched out a way to *enjoy* what I am doing. I don't think we can underestimate the power and benefit of loving what we do.

CHRISTINE GOERKE: Know your path and do not take on things too soon. I was in my mid-thirties and my first big *Jugendlich* was Chrysothemis in *Elektra*, which fit like a glove. A presenter called and said they would like me to switch parts, and I said no. And I kept saying no until I was forty. Then I sang Elektra lyrically, the way my voice required it to be sung. Once you make that step, there's no going back to Countess. Now my schedule has Dyer's Wife, Brünnhilde, and lots of Elektras. Then you have to start being careful about how many of which roles you are going to do in a year. You cannot put a high, florid role next to something that is in the basement. You have to make a road map of your year, of your season, and know what you're doing to promote longevity.

DENYCE GRAVES: By ongoing study, voice lessons, coaching, practicing, and time at the piano often. Maintaining a positive attitude, realizing that careers ebb and flow, and developing other parts of myself to bolster my creativity and to sustain myself in leaner times. I have also arrived at a point in my career where other things take precedence, like my family. This can liberate you, so that one doesn't feel obligated to accept everything, whether it's for the experience, or the venue or the artists attached to the project or the city or house or money, even though it can all be a blessing. To be able to say no is important at times. Then you can return renewed, with space between you and music and a greater appreciation, and you can offer something fuller and different to your artistry.

GREER GRIMSLEY: I would say make sure you find time to be with yourself and your family and friends. In order to be a vital communicative artist, you have to have a life outside of the stage and actually be invested in this life, just for your mental sake. Also physically, for example, I have three jobs coming up, but I have scheduled a break. It's important to think of a break and think of yourself. As Beverly Sills said, the hardest part in the career is saying no.

THOMAS HAMPSON: Many young colleagues do not get practical career advice as to what they should sing. For example, never sing an opera aria for an audition or competition from an opera you would not sing immediately. Because you can sing "Il balen del suo sorriso" does not mean you can sing *Il trovatore*. A second idea is to always sing lyrically. What I mean by that is never be more preoccupied with showing off your vocal resources. It's about singing, not sport! A lot of people in the vocal music industry today do not have any concept of whether a person they hear sing will be able to still sing that, or anything else for that matter, over a twenty- or thirty-year span. The singers who display in their late twenties a core of dramatic vocal potential are the scary ones. They need to be protected. They need to sing lyrically; they need to be allowed to sound as young as they are.

JONAS KAUFMANN: I was told this story by the great German baritone Josef Metternich, who was with the famous tenors Fritz Wunderlich and Rudolf Schock. They came to the conclusion that it's a circle. You start as a baby, you scream the hell out, and you never get tired. Then you sing in the shower, and it sounds good. Then somebody starts talking to you about technique, and this destroys the natural approach. But the circle should be

that singing is as natural as the crying of a baby. That means do not manipulate your vocal cords, do not try to sound like someone else! Use your own
voice, treat it well, and it will last for a long time. Of course, the right
repertoire and mixture are essential. I have been very judicious in the development of my repertoire. I gave myself time and experience before undertaking the most strenuous and dramatic roles.

SIMON KEENLYSIDE: Damn luck, hard work, and a deal of bloody-
mindedness. If there is a fire under your rear-end and you cannot extinguish
it, well, then you had better just get on with it. It was, and still is, that for me.
Like breakfast: I don't eat it all day, but I wouldn't want to be without it. To
some extent—and I'm almost reluctant to admit it, but the truth is inescap-
able—I sing, therefore I am. As for choices, one must be careful about what
one wishes for in this life, in case one gets it! Many sublimely gifted young
singers are washed up by their mid-thirties. They took on too much heavy
work and blew up. Many of the surprises that fate throws in front of a working
singer will be unexpectedly rewarding. I am grateful for some (not all) of those.

KATHLEEN KIM: I have to schedule well. With my repertoire, I have to
be very careful. I cannot have the high roles back to back. Also, I find enough
time to rest. Mostly I don't talk at all between performances, especially if I
have roles like Zerbinetta. But all the roles I am singing are very high, so I
sometimes have vocal rest.

ANA MARÍA MARTÍNEZ: I think that role choice and scheduling help.
If I had to do the stunts that some do with one day here, the next day in
another place, with constant jet lag, that would wear me down not only
physically but emotionally. I try to keep the hectic scheduling to a minimum. I suggest that you sing as young as you can for as long as you can. By
that I mean, sing on the lighter side of your *Fach*. In the first part of my
career, I was doing all the "-inas." The heaviest thing I did was Mimi. Also, if
you start with the big roles, you have to think about what your fee is going
to be, so start smaller and your fee will grow gradually as you add roles.

LISETTE OROPESA: I'm still young, but yes, all those things. Choice of
roles. Scheduling. Repertoire.

ERIC OWENS: Nobody knows until you are actually at the end of your
career, whenever that may be, if your choices have served you well. People
were predicting the premature demise of Plácido Domingo when he took
on the role of Otello in his thirties. On the other side, we've all seen people
with wonderful techniques and who seemingly made all the right rep
choices, but they have their career cut short by vocal problems. I liken it to
someone who has very healthy habits—is on a macrobiotic diet, jogs every
day, has regular check-ups—and dies from a heart attack at forty. On paper,
that shouldn't be happening. There's no real answer.

DIMITRI PITTAS: I have a lot of faith in my management, and I also get as much information as I can from the people I consider knowledgeable about me, my voice, and what it is I'm capable of doing. Ultimately, the decision is up to you. I think it's also really important to always sing those pieces that are kind of vocal medicines for you. Luciano Pavarotti always sang *Rigoletto*. Alfredo Kraus always sang *Lucia*. Keep those things that will just make you sing well because you have no other way of singing them except for well. As long as you keep those pieces in your repertoire that you consider healthy and that help you sing most beautifully and with the most ease, then that will help to keep the voice youthful and the career as long as it can be.

EWA PODLEŚ: I know my capabilities and I've never passed those limits of my vocal possibilities, never singing over 100 percent, rather less, like 90 percent. I am careful which roles I accept. For example, Azucena is perfect for me now. It was not so earlier in my career. Had I chosen to sing it earlier, I probably would not still be singing today.

JENNIFER ROWLEY: I am lucky because I found a team of people who are caring, watching out for me, and keeping me under their wing. When I get an offer for something, my teacher and manager talk together and decide if it's a good idea or if the timing is right. This is especially important for me right now because I've gone from being a *coloratura* soprano to a *spinto*. If I had sung some of the roles I am singing now too young, I wouldn't be here right now. These big roles are very emotional personally. The press, the media, the director, the conductor can give you a lot of stress, yet in your mind you're superwoman and can do everything, so you really do need some people to say you're not ready yet and need to wait.

GERHARD SIEGEL: Choosing the right roles is important, confidence in the teacher, and a teacher who does not want to make a career of his pupil. The same is true with the agencies. I am fortunate to have an agency that lets me make the decisions but always indicates that such-and-such could happen or this or that could happen. The danger of singing over your *Fach* is often based on false ambition. Attention: listen to your voice.

3. WHAT DO YOU FIND MOST CHALLENGING ABOUT RECORDING? WHAT ARE SOME OF THE SPECIAL CONSIDERATIONS FOR RECORDING IN THE STUDIO?

NICOLE CABELL: Microphones will capture sounds that are much more exposed than the booming acoustic of a live hall. They will capture the slightest pitch waver. Vibrato will not sail over an orchestra but will be picked up directly by the microphone and expose a wider sound (a wobble) or a flutter, whereas it might not be as evident in the theater. For all these issues, the natural beauty of the voice still cannot be captured completely. That all being said, the recording process can be extremely gratifying, as the mic will also capture the smallest, softest sound and subtlety of interpretation. In my experience, slight shadings of color are picked up beautifully by the microphone, and diction can be emphasized in a cleaner way. Smaller voices have a wonderful advantage with recording, as their transparency can be an advantage.

JOSEPH CALLEJA: Good question. Think of the microphone as your best friend and your worst enemy at the same time, in the sense that microphone singing picks up everything. When you are in good voice, don't be tempted to do a lot more than what was programmed, because you will tire the voice for the rest of the sessions. There have to be periods of the day when you are completely silent: rest, don't drink alcohol, don't socialize, and just concentrate. Singing loves sleep, rest, technique, of course, and everything else, but you have to be rested and prepared for the long three to four hours of concentrated singing in the studio.

DAVID DANIELS: I was incredibly fortunate to record with Virgin and EMI for almost a decade, and I have about twenty-two CDs and DVDs out. I'm not recording as much as I used to, but I don't think anybody is, really. The difficult part of recording is getting used to it—take after take after take. Talk about exhausting! Talk about pacing ourselves! That's crazy! The more I did it, the better I got at it. I knew what I could do and what I couldn't do, and I knew how to schedule the recording sessions in such a way that I could get it done as fast as possible.

JOYCE DIDONATO: Finding a spontaneity that occurs naturally in live performance is incredibly difficult to achieve in the studio. I've had to learn how to concentrate less on being "perfect" when the microphone is present (which is very tempting but ultimately limiting artistically) and still remember that the goal must always be *expression*, even if it's not perfect.

CHRISTINE GOERKE: I have done a bit of recording, and in the most successful things the microphone has been in the middle of the house. It is really hard to capture the true essence of my voice the way it sounds close up on a microphone. Live recordings are better. The audience is there, and you feel like you are giving a performance. I hate walking out there and seeing a microphone right in front of me.

DENYCE GRAVES: What I find most challenging is making that moment as honest and as artful as possible without being contrived and studied, and also to accept the product from that moment. Knowing a bit beforehand about the space, the mics (which are different for classical singing): is it a Pearl mic or the Neumann mic (which has been the choice for approximately sixty years)? I use the Neumann U67 when in studio. Schoeps can be used for larger spaces. I often ask for that one when I'm being miked for a concert. But get to know the space if you can, and find out what types of mics are used and experiment with them and see which one fits your voice type. Some singers carry their own mics with them. I often do.

GREER GRIMSLEY: I agree with Simon Keenlyside's definition on this, in that a recording is a different beast from a live performance. It's wonderful, but it's not a live performance.

THOMAS HAMPSON: This might surprise you, but if you're going to make a record, make a record. The recording must be honest, but achieving honesty in a recording is not the same as honesty in a live performance. One of the advantages of the digital process is that a live performance can be more exciting to record. We are in a whole new world of recording. Right now, we seem to be more preoccupied with the souvenir mentality. These beautifully engineered recordings, of which I collected several thousand, have gone the way of the dodo. The iPhone is considered sufficient. Studio work is very difficult, as it almost another art form; it is certainly a love/hate relationship.

ALAN HELD: I don't mind recording so much if it is from a live recording (which most recordings are these days). Studio work doesn't interest me too much and is tedious—it is also not as spontaneous or real. When you take away an audience and the communication that comes with that, the piece suffers (as does one's singing). If it is possible, it is most important to simply try and forget the microphone.

So many performances are recorded these days—whether professionally or by amateurs sitting out in the house. (Folks, we can see the little red lights on your recorders—it can be very distracting, you know?) You pretty much have to sing every performance knowing that your singing in Budapest will be heard online in Boston within hours. This is perhaps the hardest thing these days to get your mind around compared to not all that long ago.

JONAS KAUFMANN: Two things are most challenging to me. One is to find the right sound, because it is very difficult nowadays with all of these modern technical tools and microphones. The close miking of voices can give a very false picture of the sound of a voice. It can make lighter voices seem much more dramatic and larger than they really are, and for larger voices, the close miking does not even begin to pick up the entire body and dimension of a voice. Therefore, I prefer the old electro condenser mics since they capture more of the *Raumklang*, or hall acoustics, of my voice than the modern ones. The second challenging thing is the motivation. Because there is no audience listening, you are alone there and have only a room to address.

SIMON KEENLYSIDE: I don't like it and am no good at it. It is a very different beast to the theater. It takes special skill and practice, and I don't really have either. There is no arc, as with the theater—no preparations to assess and tinker with. The microphone sound is closer than the closest member of any audience would ever sit. No, not for me, though I am glad that many hundreds of other singers did record. I enjoy listening to them. These days, so much is "live," and the recording quality is better and better. All the same, even those do not interest me. Most of my kind are not much inclined to sit and listen to themselves. It's a bit like talking to yourself.

KATHLEEN KIM: For HD or operatic recordings, I don't like using mics. I don't think my voice sounds good with mics. There's nothing I can do about it, but I think my voice doesn't record well. I just sing the way I sing. You know, we're opera singers, not pop singers.

ANA MARÍA MARTÍNEZ: The engineers already have the microphones and the sound they want to do. I prefer when they rebalance it with the mi-

Simon Keenlyside
Born in London, Simon Keenlyside started his working life in the Hamburg State Opera, Germany. His career takes him to most of the world's major opera houses. Among the more important roles to him are the Count (*The Marriage of Figaro*), Don Giovanni, Papageno (*The Magic Flute*), Barber of Seville (Rossini), Wolfram (*Tannhäuser*), Macbeth (Verdi), Germont père (*La traviata*), Rigoletto, Posa (*Don Carlo*), Pelléas, Prospero (*The Tempest*—Adès,) Eugene Onegin, Billy Budd (Britten), and Hamlet (Thomas). In addition, song recitals are an essential component of Simon's life and take him to slightly different corners of the same parts of the world. Photo courtesy Uwe Arens.

crophone in the hall, so that you have that ambience. Not having an audience but having the microphone can sometimes be limiting because we start to listen and to judge, and it's not as free as it could be. So just close your eyes and get in the beautiful state that we all aim for—that zone when audiences are present.

ERIC OWENS: A lot of what I've done has come from live performances, which I think is a better situation. Studio recording is quite the different artistic venture. It's almost like a sport, like basketball, where if you miss the basket you can shoot again. It's not necessarily a spirit-enriching artistic endeavor. It's a bunch of people saying we need to do that again, because you're in search of perfection. It can be frustrating, and sometimes the piecemeal, producer-piloted pursuit of certain audiophilic exactitudes can leave the finished whole empty and unsatisfying. But sometimes it's really cool!

EWA PODLEŚ: A partnership with a producer and sound engineer is essential for successful recording in the studio. Delos (my label) is always very supportive, allowing me to record repertoire I would like to do at my convenience. Unfortunately, I often have no time, not even the week needed to prepare for the sessions.

JENNIFER ROWLEY: I prefer a live recording because I like audiences and I get a lot of energy from them. Studio recordings I find very difficult, because you want to be the best you can be, so your brain goes into listening mode and your technique goes away. When you listen, you sing internally, and you don't have the spontaneity you would have in a theater, where you would not be focused on your internal feelings or judgments. It can be very frustrating to listen back to what you've already done because the recording equipment can cut off the overtones, especially in a higher voice.

GERHARD SIEGEL: For this, I cannot say anything (yet) that would concern me, unfortunately. I never am concerned with recording that is made during a performance primarily because I sing for the audience in the theater where I am singing and acting.

4. SOCIAL NETWORKING, PUBLICISTS, A FREE-MARKET SYSTEM OF OUTSIDE AGENTS, AND NEW MEDIA ARE CHANGING THE LANDSCAPE OF OPERA. WHAT ADVICE DO YOU HAVE FOR YOUNG SINGERS EMBARKING ON THEIR CAREERS WITH REGARD TO THE BUSINESS OF OPERA?

STEPHANIE BLYTHE: Don't write anything in a blog, tweet, or post that you won't want to read in ten years. There is nothing wrong with social networking, but you don't have to share everything with the public. Keep some things to yourself. And *never* write negative things about your colleagues or your work situation. Everyone reads Facebook, Twitter— everyone. So post, but be smart.

NICOLE CABELL: Singers would do well knowing how to utilize technology to promote their career. Having a good website is imperative to promote oneself, as the cumbersome process of sending press kits is unnecessary; additional investments in multimedia self-promotion can only add to what a manager does. A common misconception is that managers are responsible for making a singer's career. So much is determined by connections, luck, and simply giving spectacular performances that people talk about. Being willing to audition like mad and entering as many competitions as possible are all steps you can take to boost your career. The very best thing you can do is sing the best you can and really bring something special to your performances. Have something distinctive and personal to say, and gently get the word out in as many ways as possible when you know you've done something spectacular.

JOSEPH CALLEJA: Fans love staying in contact with singers, and nowadays we have the means to do so with social media. It can also be good fun when we are in between performances or rehearsals as a means of informing people what we are doing and to interact with them and to answer questions. I treat the social media as an extension of the faculties of my communication. I am sure there is a scientific approach that would give me 20 percent more "likes," but I am not really interested in that. We are in an age as opera singers where we have to go chase our audience, so PR managers, agents, etc. are necessary. The days of staying waiting in the theater for an audience to buy tickets are over because we are competing with so many other forms of entertainment.

DAVID DANIELS: You need to be very good at social networking. It's important, because it's not going away. On my private Facebook page, I wrote that there has to be a way to keep the integrity of the art and the integrity of the music and not totally dumb down opera, music, and the art. I'm actually thinking of getting on Twitter, which makes me laugh! I keep up with my Facebook fan page, but my website is a disaster. It's being revamped now. I had a publicist for seven years, and it served its purpose, but to be perfectly honest, America will never be flocking to opera and classical music. We're not going to be on sitcoms and television. We can get our occasional article in the newspaper or the *Opera News* cover. For example, I've had two *Opera News* covers and no publicist.

JOYCE DIDONATO: I think we would be crazy if we didn't take advantage and reach out to our audiences this way, as I think it can be a very powerful way to connect to the audience. (I wonder how Mozart or Handel might have used Twitter!) But my advice about it is the same as my advice about getting a manager: a manager serves no purpose unless there is something to manage. Do not start into the convoluted PR universe until you actually have something of *substance* to promote. Superficiality, while perhaps entertaining at first, is just simply not sustainable for something as complex as opera.

CHRISTINE GOERKE: Everyone has the power now to be a critic. Don't read the stuff. I stopped reading reviews ten years ago. When you have a bad night, I bet you'll know it. When you have a good night, there will be people saying, "Oh my gosh, there was this totally great review!" and they will send it to you. Awesome. Put the quotes on your website. There's that great quote: "Opinions are like assholes. Everybody has one." I don't have a PR agent. I can think of better ways to spend my money. I have a professional page on Facebook where I just list stuff, and I just revamped my website with links to my managers, who have all the information people could need. So just decide what you need and want out of the career.

DENYCE GRAVES: I have found recently that many invitations come through Facebook, so I believe there is lots to take advantage of through social media. I would advise singers to take a business course, absolutely, and to learn as much as possible from the managers and agents about how it all works from their perspective. It's important to be entrepreneurial and learn to create your own opportunities. Take responsibility and take charge of your own destiny, and don't wait for someone else. One has to begin developing this spirit early on.

GREER GRIMSLEY: If you're inclined to use the new media and it doesn't cost you, then do it by all means. You can network, you can tweet, you can Facebook, but ultimately, at the end of the day, it only matters what the performance is like on the stage and being the best artist you can be. That is the ultimate. I am of the belief that "build it, and they will come."

THOMAS HAMPSON: I see social media as a very exciting way for the public to participate in a world of what seems to be esoterica. I don't think a lot of our public realizes how similar our lives are to theirs. However, I would advise any young colleague to respect the permanence of the Internet while at the same time being totally honest about yourself with others in the social media environment. Having a website can serve several purposes, including pedagogy; being part of social media platforms allows people to participate in your journey. The other aspect of this is that agents and PR agents are getting savvier with good, affordable packets with Twitter and Facebook management, etc. I think the real result is that artists accept more responsibility for themselves while working with the companies that represent them in this new digital world.

ALAN HELD: Whether it be through a website or Facebook page, it's all out there for good once you post it. Don't get the cart ahead of the horse. Work on your singing and develop the career slowly. Don't try to shoot to the top too quickly. Put in your time—and then your time will come. Be very careful with what you put online. Don't put recordings online unless they are recordings that you truly want to have represent your singing. Be careful with pictures as well. Most of all, consult with your manager on all things that you publish or have published. And remember, at all times, that this is a business. Make wise choices.

JONAS KAUFMANN: I think it is very important nowadays. Every major opera house has understood that this is an important way of communication. Personally, I don't want to know when people did their workout or what they had for lunch. I think this is a little bit too much. I have a Facebook site and a website and all of these things, but it's basically for information. I don't believe that with tweeting you can suddenly get sixteen-year-olds into the opera. This is not what does it. I think it's more about education than Facebook or Twitter.

SIMON KEENLYSIDE: I don't want to sound like an old, old nitwit, but none of this is for me. I can see that it is the way of the world, but it doesn't have to be the only way. I have no interest in being marketed or famous, even less in social networking or the rest. Nothing against either; but it's not for me. What might I say to young singers in this respect? Hard, since I have no experience of any of it. But be wary of its usefulness, is what I might say. Attend to the most important aspects of your trade first. Let the fickle mistress, fate, decide if your name is going onto the roster. It is better that you just get good work.

KATHLEEN KIM: Honestly, I'm really not good at this. I have a Facebook page, but I don't run it. But these days it's very important, so I think it's good to have social networking skills. And if you can do it by yourself, that's great, but you have to be careful what you put out there.

ANA MARÍA MARTÍNEZ: I have a Facebook page. The young people coming up now have this as second nature with Twitter and Facebook. A publicist told me once that if you tell people enough times, then they believe it, similar to the hype about an athlete who achieves a godlike status. A publicist is going to try to do that because you want your name in circulation, and that hasn't changed even with the new technology. You also need to stretch your repertoire. The days where a singer could perform his or her six roles, as was done in the past, are over. Social media is good, but you have to expand the information to keep yourself relevant and current.

LISETTE OROPESA: First, be aware that your image follows you wherever you go in our world. How you dress, talk, and act in rehearsals is just as important as how you behave on performance day. Be courteous to your colleagues and always show respect and kindness, but never let people walk all over you. Stand up for yourself if there is something that does not work. Learn to budget your money. You'll often be tight, so know what is worth splurging on and what can take a backseat. I, for instance, learned to cook so that I never have to eat out when I'm traveling. It saves me a ton of money.

ERIC OWENS: More than ever before, there are opportunities to put yourself out there and to be seen and heard, and one should definitely be savvy about the many pitfalls where social media is concerned. Be aware

Kathleen Kim
Korean American soprano Kathleen Kim has been heralded as "spectacular" by *Opera News* and "a revelation" and "tiny dynamo" by the *Chicago Sun-Times*. Such critical acclaim reflects the excitement Kim generates at many of the world's premiere opera houses and concert halls. At the Met, her acclaimed performances include Olympia, Zerbinetta, Oscar, and Chiang Ch'ing in the Met's iconic premiere of *Nixon in China*. Her operatic highlights worldwide include Bayerische Staatsoper, BBC Proms, Glyndebourne, and the Gran Teatre del Liceu in such roles as Lucia, Queen of the Night, and Marie in *The Daughter of the Regiment* and concert appearances with the Seoul Philharmonic Orchestra and the Oslo Philharmonic. Photo courtesy Taeuk Kang.

that you won't run into any artists who got their agent, without prior introduction, by having mailed or emailed their materials to one. Also, after having secured an agent (and, hopefully, work), you need to know when would be a proper time to seek out a press agent. It's quite saddening to come across an artist whose career seems to be one big PR campaign about absolutely nothing. It's all about timing, with the caveat that one can wait too long and miss out on opportunities due to inaction. But all of this must take place after due diligence and consultation with people who are knowledgeable about these matters.

DIMITRI PITTAS: I'm on Twitter and Facebook. An issue that I have with social media is that most people are very opinionated. If you like sharing what you feel about art and music, then it's right up your alley. But I think in general the career is changing due to the Internet. People used to wait for European singers to come across the ocean for two weeks on a boat to finally hear them, and now you can just look anybody up on YouTube and watch or listen to a clip of them. It's just up to you whether you're comfortable giving yourself away like that or not.

JENNIFER ROWLEY: Your audience wants to follow you on Twitter or Facebook and know you as a person. The more that you can let them into your life (a filtered life), the more they want to come to the opera. They want to tweet during intermission. They want to see you in your makeup chair and behind the scenes. I love connecting with people, hearing from fans, showing pictures to fans, and getting tweets that people are in the audience. You have to have a website (especially with orchestra sound clips), Twitter, a Facebook page, and Instagram with pictures. You need to have good head shots, modern and trendy. Sometimes that's what gives you the auditions! They say, "Oh, she's beautiful, so we need to hear her."

GERHARD SIEGEL: Although I use Facebook and have a website, nevertheless, I am of the opinion that the conventional, "old" way is the right one. Good vocal training, audition, agency search, audition, discipline, no pride, self-criticism, audition...

5. WHEN WORKING ABROAD, UNDERSTANDING CULTURAL AND STYLISTIC DIFFERENCES BECOMES VERY IMPORTANT. WHAT ARE SOME OF THE THINGS YOUNG SINGERS NEED TO BE PREPARED FOR?

NICOLE CABELL: Learn your languages! The usefulness of knowing what you're saying, intimately, down to the subtext, cannot be overstated. I took periods of time to throw myself into music programs overseas during the summer, but in retrospect it might have been better to divide up my time between music programs and language programs. Whenever you have an opportunity to study overseas, take it, and not only to learn how to sing but also to know how you function overseas. You can't take yourself too seriously when traveling. I've grown comfortable with looking foolish when I attempt to say something and it comes out wrong. Also, audiences can be more judgmental, and rightfully so, in Europe. After all, opera originated in Europe, and tradition runs thick.

JOSEPH CALLEJA: The best advice is to be polite, to do some research on customs, but ultimately to be yourself. People might not agree with you, but they will respect you. If they see you trying to be phony or tacky or not yourself, then they will not respect you. You do not want people on the defensive; you want them open and accepting. But this question had more relevance fifteen years ago, before the age of globalization. Everything has become one. Everybody has communication devices now and is connected constantly. We are approaching what Michio Kaku calls a Type 1 civilization.

DAVID DANIELS: There are differences, but I think experience will teach you. For example, it's annoying to come to Spain and rehearse in the morning and at night. Germany's the same way, since the orchestras have rehearsals in the morning and at night so they can have the afternoon free. So you warm up for the morning rehearsal and then you sit for five and a half hours before the evening rehearsal, when you have to do it all over again. It's not convenient and it's not ideal. One thing that drives me nuts in the States is the subscription concerts that I sing with the San Francisco, New York, Chicago, or Philadelphia orchestras. They always have the final dress rehearsal at ten o'clock in the morning of the first concert. And then you do concerts four days in a row. So for a singer, it's not ideal, but we have to adjust with the different scheduling.

JOYCE DIDONATO: It's important to have a working knowledge of life. You should be reading and watching new and old films, foreign films, going to museums, going to football games and observing the crowds, people watching! Eat the food of the region, drink the wine of the local vineyard. You need to master the languages. Get out there and learn French, German, Italian, etc. Get over there and learn in the country itself, which is truly the only way to achieve fluency. Once you have that, the text you are singing will come to life. The bottom line for me is: *be a student of life!*

CHRISTINE GOERKE: Whatever country I go to, I won't be _____ (insert here: French, German, Austrian, etc.). I'm American. Also, know that Americans are one of the best-trained groups of singers in the world. That's not to say other countries don't train their singers well; they do. But when you walk in, immediately you get the "Oh, you're American." Be open to what they're offering you, because stylistic differences are everywhere. If you get a conductor from Italy to work with you in New York, you're going to get the same thing. So don't be offended by any of it. Eat up everything you possibly can, and then you have a huge repertoire to choose from. I'm such a blatant, bubbly, loud American, and it's not like I'm going to hide it. So they either like it or it drives them bananas, and I can accept that.

DENYCE GRAVES: In terms of working abroad, this is an important education and will be on-the-job training in many cases, especially if the singer does not speak the language. In addition to studying the language, I think that singers can get a book on stage terms in several languages to help them navigate in the staging and musical process.

I always advise my students to make contact with the director and conductor before the engagement to establish a rapport. Certainly, reading as much material beforehand about the country, culture, etc. can be extremely helpful, and the natives will be more open to exchanging with you if they see that you've made an effort.

GREER GRIMSLEY: I love the 10:00 a.m. BOs—*Bühnen Orchester*, or stage orchestra rehearsals—in Germany! But seriously, keep a sense of wonder and keep your mind open. When I go abroad, I keep in mind that we are ambassadors for our country. In different places there are different rituals and customs, and be respectful of that. There are some cultural differences that are sort of fun, and you throw yourself into them and learn something, which is all part of what I mentioned before about being supple and open-minded. There is more than one way of doing things, and respect that.

THOMAS HAMPSON: It's incumbent upon any singer, whether young or old, to be adaptable. My personal discipline is completely focused on the word balance. If your rehearsal is at four o'clock in the afternoon or ten in the morning, then sing at that time. My personal experience is that you can get into any routine when you can sing pretty much at any time if you have to. Adaptability, or the German word *Umstellungsfähigkeit*, is very important today.

ALAN HELD: Be respectful at all times of different cultures and customs. I can't emphasize this enough. You are a guest in that country and in the company or with the orchestra where you are employed. Remember that things are just done differently, and don't expect things on your terms. As far as the business, understand what is coming out of your paycheck as far as taxes and fees. You are ultimately responsible for this. And, rest assured, the statements that are given to you at the end of the engagement oftentimes have errors. Handle all things within the business and, again, be respectful.

JONAS KAUFMANN: Well, of course it's important to know about certain rules. If you go to Arab countries, you should know how to behave, for instance. But on the opera stage, a lot is possible. I think you have to be aware of the differences in culture. Stylistically, I think a French opera, for example, should sound the same in France, Germany, or Russia. It is more the style of the music and not the culture.

SIMON KEENLYSIDE: The life of an itinerant musician is not easy. It is hard to spend so much time alone and in rented accommodation and hotels. Everyone has his or her own way of coping, and nobody owns up or talks about such difficulties much. All the same, we all struggle with it. I think it makes a singer's life much easier if he or she can engage in the language of that country. Sooner or later, most singers do speak, or at least understand, forced by circumstance and years in those places, to rehearse in different languages, or else just making one's way in the streets and restaurants. Making a virtue out of a hardship will bring great satisfaction and enrichment. Of course, many of the European singers already speak two, three, or four languages, which they learned from childhood. Lucky them!

KATHLEEN KIM: Prepare yourself 150 percent so that you are able and open to change and not stuck in one style. This is especially true for a young singer. You should be able to adapt. If you work in a festival, you will work with a good conductor, so you're not going to do yourself any harm. If you go to France or Germany or England, they'll have their way, so you have to be willing to accept and be open to their culture.

ANA MARÍA MARTÍNEZ: It has to start with tremendous humility on the side of the artist. Assume that you know nothing and start from that perspective to absorb as much as you can. If you're going to perform Mozart in Salzburg, then do your homework and read about it. Listen to the great Mozart singers of the past, like Steber or Schwarzkopf. I learned so much from listening to an artist like Victoria de los Ángeles.

LISETTE OROPESA: Learn to speak a language other than English. Be respectful—and don't ask for extra ice!

ERIC OWENS: You'll find quite a few procedural differences that might be shocking. These discoveries will occur after experiencing the wonderful cultural differences that make life wonderful! You'll work in places where:

1. Taxes are scarily high
2. No taxes are taken out at all
3. You can be paid in cash
4. It can take many months to be paid at all
5. Checks, from quite reputable organizations, can bounce
6. Rehearsals might not start on time (I mean, as late as an hour, and no one tells you)

7. The entire rehearsal period is three days or less
8. You receive no info as to the whereabouts of the first rehearsal
9. You receive the above information, hand-delivered by the administration, three weeks after first rehearsal
10. Hotels may *say* they have air-conditioning...

Willkommen, bienvenue, welcome!

DIMITRI PITTAS: I'm fascinated with the work ethic of the different cultures. Some countries have a big break between a morning and an evening session, and you have an entire afternoon free. When you go to Japan, their work ethic is unbelievable. They'll have two 4-hour sessions of just practice, practice, practice. Vocally, you need a break. You can't handle that. It's really important to know what it is you're capable of doing. So you have to pace yourself, not with the performances themselves, but just with the pacing of the rehearsal process and the way they work.

EWA PODLEŚ: In my opinion, not only singers, but every open-minded person, when abroad has to understand cultural and stylistic differences.

JENNIFER ROWLEY: You must know a second language, even if it's just a working knowledge. Thankfully I know Italian, and that does help me to communicate. I have been in rehearsal where there were five languages going on. You need to be able to communicate with your colleagues also. If you're in the first scene with Don Giovanni, for example, you need to tell him "This is okay" or "This is not okay." It's really important also to work on your manners and to keep a little bit of your personality a bit reserved until you've learned what is acceptable and what is not, because some cultures are very conservative.

6. CONTEMPORARY OPERA HAS BECOME A COMPETITIVE JOB MARKET, ESPECIALLY IN EUROPE. HAVE YOU ANY ADVICE TO YOUNG SINGERS FOR THE SPECIAL CHALLENGES THIS SORT OF REPERTORY CAN POSE?

NICOLE CABELL: I've turned down contemporary projects that I knew I wouldn't perform well, because I am a different kind of singer than the style I was asked to sing. Other contemporary projects are perfect for me, so I jump at them. It really depends on if the project speaks to you. Some contemporary music (atonal, for instance) is very difficult to learn, and disjointed leaps and unnatural lines can also be jarring for the physical instrument. Having a good ear and an excellent technique makes this music possible to sing, but I'd say to try to learn as much as you can and sing through as much as you can before agreeing to a project, as the demands are often more than a singer realizes at the time.

JOSEPH CALLEJA: I have never done it because most of the time it is bad for the voice. That is brutally honest. There is some nice stuff, but it doesn't measure up to what the greats have composed yet. For me, some of the greatest composers nowadays are in film music, such as John Williams or Hans Zimmer, and I would like for them to be given a go at composing an opera. Many people say that they are derivative, but Donizetti copied Rossini, Verdi copied Donizetti or Bellini. There is a limited number of intervals, after all, and, having said that, one of the composers I absolutely love is John Williams. I absolutely adore him.

DAVID DANIELS: It is something that is incredibly important right now. San Francisco Opera has just done three in the last year. The Met's doing *Two Boys*, for example, and I did *Oscar* at Santa Fe, so new music is obviously a direction that companies are going in right now which is wonderful. It's interesting because when I started my career, the new music the companies were doing was Baroque opera, so it's amazing the new operas that are being done are actually new operas!

JOYCE DIDONATO: We need composers writing music today, of that there is *no* question. Of course, we don't want to be an art form that only revives centuries-old classics—a "living museum," if you will. We need to continue to explore our lives and put our twenty-first-century fingerprint down on paper so that we can learn about ourselves, just as Beaumarchais, Mozart, or Shakespeare did. Having an audience experience *Dead Man Walking* and be forced to directly confront choices that their society is making is a *very* powerful, important experience. But as challenging as some of this music can be, I always approach it with the same *bel canto* technique. I do think composers need to treat the vocal line with care and use our instruments as they were meant to be used; we are lyrical instruments and can best serve the music in this way—not to mention that it will help us avoid irreparable damage.

CHRISTINE GOERKE: If you happen to be that singer with spectacular perfect or relative pitch; if you can just look at a piece of music and read it; if rhythm is your thing, then embrace all of this. This is very cool stuff. Often you are working directly with the composer. If something doesn't work for you, you get to shape that role, which is really cool. I actually really like this music, but I also know it requires a lot of time for learning. With my life right now, with my kids, trying to balance the two things, I am always leery of not having enough time. So know your life, know that it takes a lot more time for these projects, but if they appeal to you, go for it. They're awesome.

DENYCE GRAVES: I have done a lot of contemporary opera. As I type this on my computer, I am listening to a new opera that I am learning. I asked my pianist to record on CD the part so that I could listen to it to aid me in learning it. Basically, I think learning contemporary opera requires time and patience and repetition. Oftentimes, at least with American opera, it can be wordy, with difficult intervals that will require lots of stitching together to make it seamless, depending on the style. The bottom line is, allow yourself time and work with a coach.

GREER GRIMSLEY: I love doing new pieces. It excites me. I was in the Houston Opera studio for three years, and we workshopped tons of new operas. I'm all for it. We need to get some good stuff with interesting subjects out there.

THOMAS HAMPSON: It demands a very strong technique. I'm a big proponent of new operas, a big supporter of the avant-garde. I support composers and new music. I am very conscious of vocalism and what I would call "vocal expression" in new music. I've done a lot of modern music, but I've turned down some too, because it was either not my aesthetic or I couldn't get my vocalism around it. I am very good at learning music, even though I don't have perfect pitch. I have friends with very special ears, and they eat this stuff for breakfast and lunch. There's no question in my mind that every generation needs to embrace the creativity of its generation. Although sometimes that avant-garde can be quite nonvocal, for me it all somehow still needs to have a musical vocal expression.

ALAN HELD: No matter what the repertoire, sing with line and with your voice—what else can you do? I don't find contemporary opera so challenging. I find the productions of the operas the challenging part—and this isn't just for contemporary opera. It goes for the standard repertoire as well.

JONAS KAUFMANN: Unfortunately not. I've done many things on the way up, but it's so difficult to please everybody. Also, the opera houses don't want me to do the contemporary things. They want me to do the big hits. It's also difficult to find the time to learn these things. And unfortunately, you do them one time and never again.

SIMON KEENLYSIDE: I've done my fair share of modern opera. Some of it has been very rewarding too. Notwithstanding, some of this music can be perilous for a voice. It's funny to me to think that, barring four unauthorized performances, Wagner's *Parsifal*, for example, wasn't played outside Bayreuth until 1913. If a singer is very lucky, he will encounter great new works. That has always been the case. A singer should always be wary of any score in front of him or her. Take good care and pay attention not to hurt your voice!

KATHLEEN KIM: I treat it as the same. I don't change. It's the same technique for me as in classical repertoire. But honestly, I don't like contemporary opera. However, I love singing *Nixon in China*, and I think that's as contemporary as I could go. Although there are some exceptions—*Lulu*, for example. If it's interesting enough, I will do it.

ANA MARÍA MARTÍNEZ: I haven't done it in a while, but it is challenging, and you want to make sure that the composers have a good understanding of how the voice works. Modern opera is very important because we always need a new creation to reflect our times.

LISETTE OROPESA: All vocal music, no matter who the composer is, should be sung with the foundation of *bel canto*.

ERIC OWENS: Singing new pieces, especially ones that are written for you, can be an incredibly rewarding experience! These works tend to be quite demanding in every aspect, especially musically. You should have the type of personality that enjoys a challenge and is willing to put in the work that it takes to perform works of this nature at a high level. Also, I believe

Ana María Martínez
Grammy Award winner Ana María Martínez's dramatic range distinguishes her as one of today's most sophisticated lyric sopranos. She has portrayed leading roles on the world's biggest opera stages, including the Opéra national de Paris, Bayerische Staatsoper, the Glyndbourne Festival, De Nederlandse Opera, Royal Opera House Covent Garden, Vienna Staatsoper, Deutsche Oper Berlin, the Los Angeles Opera, the Metropolitan Opera, the Lyric Opera of Chicago, the Houston Grand Opera, and the Santa Fe Opera. Concert highlights include performances with the Filarmonica della Scala, New York Philharmonic, Puerto Rico Symphony, and BBC Symphony, as well as at the Ravinia Festival, Casals Festival, Esterházy Festival, and on tours with Plácido Domingo and Andrea Bocelli. Photo courtesy Tom Specht.

you should approach all vocal music from the *cantabile* side of things. If a composer asks you to do something that you feel is vocally unhealthy and potentially harmful, then the piece, and probably the composer, is not right for you.

EWA PODLEŚ: I am not a fan of contemporary music really, but it may be useful for young singers as they develop their careers.

JENNIFER ROWLEY: I did the very first crowd-sourced opera that was done by an Internet community. The costumes, composers, and singers were voted on by the Internet community. It was called *Free Will* and it was at the Savonlinna Opera Festival in Finland last summer. They had all of the rehearsals live online for the fans to watch every day. The performances were live-streamed and they were on Twitter and Facebook; they were everywhere. Contemporary music can be difficult from its conception, or difficult because it's not composed very well. Generally modern music can be very hard on the voice, so you have to be sure that you are vocally sound. Just as you would work on a Verdi role, you have to work on a contemporary one.

GERHARD SIEGEL: I'm not really a lover of contemporary music for singers. This does not mean that I do not like it. But I think you should be very conscious of your technique and the possibilities of your voice, since the extreme demands that are often made can cause damage if you are not careful.

CHAPTER 5

✺

On Teaching and Studying

The art of singing is a lifelong pursuit, constantly filled with new discoveries about technique, music, performing, and communication. Having a trusted teacher, vocal coach, or other person to rely on for feedback is, for many singers, essential. Stephanie Blythe stresses that studying voice "means listening to recordings, reading, studying your music, and, most importantly, getting in touch with your text." The cumulative effect of study is stressed by many artists, including Lawrence Brownlee, who says, "I've had four teachers in my life and I think that I've taken something from all of them." Interestingly, Anna Schoen-René, the teacher of pedagogue Margaret Harshaw, spoke about being required by her teacher, the legendary Pauline Viardot (the daughter of equally legendary Manuel García), to read the classics, to acquaint herself with great art in the museums, and to observe acting in the theaters in order to form a complete aesthetic sense, self-expression, and control. Even such practical advice as Simon Keenlyside gives, to learn to cook a little ("It'll save a whole lot of money and give you a gentle way to unwind on the road") and to learn "basic accountancy," go into the multitasking of being a professional singer.

1. DO YOU CONTINUE TO WORK WITH A VOICE TEACHER OR VOCAL COACH? IF SO, IN WHAT WAYS DOES WORKING WITH A TEACHER OR COACH HELP YOU AT THIS STAGE IN YOUR CAREER TO CONTINUE TO PERFECT YOUR TECHNIQUE?

STEPHANIE BLYTHE: One of the most idiotic things I have ever heard from colleagues is that they don't need to coach—they already know it all. *No one* knows it all, and no one is so good that they don't need to continue to coach and study. Our brains and bodies are constantly changing, and since the voice is a part of our bodies, we need to keep on top of those changes. You can only do that successfully with a second pair of ears and eyes.

LAWRENCE BROWNLEE: I've had four teachers in my life and I think that I've taken something from all of them. I study still with Costanza Cuccaro, as I feel that her approach to singing is one that has some credence. It works well for me.

NICOLE CABELL: Seeing a teacher on a regular basis is an excellent way to make sure you are not straying too far from correct technique or relying on the sounds inside your head. Recording yourself and listening back can also keep you in line. One doesn't simply study for a couple of years and know how to sing. I have touch-up lessons here and there with trusted and new teachers who can keep me on a healthy path as well as offering fresh ideas. Having a teacher and a coach keeps you healthy, almost like a personal trainer. Vocal coaches are essential for introducing interpretive knowledge and keeping me from adding a little too much of my personal touch to something that should also respect specific styles.

JOSEPH CALLEJA: Absolutely. This summer I have James Pearson from the Vienna State Opera coming to Malta, and I work with my teacher Paul Asciak as well, even though he is ninety now. The greatest irony of singing is that we can never truly listen to ourselves, so we have to have a teacher to listen to us. A recording does not do the whole job. It gives a good indication, but it is not the human ear, which is far more advanced than any kind of technology we have now. That is why you have to have a coach or a teacher to polish you, and cleanse you of the bad habits you have after a season of singing. Like Pavarotti, when he met Beniamino Gigli when he was eleven, said, "*Maestro Gigli, quando hai finito studiare?* When did you finish your studies?" Gigli looked at his watch and said, "*Carissimo ragazzo, venti minuti fa*—dear boy, twenty minutes ago." He was fifty-seven at the time.

DAVID DANIELS: I have a coach that I learn with. But for years (I would say the first fourteen years of my career), I would not coach. I equated coaching with bad musicianship and cheating. My thoughts were that I'm a great musician and have great piano skills. I even play cello, so I am a consummate musician. Therefore, I don't need anyone to help me. I can do it on my own or else it's weak. Isn't that crazy? But I found out I was wrong, Terribly wrong. I moved to Atlanta and started coaching with a wonderful coach in Greenville, South Carolina, Michael Rice. He could be a *répétiteur* in any opera house in the world. And I was going to engagements with the confidence and preparation that I had never had before. What was I thinking?

CHRISTINE GOERKE: I had two teachers and both were formative. Elaine Bonazzi was my first teacher. She gave me everything I had that was completely safe and wonderful. She got me into the Met program. I won lots of competitions and the Tucker Award with her. Then I just felt like I needed to start fresh with something new and went to Diana Soviero, because she knew about Italian *bel canto* technique, which, in my mind, is the only way to sing German music or you'll be dead. This is a never-ending process. So I go to my coaches to spruce up the style, and I go to my teacher to know how to sing it.

DENYCE GRAVES: I do work often with coaches and voice teachers still, and always will. Singing requires a lifetime of study, and that work is never finished. It's an ongoing process that needs adjustment as the voice grows and changes, as it will. Study also conditions your ear and keeps you in good vocal health and shape. I am still learning new things every day about myself, my voice, and my technique. That's why it's imperative to *love* what you do, because it will always be a part of your life.

GREER GRIMSLEY: My wife, Luretta Bybee, is the one I call my ears. The whole point is that what we do is all inside, and we only hear so much. Sometimes, even with recordings, you don't get a true read. I do work with certain coaches, and it's always great to get that input. That's the idea about what we do. You never get to the point where you have attained a final goal. It is always a work in progress. Luretta has helped me a great deal. She keeps me honest, which is great in that respect. It's important to have someone there, or else sometimes you've taken a wrong turn and you don't know it.

THOMAS HAMPSON: My voice teacher died in January 2013 at the tender age of ninety-nine. His name was Professor Horst Gunther. He was a visiting professor of voice at the University of Southern California when I met him. Horst and I worked together last probably ten years ago; however, it was important for me to have him hear the important challenges and repertoire expansions I did throughout the years. He was the one who gave me my professional bearings. Every role I learn I take to a vocal coach of some specialty. And over the years I have had extraordinary guidance.

ALAN HELD: I don't regularly visit my teacher or a vocal coach but on an as-needed basis. Part of this is because my teachers, Jocelyn Reiter, Wesley Snyder, Dr. George Gibson, and Richard Cross, gave me a great foundation that I haven't forgotten. I hold on to their teachings. They taught me relaxation and natural singing. Also, I have never shunned exploring my instrument and applying what I have been taught. This is the important thing I learned early on and what I try to pass along at all times in my own teaching. I have also found that teaching has made me a better singer. Working with other singers forces me to analyze what I do to get what I want, and to find the best ways to express these thoughts. This causes me to think through the process often and apply what is learned.

JONAS KAUFMANN: Now that I have been my own teacher for several years, I hope that I'm successful in continuing the work of my teacher Michael Rhodes. And thank God I've got a person on whose judgment I can trust completely. It's my wife, the mezzo-soprano Margarete Joswig. She's the first to tell me when something is wrong.

SIMON KEENLYSIDE: No, I have no teacher. I don't feel guilty. I work hard at technical issues all the time, and most of that is on feel and sensation. I confess that I do not even practice with a recording device any longer. At some point, one must be accepting of oneself and comfortable enough in one's own skin to trust that it is, at least, good enough.

KATHLEEN KIM: I work with Gerald Martin Moore. I need someone because I cannot hear myself. If I'm working for six months, I need to have a checkup to see if I'm doing everything correctly and if I'm on the right track. So I always work with a coach and voice teacher. Gerald happens to be both.

ANA MARÍA MARTÍNEZ: I recommend it because your voice is changing and your body is changing. Whenever I have a lesson with Stephen King, my jaw drops because I'm learning volumes, even when I'm working on things I have done. We discover something new in every lesson. You really stay on top of it. I can't think of an Olympic gymnast who wouldn't work with a coach.

LISETTE OROPESA: A fresh ear is always helpful. Your technique more or less stays the same, but your feeling within your body will change as you age. Listen to someone with experience and expertise and even record yourself for a different perspective. Your voice reacts to everything, so have a solid foundation, but be prepared for plan B.

ERIC OWENS: I haven't seen my teacher in years. I've been kind of policing myself and luckily I have a pretty good sense of what's going on with my voice at any particular time, but I am fortunate to work at companies that have amazing conductors, assistant conductors, and coaches, who are the best musicians you'll find anywhere and who give me wonderful guidance. It's always good to have people who can let you know what's coming across and how you sound out in the house because, very often, it's difficult to know this yourself.

DIMITRI PITTAS: Yes, I work with a coach and a voice teacher. A few years ago, I was in Vienna for my first *Lucia* and I was fortunate enough to work with a well-known singer, but I was hesitant to listen to what was said. I was at a point in my life where I thought I just needed to do what I know because that was working. Being given the same opportunity nowadays, I would approach the situation differently. I like being able to see what other people have to think. It's good to keep your mind open and try things out. If the option is there and the opportunity is there, I think it's great, which is what this book is about, so I appreciate what you're doing.

EWA PODLEŚ: All my life I have been trying to improve my technique based on what I learned from my only teacher, the wonderful soprano Alina Bolechowska at the Warsaw Academy of Music. I first met her when I was three! I was her baby in *Madame Butterfly* in Warsaw (my mother sang in the chorus). She was my only mentor. It was a beautiful relationship. I brought her with me everywhere I sang in Europe. She was always there for me whenever I needed her help.

JENNIFER ROWLEY: Renée Fleming writes in her autobiography about how she is never perfect and is constantly learning. It's important for young singers to know that the voice is going to change. Mine changed at thirty, and my teacher helped me when what I call the "trap door" opened. I suddenly had all of this voice that I didn't know what to do with. He helped me through this change. But you get older and the voice changes, and you need to have someone to help you through that. Also. when people go through weight loss, especially in this business, then the breathing will change so much. Also, if you're strengthening your core through fitness, your breathing becomes different and you have to have someone you trust who will help you with the changes.

GERHARD SIEGEL: I should, like every singer should. But for the last ten years I have been very lucky that my voice has always been at the right place and I have had no difficulties. But I have just now noticed that after a cold, which is still not cured after three weeks, I have started to *versingen*, that is, the voice seeks its own way to manage the problems rather than using technique. I had this problem before, exactly ten years ago, and hope to come to a solution by myself.

2. WHAT ADVICE WOULD YOU GIVE TO YOUNG SINGERS TODAY ON HOW TO MAKE THE MOST OF THEIR VOCAL STUDIES AS THEY PREPARE FOR A PROFESSIONAL CAREER?

STEPHANIE BLYTHE: You must learn how to listen. Simply being in a young artist program does not mean that you will have a career. Being a young artist means you have to take it upon yourself to be your own mentor and your own teacher. One of the greatest things about being a young artist at the Met came from sitting in rehearsals and watching great artists. Also, studying voice does not always mean making noise. It means listening to recordings, reading and studying your music, and, most importantly, getting in touch with your text. It does not have to do with constantly singing one aria after another. Learning how to sing songs, Lieder, or *mélodie* is extraordinarily important, along with learning about language and how it feels when you correctly recite the poem or text. When you are reciting something, it isn't just words; it is a formula to understanding.

LAWRENCE BROWNLEE: Being prepared, a good colleague, and dependable are important, in addition to knowing yourself, your limitations, and what you can do. All of these are essential to having a career. Above all these important things are having the work ethic and the drive with a sense of humility—perhaps more than anything else. Be the best and that will open doors for you.

NICOLE CABELL: Keep your trusted sources close. A voice teacher, several great coaches, advisors, and friends you trust and who will always be honest with you are worth their weight in gold. Keep learning and never become complacent.

JOSEPH CALLEJA: Simple advice: Don't fool yourself. Be honest with yourself. Don't imagine talents you don't have. Always count to fifty when you get angry. You might be abused with too many rehearsals, or picked on because you are the youngest singer. Never, ever lose your cool in an opera house. I am proud to say that in sixteen years, and even confronted with some quite difficult situations, I have never, ever lost my cool, never had any kind of diva-ish behavior. Sometimes even the best of intentions can be construed in a different manner by different people. In a recent concert performance of *Lucia*, when I cut the high note in the duet with Lucia and left the stage as written originally by Donizetti, some critic had written that I stormed off because I was angry at Diana Damrau for holding the note longer than I. I could have written a note on Facebook correcting him, but I think silence is the best. Also, surround yourself with people who are not scared to tell you the truth. You should be a person saved by criticism rather than ruined by praise. Surrounding yourself with yes-men is a recipe for disaster vocally or emotionally.

DAVID DANIELS: Don't be afraid to learn and to admit you're not a finished product or to admit you don't know everything, because you don't. I grew up in a musical family, so I was surrounded by great singing. When I was at Cincinnati for undergrad, I drove to Lexington, Kentucky, to hear Ms. Horne sing. I drove to Asheville, North Carolina, to hear Ms. Troyanos sing with Martin Katz (and I still have the program with his signature, which freaks him out). I never see college students at performances. Never! I think students are doing themselves a disservice, because they're missing out on the opportunity to evolve into something better. The day after my recital, I did a master class in Chicago with six singers, and none of them came to my recital! If you're interested in becoming a professional singer, go and support and listen to the people who are performing.

JOYCE DIDONATO: The percentage of singers who start at twenty-one who are the stars of their schools and who actually go on and make it is very, very small. There are exceptions to this, of course, but I believe slow and steady wins the race. So build your arsenal of expertise: languages! What about arriving at graduate school fluent in Italian? Save up, find a grant, and go to Europe for the summer and live, learn, study. Go to experience an opera in person, study it on the Internet, listen to the singers of the past. Opera is the culmination of everything. It is about life, breath, energy, passion, forgiveness, and betrayal. You need to know what life is about in order to put that across on the stage.

CHRISTINE GOERKE: I never took anything into lessons and coachings unless I felt like I really knew it. Did it sound perfect? No, but I knew exactly all of the rhythms, notes, and texts. I translated everything to the point that I really felt good about it. Then I took it to my teacher, and everything they said could become incorporated right away. So, do your prep at home before you bring it in front of somebody.

DENYCE GRAVES: One tool that can be helpful is to record your voice and coaching sessions and performances when possible. Often we do not hear what the audience hears, and it can be helpful to have perspective and distance from your work in order to examine it effectively. No one really enjoys hearing herself or himself (or is that just me?), but it can be very instructive. Work on languages and acting apart from singing; this too can be helpful when working on so many facets.

GREER GRIMSLEY: First of all, make sure your technique is second nature. Languages are very important. You don't have to be fluent in all the languages that opera is sung in, but having at least one of them that you can converse in is important for confidence. Acting is also very important, as is understanding how your body moves. The best thing I ever had was a movement class in Houston where a world-class fencer taught us fencing and mime. He actually taught Marcel Marceau to fence, and in exchange, Marceau taught him mime! Those mime classes were very, very helpful. You don't have to do mime—perhaps tai chi or whatever connects you to your body.

THOMAS HAMPSON: Don't take this time of your life for granted. Be disciplined. Discipline for me is the ordering of the random. Build your life's index. Use this time of your life to build your blocks of repertoire. Take your vocal development seriously. Your diction classes are wonderful and useful, but learn a language. Every singer should learn another language (or two). You're going to work as a classical singer consistently in the big four languages (English, Italian, German, and French) and now, increasingly, Russian. Treat language as a phenomenon of expression and not as an engineering design of diction. When you get out of school or your career starts, the lid comes off, and life goes a lot faster than you think.

ALAN HELD: Get to know your own voice. Spend time with it. Analyze and listen to yourself. Feel the sensations. Explore! Your teacher can only help you so far. He or she can't jump into your body, breathe for you, or produce the sound. You have to do this yourself. You have to do the work. Do it.

JONAS KAUFMANN: In school, students are treated very differently than in the professional world on the stage. So they need to know that real life is quite different. In addition, I would say a downside to study is the number of lessons. I had one coaching and one lesson per week, and of course this is not enough. If you work daily on your voice, this means that you spend more time reinforcing mistakes because you are not under supervision. Studying once a week with your teacher would have been considered ridiculous in the past. The great Italian school of singing called for daily lessons lasting many years.

SIMON KEENLYSIDE: Apart from the obvious business of making a really solid and flexible instrument (there's a piece of irrelevant advice!), be careful of having too much of a great college "career." There is sometimes a conflict of interest in what the music college will want to portray and what the best interests of the singers are. Extremely talented young singers are likely to be showcased by the college as soon as they are able to put 'em in the limelight. Young singers are liable to be flattered by that. After all, it's what they aim to do as soon as they leave the educational manger. Full-time education is short. Apart from that, I would advise any young singer to learn to cook a little. It'll save a whole lot of money and give you a gentle way to unwind on the road. That, and learn basic accountancy.

KATHLEEN KIM: I think technique is very important, but learning languages is very important too. It's easier when you're younger to learn languages.

ANA MARÍA MARTÍNEZ: Piano skills are great. I wish mine were better. I would say IPA because you're not going to hear bad diction at a major house. You don't want diction issues to hold you back from opportunity. Always have the discipline of musical preparedness and precision. Be on top of it when you go into that rehearsal. Take a lot of time for voice lessons in your studies, because when you're in a career you won't have time for lessons. Don't take lessons for granted. Don't think you have it all figured out. We are a work in progress and never finished. Never.

LISETTE OROPESA: Learn languages and at least some basic piano. Also, learn how to dress your best, not just for auditions but for everyday life. Presenting an image of success gives you confidence and a sense of purpose. Take care of your body; it is your instrument, after all! Exercise, eat healthy, sleep: all those things you're supposed to do, but seriously.

ERIC OWENS: It's necessary for young people to have a strength of character and the self-awareness to know when something is not working. I know it's hard, but we are all responsible for our own vocal development. We can't blame anyone else for our lack of advancement. However, when you're young, it's sometimes hard to know if a voice teacher is working for you and actually being helpful. I believe that you're not going to receive all the information you need from one source and that you should occasionally ask others (voice teachers or whomever) for their opinions. Ask several people, and if you start hearing the same concerns from different sources that your voice teacher doesn't seem to think is a problem, then it might be time to look elsewhere. It's very easy to become loyal because you like the teacher and you don't want to hurt him or her, which I do understand. But you have to look out for your best interests, and hopefully the teacher will understand. If the person does not understand and tries to make you feel bad because of your decision, then you don't need that type of energy in your life, and, irrespective of how good a teacher this person is, you need to move on!

DIMITRI PITTAS: One of the things that I wish I had done more as a student was just working on things that would have helped me more in per-

Lisette Oropesa
Lisette Oropesa, an award-winning soprano and a regular at the Metropolitan Opera, has sung more than a hundred performances on its stage, including eight Live in HD productions. The *New York Times* hails her as an artist with a "magnetic" stage presence and an "attractively silky, and flexible timbre," and *Opera News* asserts that "she wields a distinctive, bell-like timbre that is instantly appealing." Notable roles include Gilda in *Rigoletto* at the Metropolitan Opera, Cleopatra in *Giulio Cesare* at the Detroit Opera House, Ismene in *Mitridate* at the Bayerische Staatsoper, and Susanna in *Le nozze di Figaro* at the Santa Fe Opera. Photo courtesy Matthew Murphy.

forming: knowing the repertoire, understanding the style of the composer just by listening to it, and listening more to the music. Perhaps if you know you are going to be working with a certain conductor, go see that person conduct and listen to what he or she has to say with a score. Today it's all about data or information and the way it's processed. So the more data that you can get, the better off you are. Also, there are a lot of things that you can do that nobody's going to do for you. Learning a language is one.

EWA PODLEŚ: It is helpful for singers to find someone they can rely on, someone who will tell them honestly if something is good or not. Young singers today need to try to learn as much as they can, but keeping in mind that one day they must act on their own responsibility. Also very important is that young singers must be prepared to turn down roles that are heavier than their natural abilities. A young singer with talent and a beautiful voice will be asked to do everything. Be careful and don't accept roles that are not suitable. It can destroy the voice.

JENNIFER ROWLEY: Students focus on singing roles, and that's the wrong thing. As a young singer, you have to focus on learning how to use your voice, because you're unique. You have to figure out how your instrument works before you can take on a big full role. A lot of universities are failing in this, especially the bigger universities that have six or seven operas a year. How does someone learn how to sing if they're preparing to sing Violetta at age twenty-two?

GERHARD SIEGEL: Singing is not all there is to a career. In fact, a career includes many components, which are individual for each singer. Singing alone is not the alpha and omega. It includes a steady doggedness and a *desire* to sing. As a student, one needs to learn from the beginning to "free oneself" (acting). Teachers should increasingly take notice of diction, the alpha and omega in singing, in the singer's native language and other languages. Other aspects worth considering are humility, modesty, self-criticism, determination, and learn, learn, learn, study, study, study...and that applies not only to singing. Music history is important, as is knowledge of the body and vocal health.

3. WHAT ADVICE WOULD YOU GIVE TO TEACHERS TO HELP THEM BETTER PREPARE YOUNG SINGERS FOR A CAREER IN OPERA?

STEPHANIE BLYTHE: Teachers can get too myopic. I say that with all due respect and as someone who does a fair amount of teaching. I think that teachers need to take time to really listen to what's going on in the industry as it's happening. If you are working in a university and are necessarily and understandably mired in the bureaucracy of the institution, you may miss what is going on in the industry. I think it is very important to hear the singing that is going on today, not just for all the great things that you can take from it, but for the negative things as well. That is something the teachers could really do to help their students.

NICOLE CABELL: It's difficult to advise a young singer on a career when a teacher hasn't had a lot of experience singing in a big house. My advice is to give singers repertoire that is a little lighter than their *Fach*, but to have them sing with their authentic voice. If a singer is sensitive or prone to panicking over the pressures of the career, this must be brought to the singer's attention. The career is very demanding and can be emotionally difficult. If a singer gossips, puts down other singers, or rages against the injustice of not being cast for something, a teacher must remind the singer that this is just training for the difficult business of opera, and a student must learn to let this go and do what they do for the sake of the art.

JOSEPH CALLEJA: If you do not know what you are talking about, don't teach. You might ruin someone's life and preclude him or her from ever having a career. That borders on the criminal. Some great singers cannot be great teachers because they lack the communicative skills, but there is no great teacher who did not know what he or she was talking about. For me, the voice is an extension of myself, like touching, seeing, or hearing. If I lose it or damage it, it will be a big part of me missing.

DAVID DANIELS: Teach a healthy technique, concentrate on singing beautifully, and work on exact diction. Prepare them for the things which are most important, which is to be a good artist and a good musician. Preparing them for the market or that you have to have a twenty-inch waist— that's not as important as beautiful singing, which to me is the most important thing, no matter where social media takes us.

CHRISTINE GOERKE: You have to look at what is going on in the business, which breaks my heart a little because there is a lot that has little to do with what we actually study. I am glad that I am not teaching, because I would never want to have to stand in front of people and tell them, "You are amazing, you sound perfect, your voice is incredible, your stage presence is incredible, but you don't look as good in the costume as someone who might not have all of the same attributes that you do vocally." I would never want to have to do that to someone. That's a giant part of what's going on right now. Do look at the market and do encourage young singers to take chances, not to always play it safe, because, in fact, the ones that take chances are the ones that are remembered.

DENYCE GRAVES: I would challenge teachers to evaluate sharply how the singer could market his or her talent and to recommend repertoire that displays the singer's strongest points. Also, when appropriate, encourage singers to search themselves, so that they have a sense of purpose and know what it is they want to sing and what kind of life they envision for themselves. Many times they must take risks and take control of their own destinies instead of waiting for someone to hand it to them. One cannot escape time at the piano either. You must put in the work and be completely dedicated, and if you work diligently, we will know about you.

GREER GRIMSLEY: Teaching is a hard job because you are not only a teacher, but in some cases, a surrogate parent. The most important thing is to help the student figure out for herself or himself how to self-correct. This will begin to unlock the mystery of technique. From my first teacher, Charles Paddock, to Norma Newton and finally with Dr. Robert White, learning to self-correct was an important objective.

THOMAS HAMPSON: I have such respect for vocal teachers. I see what they do, and I do it on a limited basis. If you are a singer, be sure to keep an avenue for yourself and don't throw yourself completely on the sword. Set the standards high and with love, but with tough love—and I say this with commiseration and not instruction!

ALAN HELD: It goes without saying that each student is an individual. There is no one set technique that is going to work for all of the various students that come through the door of your studio. Use your ears. Try to feel the sensations that they are feeling while they are singing. Be patient and be a supportive teacher. Remember that you don't know everything going on in that young singer's mind, no more than he or she always understands just what is going on in yours. Find forty different ways to say the same thing. Every singer hears differently and learns in a different manner. Be open to learning yourself, and remember that you too were once a young singer very much like the one standing in front of you. I do wish it were possible to take a very hard look at the curriculum that vocal performance students have in our universities. I understand the importance of much of what is required. However, I'm not sure that it is all relevant to a singer. This would be a long and difficult process, but I think it is one worth undertaking.

JONAS KAUFMANN: Find a way to give more lessons to voice students on a regular basis. I was in the Hochschule every day for six to seven hours learning every other subject: piano, music history, theory, and so on, ad infinitum. A teacher cannot come to a student, let him or her sing, and then say it is wrong (in essence breaking the student's vocal mold) but then not have the time to put the pieces in the right order. A student has one lesson per week, and at the end of that one lesson he or she might have ten minutes of singing in a correct way. Then he or she practices mistakes the rest of the week. I would never teach because I could not do it with regularity. So maybe this book can help.

SIMON KEENLYSIDE: I wouldn't presume to give any.

KATHLEEN KIM: It's a difficult question. I would encourage my students to find more stage experience, not just opera but any type of performance, because that's what I missed when I was in college.

ANA MARÍA MARTÍNEZ: I would encourage at least two lessons a week so it keeps the student more focused. If it's just once a week, I would make sure that the student is having a coaching at least once or twice a week. Also, find a teaching language that is modified for each student coming through the door, so that you don't teach the same for all students.

LISETTE OROPESA: Don't let your students get away with silly stuff: no tension and no short-changing the importance of breath or languages. Encourage time management. Most importantly, the habits they develop in those early years are the ones that will last them a lifetime.

ERIC OWENS: The best advice I could give is to always be mindful of what is best for the student. If, after some time, the student doesn't seem to be benefiting from what you have to offer, you need to encourage and help that student find another teacher or ask a colleague to listen to the

Eric Owens
Bass-baritone Eric Owens is at home in new music, classic works, concert, recital, and opera, bringing his powerful poise, expansive voice, and instinctive acting faculties to stages around the globe. Praise from the *New Yorker*: "Owens's Alberich in *Das Rheingold* is so richly layered that it may become part of the history of the work." Owens also enjoys a close association with John Adams and was featured in the composer's *A Flowering Tree*. He performed the role of Leslie Groves in Adams's *Doctor Atomic* at the San Francisco Opera and the Metropolitan Opera, the recording of which won a Grammy. Photo courtesy Dario Acosta.

student sing and help you find the right semantics that will assist you in discerning if the problem may just be how you're putting into words what you're teaching, or if your methods themselves are not beneficial for this particular student.

EWA PODLEŚ: My advice to teachers would be to try not to be overly caring or overprotective. Also, advise students, as my voice teacher did, about repertoire, recommending works they can sing now and in the future, along with what they should never sing and why.

JENNIFER ROWLEY: Make your students independent, not code-pendent. My teacher teaches me a technique that I understand and that I can use independently of him. I continue to go back as things change, but I don't need to call him and say, "I have a big problem and I need you." This is something that doesn't start in university, but it needs to. At university, I was offered a very large role at twenty-two, but my teacher said, "I know you're going to be upset with me, but I said no. I told them you shouldn't do this. You're going to hurt yourself. You don't have a technique to sing this role." I cried for days, but now I thank him, because I *didn't* have a technique to sing and I *could* have hurt myself.

4. IF THERE WERE ONE THING YOU WISH YOU HAD LEARNED IN YOUR STUDENT DAYS THAT WOULD HAVE PREPARED YOU MORE FOR THE PROFESSIONAL STAGE, WHAT WOULD IT BE?

STEPHANIE BLYTHE: The most important thing is to know what is helpful and (I always say this to students) that if what I am saying is helpful to you, that's terrific. If not, then let it go, and don't be afraid to say that something is not working for you. Don't be afraid to let that information just pass away. On the other hand, if you hear the same technical advice from many, many different sources, then it's time to start reevaluating your own thoughts on the subject.

NICOLE CABELL: I wish I had learned the singing languages more intimately, and I wish I had spent more time learning piano skills. Playing through my accompaniment would be incredibly helpful, simply from the standpoint of learning and memorizing. Learning languages cannot be emphasized enough, if not for the art itself, then for functioning in other countries. On a psychological level, I wish I would have learned how to center myself through methods such as yoga, meditation, techniques to calm stage fright, and spiritual ways to deal with things like bad reviews and unfair politics. I eventually did learn these things (pretty much wrapped in the idea of taking life a lot less seriously), but it would have been helpful in my formative years as a singer, at a time when ambition was much stronger than purpose.

JOSEPH CALLEJA: I wish I had had the brains and experience I now have after nineteen years in the business, in order to tackle certain circumstance better, but I haven't done a bad job. The testament of that is that I am here, and I started at an early age. But I was lucky. My advice is to surround yourself with people who have your interests at heart and who will tell you the truth. My teacher Paul Asciak was like a dictator; he is an Aquarius like me and has the same character, so it is like with like. I love him to bits and he helped me a lot, not only with vocal technique, but also with how to deal with managers and agents or how to write a letter. I was lucky to have him. The mistakes I would probably have done without him I didn't do.

DAVID DANIELS: I could come up with a big list of things I didn't know, but I think it's more interesting for the artist or the student or the young professional to find all that out on their own. Everybody's experience is going to be different.

JOYCE DIDONATO: I would not change anything I did in my student years. But if I could have a conversation with my younger, petrified self, I would say, "Joyce, just breathe: it's going to be okay. Actually, you have no idea of *how* okay it's going to be!" I look at the trying process and all the difficulties I encountered, how I had to scrape and scrounge and cry and vent and suffer. I wouldn't change that for anything because it formed me into who I am today. The thing is, I did not have an easy birth in terms of trying to get started in the career, but when the dominos started to fall, they fell in a really lovely way. I vacillated between being patient and impatient, but at the right moments, and I think that is one reason why I have achieved a certain amount of success.

CHRISTINE GOERKE: Drill more languages. Not just the diction. Go take the class. Learn the grammar. Learn the language. I can't say that I am fluent in anything, including English, but I know the languages well enough to be able to pick up a piece of music and recognize 80 percent of the words. French is something that I didn't study. I studied Italian and German, but where I ended up making my debut in Europe was in Paris, and I spoke no French. They were lovely in the theater. But at the grocery store I really thought I was not going to eat the entire time I was there. The first trip was so awful I thought I would never go back.

DENYCE GRAVES: To play the piano, without a doubt. I could have saved years of worry and stress had the process of learning music come easier. Fortunately, I have a good memory, so that once it's learned, I know it forever, but the long and arduous process of learning music has been a pain in the ———!

GREER GRIMSLEY: If there were one thing, it would have been to nurture my musical instincts and to fully understand the business aspect of a career.

THOMAS HAMPSON: I never went to a music school. I never had that day-in, day-out experience. I studied political science and music at the same time. My music was pretty much directed studies or self-studies. I have a degree in political science and a degree in vocal performance. And although I wouldn't trade in my studies in the humanities, I wish I had had more musical nuts and bolts like theory, ear training, and certainly piano skills. Also, my postgraduate studies have either been directed studies or autodidactic. (Typing skills would be nice!)

ALAN HELD: It was not possible to have more language study when I was a student, but I wish that there had been. I received a degree in music education, and there was not enough time for thorough language study on top of all of my other courses. I also didn't really have acting classes. Perhaps, in some ways, that was a good thing. I learned to just be natural and relate my acting to the specific character or instance that I was performing.

JONAS KAUFMANN: I got in touch with many teachers, not only in the Hochschule, but also outside, such as Josef Metternich, James King, and Michael Rhodes. I realized that the one and only truth does not lie only in one teacher. Two or three teachers can have the exact same technique, but they describe it in different words. The first time you don't get it. The second time you think you might have understood. The third time, when the teacher just explains it with different words, then the coin drops and you say, "This is what they were all talking about. I just didn't understand." We cannot take out our instrument. We cannot observe it. We cannot show, as a teacher, exactly what we are doing. We can only describe it with images, with words, and with phrases that one singer understands and the other doesn't.

SIMON KEENLYSIDE: Aw, it's easy to be wise in retrospect. *Non, je ne regrette rien.* Not that I was right—far from it. I made a landslide of mistakes and poor decisions along the way. Neither did those mistakes inform me for the better thereafter. It's not a neat and elegant puzzle, this life or this work. It's chaos. Survival is the name of the game.

KATHLEEN KIM: For me it would have been more stage experience and studying in Europe. Going to Germany, France, or Italy for six months and learning their languages and cultures.

ANA MARÍA MARTÍNEZ: It is great to know what you want to do, but it's also frightening. Will I make it? Am I good enough? I wish I could have been more joyful about it and more fearless in my disposition. That's part of my introversion, but I'm much freer now, and motherhood has a lot to do with that.

LISETTE OROPESA: I wish I had learned more about my relationship to my body as it goes through daily activities. Everything goes straight to the voice. I also wish I had had a class on taxes!

ERIC OWENS: I wish I had spent a considerable amount of time in Europe to truly have become fluent in French, German, and Italian. There's really no substitute for total immersion if you want to be able to think in these languages.

DIMITRI PITTAS: I took two semesters of piano in undergrad, but then I decided I was going to be an opera singer, not a teacher, and so my education credits and piano studies went out the window. I wish I knew how to play the piano better nowadays.

EWA PODLEŚ: Self-confidence!

JENNIFER ROWLEY: I wish that I had learned to be independent of my teacher earlier. I don't mean to get rid of a teacher, but I mean when you're out on a job you are independent of your teacher, and if something happens and you don't feel like you're technically in the right place, you have to be able to fix the various problems.

GERHARD SIEGEL: In recent years I've just learned that, unfortunately, in Germany the administration and dramaturgy are more important than the performers. I would have liked to know that right from the start. I do not know if it would have changed what I now feel, but I would not be as disappointed as I am now.

5. MEMORIZATION IS OFTEN AN ISSUE FOR SINGERS. WHAT ARE SOME OF YOUR TECHNIQUES FOR MEMORIZING? FOR EXAMPLE, WHEN DO YOU START THE MEMORIZATION PROCESS?

STEPHANIE BLYTHE: Let me mention a memory slip and how you cannot let it affect you, as it happens to us all. Once in a recital, I came to a song I loved and knew extraordinarily well and for some reason I got a block. I had to stop and restart three times before I said to the audience, "You know what? I am just going to go and look at the music, if you will please excuse me." And I stood next to the pianist and sang the song reading over her shoulder until I felt comfortable, and then took my place back in the crook of the piano.

NICOLE CABELL: I spend a lot of time looking at the score when I'm learning a new piece, and I'm lucky enough to be a visual learner. I see the score in my head when performing, but to get there requires a lot of writing out text and staring at the score while playing through my vocal line. After

I've learned my part, I'll usually go back to recordings and listen to them ad nauseam. It's common sense that we do not copy the singers we're listening to, so I'm basically listening to the orchestra and singing over the soprano in my head or out loud, for repetition.

JOSEPH CALLEJA: I am lucky with this, as I have a really good memory. It almost borders on photographic, so learning a role and memorizing it was never a problem. I learn roles very quickly. When I was under pressure or tired, I wrote down the words; however, learning a role usually takes a week.

DAVID DANIELS: For me, it's visualizing the music and the words on the page, and then it's repetition, repetition, repetition. But I never trust myself. For example, I've sung a lot of *Julius Caesar*, but at my breaks, when I'm not onstage, I'm in the dressing room glued to the score, going through the recitatives, checking my memory. It's always amazing to me that my colleagues are out laughing and joking with the dressers or in someone else's dressing room talking, and I'm just not that way.

CHRISTINE GOERKE: Just putting pen to paper in the $4.99 notebook I mentioned in another question about learning a role. I have no idea why that works, but it does. A DVD helps me by putting movement to the phrases so I can visualize what's happening. I also do have a bit of a photographic memory. I can see what page the music is on, but I can't always remember exactly what the text is. Other than that, it is just repetition. Also, doing it for two hours and putting it away works for me. If I try to do it too many hours in a row, it just doesn't work. If I do it two hours and walk away from it, then during dinner I will just magically spout out an entire page that I thought I couldn't remember.

DENYCE GRAVES: I've never sat down to memorize. I must sing it through on my own and with a coach, and once I've sung it several times, I know it.

GREER GRIMSLEY: Often in academic situations we are told, "This is the way you do things" or "This is the process." But we don't all learn exactly the same way. Plus, our brains work in different ways. That said, you have to figure out how your brain works best. This really is a journey of constant self-discovery, your knowing yourself best and knowing how you work fastest and most efficiently. For myself, I will go through things and think about them, so that by the time I start to sing it, I have almost memorized it by itself. For some people, they have to actually sit down and sing it, but I try to find a connection so that I will remember.

THOMAS HAMPSON: I went to a deeply structured parochial school for ten years, and part of that was learning Bible verses and memorizing. I still memorize as tediously as anyone else, but I learned a structure for memorizing. Memorize in small elements: one line, one verse at a time.

There is a certain rote to it, but I have never personally memorized something because I have repeated it so often. I have to sit down and actually tear the piece apart structurally. Also, if I'm going to sing something that does not need to be memorized, I will still try to memorize it because that makes you understand the architecture so much clearer.

ALAN HELD: Memorizing for a singer is easier, to me, than just learning dialogue. We have the music that helps us with the memorization. Take away the music and the words become harder to keep in your mind. Memorize the two together. It is much easier.

JONAS KAUFMANN: I am thankful I'm a fast learner. So in two or three days I can memorize a part, but it is much more healthy to do it in a longer time. Normally, I look at the part alone, but the best way actually is when I go to a coach. I sing through the part *prima vista*, and then the whole part again maybe two or three times to get a feel for it. Then I let it sit for about two weeks. I don't do anything. Then I come back, and it feels and sounds familiar. And when I sing it again, most of it gets into my head, and I start humming some melodies, and I then realize that it is connected to my brain. So, I do it, I wait, I do it again, and then when I come back the third time, it is most probably done.

SIMON KEENLYSIDE: I'm not of the opinion that memorization *is* an issue for singers. It's a fundamental requirement. The only issue is to leave enough time to learn a new role and have it in the voice and ready for the beginning(ish) of the rehearsals. Only a young singer with a desire to be on the scrap heap early would not do that. It may be wearying at times, but so long as the excitement to get on with the role outweighs the drudgery of daily memorizing, then all will be well.

KATHLEEN KIM: I never try to memorize unless it's short notice. I only practice until it becomes memorized and it simply comes out automatically. I just use repetition. If I try to memorize and try to force the memory, after the show it goes away. But if I can put it in my muscle memory, it stays longer.

ANA MARÍA MARTÍNEZ: Even before I get out of bed, I often look at the score, then have coffee and breakfast. It seems to be sort of an alpha state of mind and helps me retain that much more. I also write things down. But learning a language I do not speak—for example, the Czech in *Rusalka*—I started at the last word, closed the book, then remembered the penultimate word, then the third to last, and so on. By the time you are at the beginning of the page, the entire page is memorized. There is something about going backward which seems to help the brain remember it better. Also, it's not really in my body until I stage it. I have a friend who gets on a treadmill with the score while reading it. If you have a physical activity, it helps in memorization.

LISETTE OROPESA: Memorizing comes from drilling and repetition and time. You cannot learn a role and expect it to be flawless in a week. I never cram my prep time. I start working on roles several months in advance. Make sure you know what every sentence means and what your character is reacting to; logic makes it easier. Again, if you know the language, it helps immensely. Don't just memorize syllables; increase your vocabulary. Note cards, pictures, funny phrases—take your pick. Practicing before bedtime is helpful, too. It gets your brain organizing while you sleep. And eat brain food, not junk!

ERIC OWENS: If I have time, I'll memorize as I go; that is, I won't move on to even familiarizing myself with a particular section without having memorized the previous section. For me, this particular process tends to etch the information permanently. A good rule of thumb is to

Dimitri Pittas
Hailed for "his rich tenor, charged with electricity and dynamism," Dimitri Pittas has appeared in such leading venues as Munich, Deutsche Oper Berlin, Vienna, Houston, and Covent Garden. His roles include Don Carlo, Riccardo in *Un ballo in maschera*, and the Duke in *Rigoletto*. A graduate of The Crane School of Music and the Lindemann Young Artist Program, he has appeared at the Met in *La bohème*, *The Magic Flute*, and *L'elisir d'amore*. On the concert stage, Mr. Pittas has been heard in performances of Verdi's *Requiem* and Beethoven's Ninth Symphony with the Concertgebouw Amsterdam and Atlanta Symphonies and has appeared in recital with the Marilyn Horne Foundation at Carnegie Hall. Photo courtesy Kristin Hoeberman.

go over smaller sections every day versus trying to cram in bigger sections and then not looking at the score for several days. Although I have friends that have photographic memories, and they're just flipping the pages of a score, and they'll have the whole thing committed to memory after having looked at it just one time! And I think, where was I when they were handing that out? Like "Morpheus, download *Tosca* for me! Thank you!"

DIMITRI PITTAS: I start at the end of the score and I work backward. A lot of times when you learn the score from the beginning, the first aria is always great and you're really solid, but then the last scene doesn't have the same understanding and security. So sometimes it's better to learn things out of sequence for the sake of having them so prepared in your mind that you can play with them when you need to. I learned, cover to cover, memorized, in two weeks, *The Rake's Progress* using that process. Then again, I started working on *Don Carlo* nine months before my performances. I could have probably done it in three months, but I wouldn't have been as comfortable or able to say as much because my mind wouldn't have been so connected to it.

JENNIFER ROWLEY: My biggest tip is red ink. It is scientifically proven that red prints something into the subconscious. So when you write out your text in red, it's like you're writing into your memory. What I do is I say the text out loud and I write the text in red pen. Usually after the second time, I know it. I use a notebook for each role and write the entire text in this notebook. Also, I don't start memorizing anything until I vocally and technically have it in me. If you're memorizing and singing at the same time, you can memorize bad habits. Sometimes I listen to the recording and write the text as fast as I can (in red).

GERHARD SIEGEL: I begin memorizing from the beginning of learning the role—in fact, as soon as I have a contract for a new role. Lately, I dare to memorize by listening to other recordings. I most decisively advise young singers not to learn in this way. Too easily one starts to imitate other voices and learns bad habits. As quickly as possible, learn the notes and text, and then even make a finished recording. At least for me, that's the way I learn the fastest.

6. WHAT IS YOUR RULE FOR DAILY PRACTICE WHEN YOU ARE NOT PERFORMING?

STEPHANIE BLYTHE: Daily practice comes in four forms: reading, listening, speaking, and singing. You can do one, some, or all. Singer's choice.

LAWRENCE BROWNLEE: I do my vocal exercises. I already start the day speaking in a place that is comfortable for me and normal and natural and not so far from where my singing voice is. As the saying goes: *Si canta come si parla.*

NICOLE CABELL: While I practice and sing consistently, I do not do so every day. I will listen to almost every genre of music but opera in my free time, because it frees me up, takes away my obsession with what I'm singing, and leaves me fresh for the times I come back to classical music. If I have a lot of new projects coming up or I need to refresh old ones, I will often write through my text on the days I'm not singing, or just peruse the score. Practicing involves many different aspects, including language study, acting, piano skills, and seeing other classical productions. When I'm practicing vocally, I try not to sing more than two hours a day. I spend less time practicing now than when I was younger, simply because I have a general idea of how to do things that would have taken me much longer to work through in the past.

JOSEPH CALLEJA: Silence and rest are very important. If you sang a performance, then rest the day after, or if possible two days. If you are not singing at all, then I would say sing two or three times a week, moving the voice each time around thirty minutes. The voice loves extended periods of rest, in my case at least. If your idea of rest is going to parties, smoking, and shouting, then the voice won't like it. But regular stuff—going to the beach, boating, having a glass of wine, even the occasional cigar—is not going to harm you. The human body is adaptable, and it is fine when you give the regenerative factor time to work.

DAVID DANIELS: If I really have time off, I won't sing at all. But it does take me a good four or five days to get where the voice is connected again to the breath. I have no fear of not singing. If I go to Vegas, I don't think about singing. I just think about blackjack.

CHRISTINE GOERKE: I don't have one. Usually if I am about three weeks out from doing something, I have to be working on it a certain amount of time. If it's something new, I might start a bit earlier. I happened to luck out this year: I have most of July and August at home with my kids. But I won't lie. I have the panic singer moment: "Oh my God, what if it's broken?" And then I tell myself, "You have been doing this twenty years. You didn't break it. It's still in there. You know how to do this." Of course I start singing and it is fine, but sometimes it's really good to give yourself a break. So, know thyself.

DENYCE GRAVES: My daily rule for practice is this: whether you're singing or not, be in music somehow, either by reading the text of your material, translating, phoneticizing, listening, or mentally singing, I have sometimes had great breakthroughs not singing at all, just by watching my breathing or thinking through music.

GREER GRIMSLEY: Pavarotti said you take one day off singing and nobody notices. Two days off, maybe you notice, but three or four days off, other people start noticing. Personally, I think at least touching it on a regular basis, or every other day, is good enough. But there are times when after a long series of operas, I just take a couple of weeks and I say I'm not going to sing. Sometimes it's more important to be with my family than to sing. But you know that when you start to sing again, it's going to feel awful to you and it's going to sound not at its optimum. You haven't forgotten how to sing; it's just reconnecting the muscles of singing. It is important to know that you're not going to take a couple of weeks off and go straight to rehearsals. Plan accordingly.

THOMAS HAMPSON: The first thing I would say is, if you're resting, rest. There is real value to "resetting the computer" in every way. However, if you're practicing, it is for performance, i.e., work. The simplest advice is to always warm your voice up. Don't just start working away. I always like to keep my personal resonance focused and agile; you might even hear me humming on the golf course.

ALAN HELD: At this point, I don't have to sing as long every day to keep the voice in shape. However, if I take much time off, I notice it. I do a little singing every day. Before the next engagement begins, I do have to spend time getting my voice back in shape. In addition, there seems to always be a new role to learn (or an old role to relearn). My practice sessions are not really sessions and haven't necessarily changed. If I am learning a new role, I'll have to spend more concentrated time and effort. If I have the role learned, I often will simply just pass by the piano and try out a phrase here and there to make sure it is all working as I planned.

JONAS KAUFMANN: I treat singing almost like a sport. It's about muscle memory, and if you don't train the muscles, you lose that memory. It is like the violinist before he puts the bow on the string: he has his finger on the position, and that is what our voice does, just like that. The daily vocalizing can be as little as ten to fifteen minutes, but doing it every day helps. Of course, I also have holidays where I don't do anything, but then it takes several days to get back up to a performing level. If I am in a rehearsal or performance series, I will adjust accordingly. For example, I had a performance yesterday [*Parsifal* at the Met], and I will have a performance in two days, so I will practice tomorrow.

SIMON KEENLYSIDE: The amount of practice I do when not performing depends on the nature of the role that I'm singing. If that role is tiring on the voice but not particularly lyrical, then I'll sing something else. I do that for stamina and to keep the muscles elastic. If the role is lyrical and tiring, then I will do almost no practice, because I will already be doing enough singing of the "right" type. If it is holiday time, I will take around two weeks completely off, after which I'll do around half an hour a day thereafter of gentle practice. If this baritone did not do that, then it would take me too long (in the region of two weeks) to get the voice back in any sort of usable shape. We are all made differently. I suspect that even the way one speaks will impinge on such matters.

KATHLEEN KIM: If I don't have any performances, then I practice three or four days a week. Then I have a couple of days' rest, and practice again after the rest. When I practice, I work on upcoming roles.

ANA MARÍA MARTÍNEZ: A few minutes a day is great—some scales and passages from the arias. I stay physically active even if I'm not singing. I'm going to be running or doing things that keep me limber. But if I am not singing or I have jet lag, then I don't like that feeling, because the voice is a part of me and I need to keep it limber and fresh.

LISETTE OROPESA: When I'm not performing, rehearsing, or learning a role, I take time off singing. It's rare, so I do enjoy it. I sing all the time without meaning to—while working around the house and in the shower—so I'm definitely not silent, but I do take advantage of time to rest. Nine times out of ten there is new music to be learned, so if and when I can have a chance to regroup, I take it.

ERIC OWENS: LOL! Unless I have something new to learn during that time, I will not be in a practice room. Sometimes you just have to forget about work and have some fun! But for young people who are in the process of building a technique, I think you need to practice at least every other day, if possible, no matter if you're performing or not! But, even during the early years, I think it's important to have fun.

DIMITRI PITTAS: I do at least thirty minutes of vocalizing with a specific goal. A goal is just something like "Make sure that you're focused for the next half hour." If you can, get in two times a day: do half an hour of vocalizing in the morning, go out, have your day, come back, and before dinner then another half hour, just for maintenance's sake. Also, you never know what's going to happen because you might get a call saying, "Someone dropped out and we need you next week," and you've got to be in the zone.

JENNIFER ROWLEY: There are many different aspects of practicing that do not involve singing. This includes language, research, or writing texts. I consider all of that practice time. I usually combine singing with my workouts. I usually do two days on, then a day off. When I'm working, that's often what my performance schedule looks like, too. So, I like to go do my workouts, come back, shower, and sing. On vacation you can take your iPod with you and learn something.

GERHARD SIEGEL: If I have a lot of rehearsals and performances, I do not need daily vocal practice, since one is constantly warmed up anyway. However, I think the voice needs calm and rest for longer periods. That said, I'm lazy between productions.

CHAPTER 6

✧

Extras from the Experts

Dealing with nerves and competition, singing through illness, and staying vocally healthy and fit are things almost every professional singer can discuss. Even soprano Renée Fleming has often spoken of having had stage fright and the difficult time she had with it. Amusingly, Kiri Te Kanawa has said, "There is nothing like being up on that stage and looking at that audience looking back at you...and for a split second you wonder if you should Sing or Run."

Following are thoughts not only on overcoming performance anxiety or stage fright but also on learning what your voice can do even through illness. In addition, the artists offer ideas on vocal hygiene and finding one's place amidst the competition. As Alan Held advises, "You've got to be willing to enter into the fray, take the hits along with the success, and keep going." Knowing yourself and your strengths is also essential, as Joseph Calleja reasoned: "Be honest with yourself. Don't imagine talents you don't have." Perhaps most important is developing an attitude of love for sharing music and a gratefulness for the extraordinary opportunity to be on the stage and perform. As Gerhard Siegel exhorts, "Go out and sing and have fun!"

1. WHAT ARE SOME OF THE THINGS YOU DO TO STAY VOCALLY HEALTHY AND FIT?

STEPHANIE BLYTHE: If you don't take time to recharge those batteries, it can really affect you. Now, there are some people who are like sharks. If they stop swimming, they die, so they just keep going. That's fine, and for those people, I salute them. I've had to force myself to take time in between things, and I have had to actually cancel things that I didn't want to cancel because I simply knew that I would be spending resources that I didn't have and that would negatively affect the next job that I did or my life. I like my life very much, and I like living a normal life as much as possible whenever I can.

LAWRENCE BROWNLEE: You need to be sure that you are not singing beyond who you are. As the voice and the body mature, it's not necessarily about the overwhelming amount of sound but the color of the voice and how you produce it. I always try to keep in mind that I approach new roles with the way that I sing. Next year, I will be doing *I Puritani* at the Met. I know people have been really more heroic, but I've done it twice, and I feel that it is a role that is appropriate for my voice. I will approach it my way; there's definitely a difference in the way Corelli sang it, or Kraus. By carefully choosing my roles, I keep my voice in good shape.

NICOLE CABELL: I stay hydrated, do yoga, jog, and get plenty of sleep. I've begun to monitor what I eat, which seems to make a bigger difference than I ever thought. When I can, I meditate and do breathing exercises, which calms my nerves and gives me energy. The trick is not to push myself too hard at any point, and to maintain a balance in every aspect of life. Staying away from excessive alcohol and smoking is key, and maintaining a positive attitude keeps me healthy.

JOSEPH CALLEJA: Yoga, gym, and weight training for a man and two to three times a week of jogging. I run three times a week, forty minutes each. You are not trying to have a six-pack and be Schwarzenegger. You are trying to be healthy for your voice. I do not work out with weights the day of nor the day before, because singing is a workout. It really is. Yesterday with *Rigoletto* at the Staatsoper in Munich, I lost at least three liters of sweat, it was so hot on the stage. You move, you use your diaphragm, you sometimes carry sopranos, you climb steps. It's physical.

DAVID DANIELS: I'm up and down with my weight or whether I'm exercising or not. I played varsity basketball in high school, and it's still something I love to do, but it's hard to find pickup games. I played with Lucas Meachem and a bunch of young artists at Santa Fe, and we had a great summer because Lucas is quite a basketball player and I'm not bad. But in regard to vocal health, it's really about sleep and hydration. And I'm a major believer in silence. It's amazing what twenty-four hours of silence can do for the vocal folds. I often don't talk from about three in the afternoon the day before the performance until after the show. That's about seventeen to eighteen hours of silence.

JOYCE DIDONATO: Welcome to the world of an opera singer, where everything is discipline: your practice regime, your diet, your physical exercise, your mental health. If you are really disciplined about all of that, you're going to be in good shape. The approach to my body, which is my instrument, is vitally important. I am a big fan of yoga and a recent convert to the Alexander Technique. Obviously the diet is best made up of fresh foods and moderation. (Although I do drink a diet drink before I sing!) The question is, what kind of instrument do you want to be singing with? The more attention you pay to your overall health, the stronger, more vibrant your instrument can be. However, I am not a slave to this discipline either. As in life, moderation and balance are key!

CHRISTINE GOERKE: I try to get sleep. I try to drink a lot of water. That's my thing. I don't succeed in either of them with my children, but those are the things I try to do. I am on and off with the exercise regimen. I am also a gigantic klutz, so at any given time I usually have a sprained something. I don't generally think about a vocally fit thing. I try not to get sick. That's the best I can do.

DENYCE GRAVES: I continue with my voice lessons and coaching. I try physical exercise when I can. I'm learning new material that challenges me to grow differently. I go to concerts of all kinds and always learn something.

GREER GRIMSLEY: I try to exercise as much as possible. By that I mean walking, going to the gym, but not in a ridiculous manner. Our bodies are just as much part of our instrument as anything else, and keeping that working at an optimum is important. If knee problems are hereditary, you might just do walking instead of jogging. As singers, I would say anything aerobic is a plus.

THOMAS HAMPSON: My personal routine is based on yoga and to some extent Pilates, and I add to that vocalizing to feel the edges of the vocal cords vibrating cleanly, so that even if I'm not singing a lot but I am speaking more than usual, my voice is clean and functioning healthily. The alpha and omega of my vocal health are sleep for regeneration. If you've had a big sing or a big rehearsal, then know that you need equal time for regeneration. Try to speak and sing in the same place with a lighter and focused resonance. Your voice has muscles like everything else, so pay attention to how you use them and how much you use them.

ALAN HELD: I enjoy working out in many different manners. I like treadmills, cycling, playing basketball, or just about any other kind of sport you can name. As I have gotten older, obviously, I've had to take some things a bit easier. My breath support is better for having taken reasonable care of my body. I try never to abuse it.

Singers need plenty of sleep in order to maintain their voices and to keep their minds sharp for rehearsals and performances. As far as foods—everyone's body is different. If you have reflux, avoid the foods that cause you problems. The important thing is to simply take care of your instrument.

JONAS KAUFMANN: When you are studying, you never hear about the physical side of singing. I've never heard that anywhere, and I have spoken with many students from other countries and universities. Your body has to be in shape somehow. I'm not saying that you need to do sit-ups or go to the gym. This is actually wrong and counterproductive because the muscles will be too tight and lose their flexibility. The body needs to be relaxed, and with too much muscle you can't be relaxed. You just want to warm up your body, to feel that your body and breathing are awake. Yoga, for example, is a good warm-up, as you are always stretching and breathing in and out. Wake up the body before you wake up the voice, and then instead of an hour, you need five to ten minutes to wake up the voice.

SIMON KEENLYSIDE: Be normal. Do your work in time. Practice when you see fit, and in the right way, but be as normal as you can be in daily life—as few fussy regimes as possible, and try to keep them to a minimum. To give in to a host of mannerisms would be to build a gilded cage around your life, which you are bound to regret later.

If I am under vocal pressure, there are two things I will regularly do. It depends how well my voice is coping with that strain. I steam, either with a mask or in a steam room. Second, and only as a last resort, I will have a day of quiet or even silence, even if I have to skip a day at work. Both measures are utterly boring, but desperate times require sensible measures, something like that. They work for me.

KATHLEEN KIM: I just don't talk much and I do some exercise. I am in the process of learning yoga, but with so much traveling, I find it hard to keep it up. I try to do any possible physical exercise I can, including some running.

LISETTE OROPESA: I sing plenty for my job, so I make the most of my time off! I run, practice yoga, hike, cook, read, and even compose my own songs. It is important to make time for personal well-being.

ERIC OWENS: Everyone is different. Sometimes, knowing what to do involves going through some rough periods, retracing what led you to those points, and figuring out what you must not do. This is in addition to all of the common-sense measures of washing your hands often, drinking plenty of water, taking vitamins, etc. But beyond these, you'll figure things out with experience.

DIMITRI PITTAS: Lamperti, in *The Technics of Bel Canto*, states not to sing after a fatty meal, and I agree. Therefore I can make the correlation that if I feel well, I sing well. Try to live a healthy lifestyle, which includes a lot of activity, a lot of water, and a lot of rest. Just by focusing on those three things, I notice a big difference in my singing. You're healthier and happier because you've got more endorphins in your body. Having said that, I've also lost close to twenty pounds. I'm not doing it just because that's where the business is going, but the fact of the matter is it is.

EWA PODLEŚ: I do not do special exercise programs nor follow special diets. Because I never overdid it, my voice is in very good shape. I never worried about turning down roles that were not right at the time. I wanted to succeed and to get everything, but in the right time.

JENNIFER ROWLEY: Cardio, cardio, cardio, cardio. You have to be in shape for this business now. They want you to look a certain way and you need to be fit, because you may have to run around like a chicken with your head cut off and not be winded and still be able to sing. This summer at the Savonlinna festival there were more obstacles backstage in the castle than on the stage! You have to climb upstairs and crawl through small openings, and you are getting winded just climbing the stairs to get to the stage.

Ewa Podleś
Endowed with a wide vocal range, Ewa Podleś is considered to be one of the rare true contraltos of our time. Winner of many great competitions, she completed her musical education exclusively at the Fryderyk Chopin Academy of Music in Warsaw. Her repertoire spans from baroque to Penderecki. She has performed on such stages as La Scala, Metropolitan Opera, Covent Garden, Le Châtelet, Deutsche Oper, Gran Teatre del Liceu in Barcelona, and Teatro Real Madrid. An avid recitalist, she has made successful appearances at Carnegie Hall and Lincoln Center, Wigmore Hall, Théâtre des Champs Elysées, and the Warsaw Philharmonic. Her numerous CD recordings have received prestigious prizes. Photo courtesy Andrzej Świetlik.

What's going to happen when you get on the stage? Combine your workouts with your singing; do lip trills while you are running or on the elliptical. Your breath line will be longer and stronger.

GERHARD SIEGEL: Honest answer or constructed response? Since I started in the profession blithely unaware of the problems of singing, I have never taken the word *overdiscipline* seriously. It is important to have a lot of sleep, no (almost no) smoking, and avoid excessive alcohol. The rest of it you can manage to discover yourself. As I said earlier, I try not to torture myself and not lose the fun in life by limitations. Happiness is an important pillar of good singing.

2. HAVE YOU ANY SPECIAL THINGS YOU DO THAT HELP YOU TO PERFORM THROUGH ILLNESS?

STEPHANIE BLYTHE: I would avoid singing during illness, but if you must, then you need help, especially from the conductor, for example. I remember once singing *Falstaff* at the Bastille. I had lost my voice, and there was no cover. James Conlon was conducting and is an incredibly savvy opera conductor, and he was so with me in every moment that regardless of what I could give him, he was there and supporting me. If I had to sing a passage down an octave, he'd bring the orchestra down to a volume where I could be heard. He used the orchestra as one big instrument that night so that even though I was only at half of my vocal powers, I was still able to give an effective performance.

NICOLE CABELL: Occasionally I've decided to sing through an illness. If I'm singing a role like Micaela in *Carmen*, I can sing through almost any illness, as I don't have a lot of high-wire singing to do. Singing Giulietta in *I Capuleti e i Montecchi* is another case, where the role is fraught with high singing and long lines that require optimum vocal health. I may need the help of a doctor who can provide vitamins or a prescription to eliminate an illness, but I usually avoid this, as I believe taking antibiotics or steroids on a regular basis can be very dangerous for the body. I will refrain from doing any excessive speaking, as this can make me vocally tired, and I will stay obsessively hydrated. Concentrating on my technique is the only way to get through these performances—basically being diligent about keeping my voice out of my throat.

JOSEPH CALLEJA: If it is just a slight cold in the nose, you might get away with it. However, my rule of thumb is to cancel. I have, in sixteen years, taken some medication in order to clean my nasal passages, of course only with a doctor's prescription, but I never took an injection in order to sing a performance. The worst thing you can do is to mask the symptoms. You can sing with an ear infection, sinus problem, or cold, but you can't sing if your larynx or pharynx is compromised. If you do it, you are asking for severe trouble, possibly career-ending, because no technique can sing through an inflamed larynx. People who tell you they can are lying and will pay the price afterward.

DAVID DANIELS: It's horrible to sing when you're under the weather. There's nothing worse than that day when you're getting the sore throat and you know in a few days you're going to be so ill, but you usually are in amazing voice. Nobody can tell us why.

JOYCE DIDONATO: I can tell this story of a positive result in spite of injury. I broke my fibia at Covent Garden during the premiere for *Barber of Seville* and had to finish the run in a wheelchair. As un-ideal as this was, the idea came to me that Rosina is such an independent, feisty girl that she could not be pushed around by somebody (the original thought of the directors), so I said, "Let me do it myself!" I improvised a new staging of *The Barber of Seville* with Rosina on wheels. Being thrust into the restraint of a wheelchair was the first time I physically felt her frustration and confinement. But it taught me that improvisation is often necessary in live theater, and working around obstacles just requires a bit of imagination!

CHRISTINE GOERKE: For me the rule is if it's chest up, I'm okay. If it's chest down, I cancel. I'm prone to bronchitis when I get a cold. I had walking pneumonia years ago, so the chance that a cold will drop directly into my chest is good. Anything that produces coughing inflames your cords, so singing on cords that are gigantic already just does more damage. But if I have a cold? It's annoying as hell, but that's why God made handkerchiefs.

DENYCE GRAVES: Ah, yes, performing through illness—it will happen in one's career many times. It depends on how serious the illness, but if it's a cold or allergies or sore throat, the first thing that I do is separate myself from everyone and get quiet. I start texting (which I prefer anyway) and emailing. Then I might gargle, take Mucinex (depending again on what the problem is), drink lots of water, use the neti pot, eat cleanly, and sleep or rest as much as possible. I keep a humidifier going and will often steam on and off throughout the day of a performance. I would also warm up lightly, humming or doing massaging types of vocal exercises in ten-minute intervals a few times per day, but very lightly, and then, of course, *pray*. These precautions often make a huge impact on the success of the evening and are good practices anyway.

GREER GRIMSLEY: That's when you rely on the things you have learned. That's when you can tip more toward technique with what you're going to do. It's amazing what you can do when you're under the weather, but the hardest time is when you realize it isn't going to work. That, on this particular night, it's not going to happen. Knock on wood, but up to now, I've not had to cancel where there wasn't a cover. It's about living to fight another day.

THOMAS HAMPSON: For one thing, if you're only slightly ill and you're in a rehearsal, use that time to teach yourself what you may get stuck with sometime and you can't do anything about. My rule of thumb is if you are sick in your throat and on your vocal cords, shut up. Having said that, we are under enormous pressure as public figures to perform, but we also live in a world where the adage "You're only as good as your last performance" is somehow true. On the other hand, we also have too many vain cancellations today. You can experiment so that even if you're not at what you feel your 100 percent is, your 90 percent or your 85 percent achieves the level that is worthy of what you're singing.

In general, I prefer alternative medical methods such as homeopathy to the world of easily dispensed "drug Band-Aids."

ALAN HELD: Technique is what you have to rely on when you have to sing during an illness. In addition, again, stay hydrated. Ultimately, try to avoid germs as much as possible and keep your hands clean! Also, be good colleagues, and if you're ill, don't infect others.

JONAS KAUFMANN: If you have a slight cold, it takes some experience to find out when you can perform and when you need to cancel. I wouldn't take any risks. Very often people put pressure on you, saying this is the most important performance and you have to do it, or it is so important for your career, but nothing, nothing can be as important as your instrument. So, never harm your instrument by singing when you shouldn't. I am very sad when I am forced to cancel a performance, as I know many people will have bought their tickets long in advance and often even traveled great distances to hear me. But I would be even more unhappy were I to sing ill and then to give a performance which did not allow me to give the public what I am always hoping to give—and that is my best.

SIMON KEENLYSIDE: In addition to the periodic courses of antibiotics, which only help at the tail end of a bug in any case, I cancel. If you're sick, then don't sing. Easy to say, painful to do. There's probably a chance at the beginning of a cold that you'll still be able to perform—a small window of opportunity, perhaps? There may be pressure for you to show up and sing. Personally, I have always regretted giving in to those pressures. Even if you can get through the evening without embarrassment (at the least) or hurting your voice (at worst), well then, what state will you be in for the subsequent show in three days' time? It's not worth it. We all get sick and we all have to cancel.

KATHLEEN KIM: I don't have any special tricks. You know where the problem is. If the problem is on the vocal cords, then cancel. But it all depends. You have to do what you have to do, and you learn by doing.

ANA MARÍA MARTÍNEZ: I was so sick with bronchitis in Amsterdam and I remember just coughing and telling the baritone that we can't make out tonight. So we did all that we could but without touching too much. If you can go on without compromising the vocal cords, it's okay. Sometimes I just take two Advil and go on. I know there are some singers who do not like to take Advil because it thins your blood. They worry that it might rupture a blood vessel in the cords. So it's a judgment call, but if it's a low-grade fever, then go ahead. Otherwise, cancel.

LISETTE OROPESA: Technique is important and can get you through a rough night. But if you lose your voice completely, it's best to rest and recover. I don't take medicines other than vitamins or natural supplements. Healthy diet, rest, and patience are the only answers. We are human, after all.

ERIC OWENS: It's something you're going to have to find out, unfortunately, through trial and error. Everyone is different. For instance, I now know what's going on with my body when it's telling me I can sing through an illness and not have to worry about damaging my voice, and I now know what it feels like when I absolutely need to cancel, either because I know that I will be damaging my instrument or the performance will not be worthy of the professional situation at hand. But if I'm in a position where the company doesn't have a cover or there's no way of finding a replacement, I'm going to do everything in my power to work with them to come up with a solution that doesn't involve them canceling a performance and which doesn't involve me leaving my voice on their stage! I don't take canceling performances lightly!

DIMITRI PITTAS: I have been through both of them: illness and cancellation. Actually, my last performance of my recent *Don Carlo*, I woke up with a terribly swollen throat. I sang the entire performance that way. But when you're under the weather, you actually sing better because you focus a little bit more on the technique. I just say rely on the work that you've done beforehand and what it is that you're capable of doing, and be honest with yourself. The body and the mind are very strong things when they work together. However, I think that if you're constantly singing on sick cords, you can have long-term damage.

EWA PODLEŚ: I do not perform through illness. I cancel. However, it is extremely rare to be in ideal condition for any performance, which most singers would agree with.

JENNIFER ROWLEY: This past season for four performances I was ill. I had food poisoning for two and a terrible sinus infection for two. If you don't sing, you lose money and you have to be paid! I know when I'm sick I have to steam, rest, and drink a ton of water. Steam is going to clear up anything that I have on the cords. I also know I can take antibiotics and it doesn't bother me. I cannot take ibuprofen because it restricts my voice. So if you're sick, figure out what you can take. If it is a cold, I take Tylenol and sing. My manager says to just sing on the computer when you're sick, that is to say you need to sing using technique and muscle memory. I tend to sing better when I'm sick. Actually for singers, sometimes sick performances tend to be the better performances.

Jennifer Rowley
Emerging international artist Jennifer Rowley has received top prizes from the Gerda Lissner Foundation, the Opera Index Awards, the Licia Albanese Puccini Foundation, and the William Matheus Sullivan Foundation; she also received the Richard Tucker Career Grant Award. *Opera News* calls her "a real star," and the *New York Times* says, "Soprano Jennifer Rowley holds nothing back in her scenery-chewing, vocally visceral portrayal." Her international credits include the New York City Opera, Caramoor Music Festival, Norwegian National Opera, Savonlinna Festival in Finland, Spoleto Festival USA, Teatro Communale di Bologna, and Opera Hong Kong, with upcoming performances at the Metropolitan Opera, Covent Garden, and the Semperoper Dresden. Photo courtesy Arielle Doneson.

GERHARD SIEGEL: No, unfortunately not. I have a cold right now and am having problems getting around it.

3. NERVES, PERFORMANCE ANXIETY, OR STAGE FRIGHT CAN BE ISSUES SINGERS STRUGGLE WITH THROUGHOUT THEIR STUDIES AND CAREERS. WHAT ADVICE DO YOU HAVE FOR OVERCOMING THESE CONDITIONS?

STEPHANIE BLYTHE: The interesting thing about stage fright and performance anxiety is that I never had it. I think the most important thing about stage anxiety is that you have to understand that fear feeds upon itself when it comes from the unknown. If you are able to diagnose why you are afraid, then the likelihood of being afraid is lessened enormously. Are you afraid of the audience, the conductor, the piece? Remember, there is no shame in it; you are not the only one. There are professionals who are trained to help you deal with it. If we are able to accept certain foibles about who we are and not let them become bad habits that take over our lives, then we can go on and have wonderful careers and have wonderful experiences onstage. But I will tell you that there were great artists who had very long careers, and artists who are singing today who do so and are terrified when they get on that stage. So it is possible to have a career full of stage fright. I just don't think it's a happy one.

NICOLE CABELL: I've struggled with stage fright over the course of my training and career. Mental exercises like visualization, meditation, and affirmations help immensely, as well as physical exercises like breathing and yoga. We tend to reflect on that negative experience and become more and more nervous for future performances. I know singers who've developed more stage fright through the years because of a few negative experiences that were so traumatic they project them onto future performances. There is so much psychological baggage behind stage fright that can be eliminated through simple methods, which all lead to keeping the mind quietly in the present and to keeping the focus sharply on what a singer is supposed to be doing technically.

JOSEPH CALLEJA: I suffer from stage fright, but I cover it. I suffer from incredible nerves before a performance. However, I prepare and have everything as good as possible. Then when I get onstage, adrenaline and training and schooling kick in and I give a good performance. There is no quick fix. Preparing months, weeks, and days in advance so that you will give a good performance helps everyone. But in the bigger picture, it is not important, not the way a football player in the World Cup pulls a muscle and it's over. And they are using bigger muscles than we are; we are just using these small muscles of the throat, and it is much easier to go wrong.

DAVID DANIELS: I started yoga about six months ago and I love it. But I don't do it for stage fright, but because I felt like my body was seventy-seven years old. My advice is to just get out onstage and do it. If I know the voice is there and I've warmed up successfully, then there is an excitement about walking on the stage. I don't have a fear.

JOYCE DIDONATO: That horrible, critical inner voice can be a crippling factor for a lot of singers and musicians, because we often feel we are being studious and responsible by constantly critiquing and debasing ourselves. My question is, "How beneficial is that voice if it is destroying your basic artistic expression?" It is often debilitating, paralyzing. When you sing, think about what you are expressing and there will be no space for that destructive inner voice. If you are fully engaged in *being* your character, there is no chance for your voice to interrupt. I would invite you to ask yourself if you would *ever* speak to another human being in the manner in which you speak to yourself! Ask yourself if you want to mentally imprison yourself. I prefer not, so I put the voice on hold until after the show, when I can objectively analyze my performance. I just think it's simply more humane.

CHRISTINE GOERKE: Just trust that you are there for a reason and that you can do this. My stage fright is pretty stupid, actually. Even if I have just sung the dress rehearsal the day before, I will have no idea what my first words are and will have to go over to the stage manager and say, "Can I see your book?" And they just look at me and I say, "Shut up. Just give me your book. Oh, those are the words." But I cannot remember my first lines of any scene. I just have to hope I will go out there and the words will be there. Other than that stupid little word thing, I just have the best time and think I have the best job in the world. It is so much fun to be up there and be paid to pretend! And the music! A bonus!

DENYCE GRAVES: This is intensely personal. I think that the best way to overcome or manage stage fright or nerves (which I most certainly have had my entire career) is to just keep doing it. Performance practice is the key, and also working so that you know the material cold. This will help so much in terms of your confidence.

GREER GRIMSLEY: It's not so much overcoming it. It's how you look at it. We respond to a performance with a rush of adrenaline. In some cases, negative thoughts will go through your mind. Let them pass through and stay focused on the task at hand. Learn to welcome this feeling; your body is getting ready to perform. Instead of being compromised by this energy, harness it. As with anything, you must practice this to use your performance energy. Once you master this, you will find it will feed your performances in a positive way.

THOMAS HAMPSON: There is no question that what we do is in a heightened nervous state; otherwise it wouldn't be interesting. But if you go out and sing *at* people, you're going to be nervous. If you come onstage and think you have to prove or convince your audience of something, that is, the piece, the language, etc., you're going to be nervous. Get out there and get into your world as soon as possible. Come onstage, for example, to sing *Frauenliebe und -leben* and that creation of Chamisso and Schumann is what you're all about in that moment, and you're not going to be nervous after the first minutes of the first song. You're going to be in your world. I think a large percentage of one's nervousness or the stuff that pulls you off your mark is wrong thoughts about why you are there.

ALAN HELD: I always try to keep this in mind: I want to be a singer. I want to sing. If I want to do this, why am I so nervous about this? If the nerves are affecting my performances in a way that is detrimental, then I am not wanting to sing for the right reasons. I have also learned to remind myself over the years that, for the most part, audience members are out there wanting you to do your best. They are pulling for you. They are not your enemy. Nerves are controlled in your head. The head is part of your vocal instrument. It's been part of your instrument since day one in the studio. Nothing has changed. Just do it.

JONAS KAUFMANN: The first and most important ingredient would be to reach the point where you are the master of your instrument and its possibilities. It is impossible to be confident without this. Technique is what frees the singer to fully express himself as an artist. But aside from that issue, the best way to keep a positive attitude is to remain focused, not on competition but on your own path, your own voice, and by that I mean not just your singing voice but your inner voice as well. And I would say to every young artist: Always hold on tightly to the reasons which made you become a singer in the first place—your love of the art, your love of music, your desire to contribute to it through your own expression. Keep that as your anchor.

SIMON KEENLYSIDE: It's not enough that one must merely be on top of the practical things: the fear that the work is not sufficiently memorized, for example. It's perhaps equally glib to say that building a robust technique will overcome nerves so that you have a voice which, sickness aside, is predictable and workable in most circumstances. How can you best focus and fire those arrows of inflection, sound, and color into the auditorium? Think! I would venture to say that the more a young singer throws himself into all of this, the less time that there will be to worry about nerves. Nerves can be a form of vanity, in that you are too much occupied in yourself and too little in the business at hand (easy to say). Fake it till you make it!

KATHLEEN KIM: I always get nervous before my performances. You just have to have confidence that you know it and just do it. That's why rehearsal is very important, because if you can do it in the rehearsal, you're doing it right and you can do it onstage. Trust yourself. And have a big breath before you enter.

ANA MARÍA MARTÍNEZ: I get the normal butterflies before the show, but once a show starts, I'm fine. It's just the anticipation beforehand, I think, since we feel alone and vulnerable. Then suddenly you go on automatic pilot, and your body knows what to do. A colleague once told me to think we are standing in God's hand, and why should you be nervous when you're standing there in the center? You can call it the center of strength or purpose if you don't want to call it God. And something else that disarms fear is that I try to look in as many faces as possible in the audience and think of them as being special in their own way.

LISETTE OROPESA: Nerves are normal. They may never go away, but with experience you will learn to focus and project confidence and security. (Though you may never feel them inside!) Enjoy the spike of adrenaline. Always know, though, that you are a living, breathing entity. Center yourself with breath and a positive mind-set. Let the music fill your heart. It will come through to the public, and the applause comes soon after.

ERIC OWENS: I still get nervous from time to time. But, the ultimate antidote for nerves is preparation!

DIMITRI PITTAS: There's a dichotomy of being in control and letting go. Only when you are in complete control of everything can you let go and make yourself most vulnerable. The only way that you can be in control is by doing the work beforehand and by being prepared. Then I can say, "Hey, dummy, you've been through this before and you got through it with no problem, so it shouldn't be any big deal now." But you can only do that to yourself and flick off those little devils sitting on your shoulder if you've been through those situations before. And the only way to be through those situations is to put yourself through them. So, prepare yourself as much as possible so that when those moments of stress do come up, you can recognize that you've been in those positions before and you know how to deal with them.

EWA PODLEŚ: All of this belongs to the artist's lot: stage fright or performance anxiety. Only way to overcome stage fright, as I see it, is to fight it.

JENNIFER ROWLEY: You have to be confident and believe in yourself before you get on that stage. If you have to sing the first-act aria in your dressing room to prove to yourself that your voice is ready to go, then do it, if that's what you need to control the mind. You have to do something to combat fear. I actually do boxing. My personal trainer bought me a pair of boxing gloves, saying, "You have to get over fear and learn how to box!" It gave me the strength to learn how to combat fear in the theater. I also do yoga.

GERHARD SIEGEL: I'm sorry, I have no recipe, no prescription. Go out and sing and have fun!

Gerhard Siegel
German tenor Gerhard Siegel began his music career as an instrumentalist and composer. He won the International Belvedere Singing Competition in Vienna, after which he made his debuts at the Munich and Vienna State Operas. Since then, his roles include Tristan, Florestan, and Siegfried at venues such as Brussels, Barcelona, London, and Madrid. One of his most acclaimed roles ("the standout of the show," "a miracle") is Mime in *Das Rheingold* and *Siegfried*, which he has performed at the Metropolitan Opera, the Bayreuth Festival, Covent Garden, and Tokyo. The 2012 Metropolitan Opera recording of Wagner's *Ring* cycle, with Gerhard Siegel, was awarded a Grammy for Best Opera Recording. Photo courtesy Claudio Hiller.

4. YOUNG SINGERS OFTEN STRUGGLE WITH CONFIDENCE AND FINDING THEIR OWN PLACE AMONG THE COMPETITION. HOW DID YOU HANDLE THAT AND KEEP A POSITIVE ATTITUDE—INDEED, A WINNER'S MIND-SET?

STEPHANIE BLYTHE: For self-confidence, the most important advice I can give is be prepared and listen and you will master any rehearsal and performance situation. I think that one of the most terrifying experiences I had working with a conductor for the first time was with James Levine, and just being overwhelmed by him. Because I had grown up watching this man conduct and listening to his concerts, I arrived prepared. He was extraordinarily supportive, especially of young singers. I could have been the type of singer who came in thinking I knew everything there was to know; I would never have been able to glean anything from what he said to me. I kept an open mind and an open heart and I was able to hear him, and he was able to help me.

NICOLE CABELL: Comparison is just about the worst thing you can do, and yet we are all prone to it. It's about working through the ego. So, that winning attitude is an internal thing. I can't deny that I was competitive and ambitious at one time in my life. The singing business is a roller coaster, and if you don't want to get sick over and over with the craziness of it all, it's best to watch it from a distance and not ride on it. Being smart about who you listen to is also helpful. Realize that many critics and bloggers, fellow singers, even coaches, teachers, and conductors are simply bullies. What would you do when encountering a bully at school? Choose the people you listen to very carefully, and don't indulge in who's writing or saying what about you.

JOSEPH CALLEJA: You have to have the talent. If you do not have the talent, then you are not going to succeed and will be in a vicious circle of lessons, master classes, and competitions. In my life I did literally three auditions. That is all. I was naturally gifted and had the talent and the schooling at an early age. If you do have it all together, then believe in yourself. Do everything necessary to prepare yourself psychologically for the audition. If you go to an audition and you are conscious you have been good to yourself, in that you slept, ate well, and are rested, then you should have confidence in yourself. The best is to be prepared and have the mental frame of mind to be a success. If it doesn't work, then shit happens. You can't do more than you can do.

DAVID DANIELS: When I was first starting out, I was so confident. I was just stupidly oozing confidence because I felt that I had a countertenor sound that nobody had heard before and I was going to show everybody what I could do. Yet I didn't get everything. I never won the Met auditions. I couldn't get past South Carolina. It wasn't all amazing. Disappointment is tough, but you just have to know that when the right thing will happen, it will happen when it's the right time. It's part of being a human being to learn how to deal with frustration and rejection and being positive that something good is around the corner.

JOYCE DIDONATO: I think it was a process of realizing that a performance is not about "me." It must be about the art: the character, the music, the expression, the message—it is ultimately about genuine *connection*. That has always been my salvation when nerves or a sense of being overwhelmed get in the way. I think if young singers can embrace that, they will find a freedom and a joy in their singing that will bring infinite rewards.

CHRISTINE GOERKE: I had to learn how to audition again. I was great at it the first time. After being out there, winning awards, and singing all over (I won two Grammys), I had to start auditioning again. I had to start proving to everybody that I wasn't broken. I was scared. And I've never been scared before. I actually decided that I had an audition character that I walked in the door with. I was very friendly, really, but it was very much, *You're so lucky I'm here. I only have fifteen minutes. What would you like to hear?* I didn't say that, but I immediately became somebody else for those fifteen minutes. I didn't have to do it very long and I got my confidence back, but it was a trick that really worked.

DENYCE GRAVES: I never really worried or concerned myself with what other singers were doing. I didn't as a student and don't now. I really don't care. I figured I have so much work to do on my own that that occupied my time, energy, and thoughts, and I set out to do the best that I could do. I never really listened to other singers too often. I just came from my own heart and had it inform my music making. It can be a challenge to keep a healthy mind-set, especially if you've been "out there" struggling to be heard, but again I go back to creating your own opportunities, being creative, and having personal goals, and that should keep you engaged enough not to worry about anyone else.

GREER GRIMSLEY: You have to look at it as a bank account and not necessarily what builds confidence. Just being at the audition, that's one step. If someone is very interested in you at the audition, another notch. Then you may get hired, that is another deposit. You keep adding these deposits that seem insignificant until you have a huge bank account. Don't go back to square one every time you perform or audition. Everything you do is a building block.

THOMAS HAMPSON: The only barometer you really can control for yourself is whether you feel you have done as well as you can. What we do as artists and singers has no guarantees. It has no formula, no scoreboard. It is horribly, unfairly, unjustifiably subjective. So all you can really achieve is to have represented yourself to the best of your ability in the service of the great art you have chosen to sing. And if you then get the job, *mazel tov!* If you then win the competition, treasure its rewards. Our lives are about auditioning and performing and being assessed whether we're ready for the next level or challenge. There is seldom a controllable result to that, so the more you can keep that in your mind in those unavoidable dark moments of doubt, the healthier you will be. It's not about us. It's about Art. It's not easy. It is worth it.

ALAN HELD: Confidence in singing, as in all things, comes through time and preparation. My first engagement at the Met was as a cover in *Lulu*. When I finally got my chance to sing the "Prolog" of the opera in rehearsal, it nearly brought the room to a standstill and applause broke out when it was over. That brought confidence—knowing that I could put in the work and get the reward in the end. And the biggest reward was having other contracts offered after that. If you're not confident in those things, then maybe you need to look at your effort—or perhaps this is not the business for you. And this is a *very* competitive business. You've got to be willing to enter into the fray, take the hits along with the success, and keep going.

JONAS KAUFMANN: This is difficult because I don't know how you achieve that; once you know how to sing you have it. As long as you don't know how to sing, you don't have confidence. So, be prepared.

SIMON KEENLYSIDE: A lack of confidence is something that most singers struggle with from time to time. We all know hugely gifted professionals who still suffer the torments of the damned. Your greatest competition is not from without but from within, overcoming your own demons to become the best singer that you can be (and not just in the garden). It's an inquiring and investigative and passionate mind you need in order to be an artist, not a "winning" mentality. Be just that—an artist and not just a singer.

KATHLEEN KIM: I also had to do millions of auditions. You just keep doing it until someone finds you. If you are ready, then the time will come. Competitions are different because some people have three or four arias ready and sing them so well, but onstage, it's going to be different. Competitions are important to get exposure, but getting a job is more important than winning the competition.

ANA MARÍA MARTÍNEZ: The most beautiful definition of freedom is the ability to reach the highest capability without hurting anyone else, because there's room for everybody. So take a deep breath and trust you are prepared. If you're doing a competition, remember that every aria has to be perfectly prepared and equally polished. I did a competition once, and the first aria was impeccable but my second aria wasn't quite as polished, which disqualified me. Also, when I started out auditioning I thought of a color. Let's say I was a beautiful, vibrant purple. I hoped they were looking for that color, but maybe they were looking for an orange. I will continue perfecting my purple until they accept that color. The whole networking that occurs in the competition circuit is phenomenal. In one contest I didn't win but I got a manager recommendation, which started my career.

LISETTE OROPESA: Don't compare yourself to other people. That leads to bitterness and negativity. You are unique and there is only one person with your sound, personality, and being. Be thankful for the gift that is music that gets to flow through you. Happiness is cultivated within. Music may be your living, but make time for other things that inspire you: hobbies, nature, relationships, and love. Life is full of chances to grow, and most of them happen off the stage.

ERIC OWENS: In any situation, whether an audition or public performance, you should know that the people sitting there, on the other side of the table or out in the house, want you to do well. Live in that positive space with the knowledge that they're rooting for you. They are not going to sit there for hours wanting people to sing poorly. They are with you. So, try to recognize and pick up on that energy.

EWA PODLEŚ: I am always trying to do my best, which helps me to keep confident.

JENNIFER ROWLEY: Know what you do better than everyone else. If you are stunningly beautiful, exploit it. If you have the best high A-flat in the world, exploit it. You have to believe in you more than anybody, because if you don't, no one else will. Your audition starts the minute you enter the room, so walk in with confidence ready to perform. It is important to love your audition repertoire. You cannot go with pieces on your list that you hope they don't pick, because they will pick that piece. The mind plays a big role in an audition. It can make you or break you. I have seen people crash and burn because they walk into the audition insecure because so-and-so's in the hallway.

GERHARD SIEGEL: I must confess that I did not feel that. Because there was in my *Fach,* as a character tenor or young heroic tenor, always enough work without having to come up against extreme competition. Also, especially in German and heavier vocal categories, rather more respect prevails than jealousy because everyone knows how hard it is to sing Siegfried for five hours. A positive attitude is always important.

REFERENCES

CHAPTER 1. ON THE CRAFT OF SINGING

Lamperti, Giovanni Battista. *Vocal Wisdom: Maxims of Giovanni Battista Lamperti, Recorded and Explained by His Pupil and Assistant William Earl Brown.* Boston: Crescendo, 1931.

CHAPTER 2. ON THE OPERATIC STAGE

The quote by Janet Baker is from:

Watson, Derek, editor. *The Wordsworth Dictionary of Musical Quotations.* Edinburgh: Wordsworth Reference, 1991.

CHAPTER 4. ON MAINTAINING A CAREER

The quote by Margaret Harshaw is from:

An International Symposium in Collaboration with Opera News: Celebrating the Metropolitan Opera Guild's Fiftieth Anniversary: New York, November 1 and 2, 1985. New York: Central Opera Service, 1986.

CHAPTER 5. ON TEACHING AND STUDYING

West, Stephen. "The Traditions of Fine Singing: An Interview with Mme. Anna E. Schoen-René." *The Etude,* November 1941.

CHAPTER 6. EXTRAS FROM THE EXPERTS

The quote from Kiri Te Kanawa is from: http://www.kiritekanawa.org.

INDEX

ARTISTS AND COMPOSERS

Asciak, Paul, 116, 129
Ameling, Elly, 70

Bach, Johann Sebastian, 73
Baker, Janet, 34
Bicket, Harry, 60
Bellini, Vincenzo, 111
Björling, Jussi, 39, 50
Bolechowska, Alina, 119
Bonazzi, Elaine, 117
Bonney, Barbara, 15, 65
Borge, Victor, 55
Brahms, Johannes, 15, 82
Brown, Oren, 21
Bybee, Luretta, 90, 117

Caballé, Montserrat, 87
Carreras, José, 50
Caruso, Enrico, 50
Castel, Nico, 10
Conlon, James, 145
Corelli, Franco, 50, 141
Cross, Richard, 117
Crutchfield, Will, 63
Cuccaro, Costanza, 116

Damrau, Diana, 120
de los Ángeles, Victoria, 109
di Stefano, Giuseppe, 50
Dobner, Gabrie, 78
Domingo, Plácido, 55, 60, 62,
    69, 96
Donizetti, Gaetano, 39, 111, 120
Dudamel, Gustavo, 62, 69

Fleming, Renée, 93, 119, 140
Freni, Mirella, 38

García, Manuel, 115
Gershwin, George, 79
Gibson, George, 117
Gigli, Beniamino, 116
Grieg, Edvard, 82
Gruberova, Edita, 31
Gunther, Horst, 117

Hagen, Uta, 59
Handel, George Frideric, 24, 71, 94, 102
Harnoncourt, Nikolaus, 61
Harshaw, Margaret, 88, 115
Horne, Marilyn, 120

Isokoski, Soile, 65

Jones, Warren, 75, 76
Joswig, Margarete, 118

Kaku, Michio, 107
Katz, Martin, 75–76, 120
King, Stephen, 118
King, James, 130
Koldofsky, Gwendolyn, 76
Korngold, Erich, 82
Kraus, Alfredo, 35, 97, 141

Lamperti, Giovanni Battista,
    1, 143
Levine, James, 60, 61, 155
Luisotti, Nicola, 54

Mahler, Gustav, 81
Malas, Marlena, 29
Marceau, Marcel, 121
Meachem, Lucas, 141
Mehta, Zubin, 60
Melchior, Lauritz, 87

Metternich, Josef, 95, 130
Misslin, Patricia, 24
Moore, Gerald Martin, 118
Mozart, Wolfgang Amadeus, 27, 39, 44,
    75, 94, 102, 109, 111

Newton, Norma, 126

Offenbach, Jacques, 22
Olivero, Magda, 50

Paddock, Charles, 126
Pappano, Antonio, 60
Pavarotti, Luciano, 20, 50, 87, 97,
    116, 137
Pearson, James, 116
Plishka, Paul, 39
Ponselle, Rosa, 87
Porter, Cole, 79
Price, Leontyne, 87
Price, Margaret, 87
Puccini, Giacomo, 29

Reiter, Jocelyn, 117
Rice, Michael, 116
Rhodes, Michael, 32, 118, 130
Rossini, Gioacchino, 94, 111

Sawallisch, Wolfgang, 61
Schock, Rudolf, 95
Schoenberg, Arnold, 82
Schoen–René, Anna, 115
Schreker, Franz, 82
Schubert, Franz, 81, 82
Schwarzkopf, Elisabeth, 17, 109
Sills, Beverly, 95
Snyder, Wesley, 117
Souzay, Gérard, 70
Soviero, Diane, 25, 117
Steber, Eleanor, 109
Strauss, Richard, 68, 81, 82
Summers, Patrick, 62

Tate, Jeffrey, 61
Te Kanawa, Kiri, 140
Traubel, Helen, 87
Troyanos, Tatiana, 120

Verdi, Giuseppe, 39, 44, 51, 75,
    111, 114

Viardot, Pauline, 115
von Karajan, Herbert, 58

Wagner, Richard, 34, 52, 73
White, Robert, 126
Williams, John, 111
Wolf, Hugo, 74
Wunderlich, Fritz, 95

Zimmer, Hans, 111

**OPERAS, ROLES, AND OTHER
WORKS CITED**
Operas and Other Works
Barber of Seville, The, 46, 52, 146
Carmen, 145
Dead Man Walking, 111
Dichterliebe, 81
Die Frau ohne Schatten, 29, 41
Don Carlo, 53, 135, 148
Enchanted Island, 83
Elektra, 94
Eugene Onegin, 57
Falstaff, 59, 145
Flying Dutchman, The, 47
Frauenliebe und -leben, 152
Free Will, 114
I Capuleti e i Montecchi, 145
I Puritani, 50, 141
Il trovatore, 54, 95
Julius Caesar, 83, 132
Lucia di Lammermoor, 97,
    118, 120
Lulu, 113, 157
Macbeth, 87
Madame Butterfly, 58, 119
Nixon in China, 113
Oscar, 35, 111
Otello, 60
Parsifal, 73, 112, 137
Peter Grimes, 56
Rake's Progress, The, 135
Rigoletto, 47, 97, 141
Ring Cycle, The, 42, 61
Rusalka, 133
Symphony No. 9 (Beethoven), 71
Tales of Hoffmann, The, 22
Tosca, 57, 135
Two Boys, 111
Winterreise, 51, 57, 74, 81

Roles
Amneris, 51
Antonia (*The Tales of Hoffman*), 22
Azucena, 54, 97
Brünnhilde, 95
Butterfly, 29, 58, 62
Chrysothemis, 94
Count Almaviva (*The Barber of Seville*), 55
Don Giovanni, 110
Donna Anna, 49
Dyer's Wife, The, 29, 41, 95
Elektra, 41, 94, 95
Ellen Orford (*Peter Grimes*), 56
Eugene Onegin, 57
Faust (Busoni), 52
Giulietta, 145
Hans Sachs, 37
Iago, 52
Juliette (Gounod), 50
Julius Caesar, 35, 83
Kundry, 47
Lucia, 120
Madame Mao, 29
Mandryka (*Arabella*), 52
Marschallin, 65
Micaela, 145
Mimi, 29, 96
Octavian, 65
Oscar Wilde, 35
Otello, 96
Parsifal, 64
Rosina, 146
Scarpia, 30
Siegfried, 64, 158
Siegmund, 64
Stolzing, 64
Susanna (*Le nozze di Figaro*), 53
Tosca, 30
Tristan, 64
Violetta, 124
Zerbinetta, 29, 43, 96

TOPICS
Chapter 1: On the Craft of Singing
Breathing, 1–6
Color, 14–19
Diction, 6–11
Men: High Voice, 30–33
Passaggio, 19–23
Placement, 11–14

Technique, 24–28
Women: Chest Voice and
    Flageolet, 28–30

Chapter 2: On the Operatic Stage
Conductors, 59–64
Integrating singing and acting, 54–59
Learning a role, 34–39
Pacing, 49–54
Projection, 64–68
Stage direction, 44–49
Warming up, 39–44

Chapter 3: On the Recital and Concert Stage
Collaborating with a pianist, 75–78
Programming, 79–82
Recital stage vs. operatic stage, 70–74
Singing for the camera, 83–87

Chapter 4: On Maintaining a Career
Attributes for success, 88–93
Contemporary opera, 110–14
Longevity, 93–97
Recording, 97–101
Social media, 101–6
Working abroad, 106–10

Chapter 5: On Teaching
Memorization, 131–35
Practicing, 135–39
Professional preparation, 128–31
Teaching, 124–28
Vocal studies, 119–24
Working with a teacher or coach, 115–19

Chapter 6: Extras from the Experts
Competition, 155–58
Health tips, 140–45
Performance anxiety, 150–54
Performing through illness, 145–50

ARTISTS INTERVIEWED
Blythe, Stephanie
    Attributes for success, 88–89
    Breathing, 1–2
    Chest voice, 28
    Collaborating with a pianist, 75
    Color, 14–15
    Competition, 155

Conductors, 59
Diction, 6
Health tips, 140–41
Integrating singing and acting, 54
Learning a role, 34
Longevity, 93–94
Memorization, 131
Pacing, 49–50
Passaggio, 19
Performance anxiety, 150
Performing through illness, 145
Placement, 11
Practicing, 135
Professional preparation, 128
Programming, 79
Projection, 64
Recital stage vs. operatic stage, 70
Singing for the camera, 83
Social media, 101–2
Stage direction, 44–45
Teaching, 124–25
Technique, 24
Vocal studies, 119–20
Warming up, 39
Working with a teacher or coach,
    115–16

Brownlee, Lawrence
Attributes for success, 89
Breathing, 2
Color, 15
Conductors, 59–60
Diction, 6
Health tips, 141
High voice, 30
Integrating singing and acting, 54–55
Learning a role, 34–35
Pacing, 50
Passaggio, 19
Placement, 11
Practicing, 136
Programming, 79
Projection, 64
Recital stage vs. operatic stage, 70
Stage direction, 45
Technique, 24
Vocal studies, 120
Warming up, 39
Working with a teacher or
    coach, 116

Cabell, Nicole
Attributes for success, 89
Breathing, 2
Chest voice, 28–29
Collaborating with a pianist, 75
Color, 16
Competition, 155
Conductors, 60
Contemporary opera, 110–11
Diction, 6–7
Health tips, 141
Integrating singing and acting, 55
Learning a role, 35
Longevity, 94
Memorization, 131–32
Pacing, 50
Passaggio, 20
Performance anxiety, 150
Performing through illness, 145
Placement, 11
Practicing, 136
Professional preparation, 128–29
Programming, 79
Projection, 64–65
Recital stage vs. operatic stage, 70
Recording, 97–98
Singing for the camera, 83
Social media, 102
Stage direction, 45
Teaching, 125
Technique, 24
Vocal studies, 120
Warming up, 39
Working abroad, 106–7
Working with a teacher or coach, 116

Calleja, Joseph
Attributes for success, 89
Breathing, 2
Collaborating with a pianist, 75
Color, 16
Competition, 155
Conductors, 60
Contemporary opera, 111
Diction, 7
Health tips, 141
High voice, 30–31
Integrating singing and
    acting, 55
Learning a role, 35

Longevity, 94
Memorization, 132
Pacing, 50
Passaggio, 20
Performance anxiety, 150–51
Performing through illness, 145–46
Placement, 11–12
Practicing, 136
Professional preparation, 129
Programming, 79
Projection, 65
Recital stage vs. operatic stage, 70–71
Recording, 98
Singing for the camera, 83
Social media, 102
Stage direction, 45
Teaching, 125
Technique, 24
Vocal studies, 120
Warming up, 39–40
Working abroad, 107
Working with a teacher or coach, 116

Daniels, David
Attributes for success, 89
Breathing, 2
Collaborating with a pianist, 75–76
Color, 16
Competition, 155–56
Conductors, 60
Contemporary opera, 111
Diction, 7
Health tips, 141
High voice, 31
Integrating singing and
    acting, 55
Learning a role, 35
Longevity, 94
Memorization, 132
Pacing, 50–51
Passaggio, 20
Performance anxiety, 151
Performing through illness, 146
Placement, 12
Practicing, 136
Professional preparation, 129
Programming, 79–80
Projection, 65
Recital stage vs. operatic
    stage, 71

Recording, 98
Singing for the camera, 83–84
Social media, 102
Stage direction, 45
Teaching, 125
Technique, 24–25
Vocal studies, 120–21
Warming up, 40–41
Working abroad, 107
Working with a teacher or coach,
    116–17

DiDonato, Joyce
Attributes for success, 90
Breathing, 3
Chest voice, 29
Color, 16
Competition, 156
Conductors, 60
Contemporary opera, 111
Diction, 8
Health tips, 142
Integrating singing and acting, 55–56
Learning a role, 35–36
Longevity, 94
Performance anxiety, 151
Performing through illness, 146
Professional preparation, 129
Projection, 65
Recording, 98
Singing for the camera, 84
Social media, 102–3
Stage direction, 46
Technique, 25
Vocal studies, 121
Warming up, 41
Working abroad, 107

Goerke, Christine
Attributes for success, 90
Breathing, 3
Chest voice, 29
Color, 17
Competition, 156
Conductors, 60–61
Contemporary opera, 111
Diction, 8
Health tips, 142
Integrating singing and
    acting, 56

Learning a role, 36
Longevity, 94–95
Memorization, 132
Pacing, 51
Passaggio, 20–21
Performance anxiety, 151
Performing through
   illness, 146
Placement, 12
Practicing, 136
Professional preparation, 129
Programming, 80
Projection, 65
Recital stage vs. operatic
   stage, 71
Recording, 98
Singing for the camera, 84
Social media, 103
Stage direction, 46–47
Teaching, 125
Technique, 25–26
Vocal studies, 121
Warming up, 41
Working abroad, 107–108
Working with a teacher or coach, 117

Graves, Denyce
Attributes for success, 90
Breathing, 3
Chest voice, 29
Collaborating with a pianist, 76
Color, 17
Competition, 156
Conductors, 61
Contemporary opera, 112
Diction, 8
Health tips, 142
Integrating singing and acting, 56–57
Learning a role, 36
Longevity, 95
Memorization, 132
Pacing, 51
Passaggio, 21
Performance anxiety, 151
Performing through illness, 146
Placement, 12
Practicing, 136–37
Professional preparation, 129
Programming, 80
Projection, 66

Recital stage vs. operatic stage, 71
Recording, 98–99
Singing for the camera, 84
Social media, 103
Stage direction, 47
Teaching, 125–26
Technique, 26
Vocal studies, 121
Warming up, 41
Working abroad, 108
Working with a teacher or
   coach, 117

Grimsley, Greer
Attributes for success, 90
Breathing, 3
Collaborating with a pianist, 76
Color, 17
Competition, 156
Conductors, 61
Contemporary opera, 112
Diction, 8
Health tips, 142
High voice, 32
Integrating singing and
   acting, 57
Learning a role, 36
Longevity, 95
Memorization, 132
Pacing, 51
Passaggio, 21
Performance anxiety, 151–52
Performing through illness, 146–47
Placement, 12–13
Practicing, 137
Professional preparation, 130
Programming, 80
Projection, 66
Recital stage vs. operatic
   stage, 72
Recording, 99
Singing for the camera, 84
Social media, 103
Stage direction, 47
Teaching, 126
Technique, 26
Vocal studies, 121
Warming up, 41–42
Working abroad, 108
Working with a teacher or coach, 117

Hampson, Thomas
Attributes for success, 90–91
Breathing, 3–4
Collaborating with a pianist, 76
Color, 17
Competition, 156–57
Conductors, 61
Contemporary opera, 112
Diction, 8–9
Health tips, 142
High voice, 32
Integrating singing and acting, 57
Learning a role, 36–37
Longevity, 95
Memorization, 132–33
Pacing, 52
Passaggio, 21
Performance anxiety, 152
Performing through illness, 147
Placement, 13
Practicing, 137
Professional preparation, 130
Programming, 80–81
Projection, 66–67
Recital stage vs. operatic
    stage, 72
Recording, 99
Singing for the camera, 85
Social media, 103–4
Stage direction, 47
Teaching, 126
Technique, 26
Vocal studies, 121–22
Warming up, 42
Working abroad, 108
Working with a teacher or coach, 117

Held, Alan
Attributes for success, 91
Breathing, 4
Collaborating with a pianist, 76
Color, 17–18
Competition, 157
Conductors, 62
Contemporary opera, 112
Diction, 9
Health tips, 142–143
High voice, 32
Integrating singing and
    acting, 57

Learning a role, 37
Memorization, 133
Pacing, 52
Passaggio, 21–22
Performance anxiety, 152
Performing through illness, 147
Placement, 13
Practicing, 137
Professional preparation, 130
Programming, 81
Projection, 67
Recital stage vs. operatic stage, 72–73
Recording, 99
Singing for the camera, 85–86
Social media, 104
Stage direction, 47
Teaching, 126
Technique, 26
Vocal studies, 122
Warming up, 42
Working abroad, 108
Working with a teacher or coach,
    117–18

Kaufmann, Jonas
Attributes for success, 91–92
Breathing, 4
Collaborating with a pianist, 76–77
Color, 18
Competition, 157
Conductors, 62
Contemporary opera, 112
Diction, 9
Health tips, 143
High voice, 32
Integrating singing and acting, 57–58
Learning a role, 37
Longevity, 95–96
Memorization, 133
Pacing, 52
Passaggio, 22
Performance anxiety, 152
Performing through illness, 147
Placement, 13
Practicing, 137
Professional preparation, 130
Programming, 81
Projection, 67
Recital stage vs. operatic
    stage, 73

Recording, 99
Singing for the camera, 86
Social media, 104
Stage direction, 47–48
Teaching, 126
Technique, 27
Vocal studies, 122
Warming up, 42
Working abroad, 108–9
Working with a teacher or coach, 118

Keenlyside, Simon
Attributes for success, 92
Breathing, 4
Collaborating with a pianist, 77
Color, 18
Competition, 157
Conductors, 62
Contemporary opera, 112
Diction, 9
Health tips, 143
High voice, 33
Integrating singing and acting, 58
Learning a role, 37
Longevity, 96
Memorization, 133
Pacing, 52
Passaggio, 22
Performance anxiety, 152–53
Performing through illness, 147
Placement, 13
Practicing, 137–38
Professional preparation, 130
Programming, 81
Projection, 67
Recital stage vs. operatic stage, 73
Recording, 100
Singing for the camera, 86
Social media, 104
Stage direction, 48
Teaching, 127
Technique, 27
Vocal studies, 122
Warming up, 42–43
Working abroad, 109
Working with a teacher or coach, 118

Kim, Kathleen
Attributes for success, 92
Breathing, 5

Collaborating with a pianist, 77
Color, 18
Competition, 157
Conductors, 62
Contemporary opera, 113
Diction, 10
Health tips, 143
Integrating singing
    and acting, 58
Learning a role, 37
Longevity, 96
Memorization, 133
Pacing, 52–53
Passaggio, 22
Performance anxiety, 153
Performing through illness, 148
Placement, 14
Practicing, 138
Professional preparation, 130
Programming, 82
Projection, 67
Recital stage vs. operatic
    stage, 73
Recording, 100
Singing for the camera, 86
Social media, 104
Stage direction, 48
Teaching, 127
Technique, 27
Vocal studies, 122
Warming up, 43
Whistle tone, 29
Working abroad, 109
Working with a teacher or coach, 118

Martínez, Ana María
Attributes for success, 92
Breathing, 5
Chest voice, 29–30
Collaborating with a pianist, 78
Color, 18
Competition, 157–58
Conductors, 62
Contemporary opera, 113
Diction, 10
Flageolet, 14
Integrating singing and
    acting, 58
Learning a role, 37–38
Longevity, 96

Memorization, 133
Pacing, 53
Passaggio, 22
Performance anxiety, 153
Performing through illness, 148
Placement, 14
Practicing, 138
Professional preparation, 130
Projection, 67
Recital stage vs. operatic
    stage, 73
Recording, 100–101
Singing for the camera, 86
Social media, 104
Stage direction, 48
Teaching, 127
Technique, 27
Vocal studies, 122
Warming up, 43
Working abroad, 109
Working with a teacher or coach, 118

Oropesa, Lisette
Attributes for success, 92
Breathing, 5
Chest voice, 30
Collaborating with a pianist, 78
Color, 18
Competition, 158
Conductors, 63
Contemporary opera, 113
Diction, 10
Health tips, 143
Integrating singing and
    acting, 58
Learning a role, 38
Longevity, 96
Memorization, 134
Pacing, 53
Passaggio, 22
Performance anxiety, 153
Performing through illness, 148
Placement, 14
Practicing, 138
Professional preparation, 130
Programming, 82
Projection, 68
Recital stage vs. operatic
    stage, 73
Singing for the camera, 86

Social media, 105
Stage direction, 48
Teaching, 127
Technique, 27
Vocal studies, 122
Warming up, 43
Working abroad, 109
Working with a teacher or coach, 118

Owens, Eric
Attributes for success, 92
Breathing, 5
Collaborating with a pianist, 78
Color, 18–19
Competition, 158
Conductors, 63
Contemporary opera, 113–14
Diction, 10
Health tips, 143
High voice, 33
Learning a role, 38
Longevity, 96
Memorization, 134–35
Pacing, 53
Passaggio, 23
Performance anxiety, 153
Performing through illness, 148
Placement, 14
Practicing, 138
Professional preparation, 130
Programming, 82
Projection, 68
Recital stage vs. operatic
    stage, 74
Recording, 101
Singing for the camera, 86
Social media, 105–6
Stage direction, 48–49
Teaching, 127–28
Technique, 27–28
Vocal studies, 123
Warming up, 43
Working abroad, 109–10
Working with a teacher or coach, 118

Pittas, Dimitri
Attributes for success, 93
Breathing, 5
Collaborating with a pianist, 78
Color, 19

Conductors, 63
Diction, 10
Health tips, 143–44
Integrating singing and
    acting, 58
Learning a role, 38
Longevity, 97
Memorization, 135
Pacing, 53
Passaggio, 23
Performance anxiety, 153
Performing through illness, 148
Practicing, 138
Professional preparation, 130
Programming, 82
Projection, 68
Recital stage vs. operatic stage, 74
Singing for the camera, 87
Social media, 106
Stage direction, 49
Vocal studies, 123–24
Warming up, 44
Working abroad, 110
Working with a teacher or coach,
    118–19

Podleś, Ewa
Attributes for success, 93
Breathing, 5–6
Chest voice, 30
Collaborating with a pianist, 78
Competition, 158
Conductors, 63
Contemporary opera, 114
Diction, 10
Health tips, 144
Learning a role, 38
Longevity, 97
Pacing, 53
Performance anxiety, 154
Performing through illness, 148
Professional preparation, 130
Programming, 82
Projection, 68
Recital stage vs. operatic stage, 74
Recording, 101
Singing for the camera, 87
Stage direction, 49
Teaching, 128
Vocal studies, 124

Warming up, 44
Working abroad, 110
Working with a teacher or coach, 119

Rowley, Jennifer
Attributes for success, 93
Breathing, 6
Chest voice, 30
Color, 19
Competition, 158
Conductors, 63–64
Contemporary opera, 114
Diction, 10–11
Health tips, 144–45
Integrating singing and acting, 58–59
Learning a role, 38–39
Longevity, 97
Memorization, 135
Pacing, 54
Passaggio, 23
Performance anxiety, 154
Performing through illness, 149
Placement, 14
Practicing, 138–39
Professional preparation, 130
Programming, 82
Projection, 68
Recital stage vs. operatic stage, 74
Recording, 101
Social media, 106
Stage direction, 49
Teaching, 128
Technique, 28
Vocal studies, 124
Warming up, 44
Working abroad, 110
Working with a teacher or coach, 119

Siegel, Gerhard
Attributes for success, 93
Breathing, 6
Collaborating with a pianist, 78
Competition, 158
Conductors, 64
Contemporary opera, 114
Diction, 11
Health tips, 145
High voice, 33
Integrating singing and
    acting, 59

Learning a role, 39
Longevity, 97
Memorization, 135
Pacing, 54
Passaggio, 23
Performance anxiety, 154
Performing through illness, 150
Placement, 14
Practicing, 139
Professional preparation, 130
Programming, 82

Projection, 68
Recital stage vs. operatic
    stage, 74
Recording, 101
Singing for the camera, 87
Social media, 106
Stage direction, 49
Technique, 28
Vocal studies, 124
Warming up, 44
Working with a teacher or coach, 119